Winter-flowering **Shrubs**

Daphne bholua 'Jacqueline Postill'.

Winter-flowering **Shrubs**

Michael W. Buffin

Timber Press

For Carla, Zoë, and Joshua

Published in 2005 by
Timber Press, Inc.
The Haseltine Building
133 S.W. Second Avenue, Suite 450
Portland, Oregon 97204-3527, U.S.A.
www.timberpress.com
For contact information for editorial, marketing, sales, and distribution
in the United Kingdom, see www.timberpress.com/uk.

Designed by Dick Malt
Printed through Colorcraft Ltd., Hong Kong

Library of Congress Cataloging-in-Publication Data
Buffin, Michael W.
  Winter-flowering shrubs / by Michael W. Buffin.
      p. cm.
  Includes bibliographical references and index.
  ISBN 0-88192-722-8 (hardcover)
  1. Flowering shrubs. 2. Plants in winter. I. Title.

  SB435.B83 2005
  635.9'76–dc22

                          2005005399

A catalogue record for this book is also available from the British Library.

Contents

Preface 7

Introduction 9

Designing for Winter 29

A-to-Z of Winter-flowering Shrubs 83

Where To See Winter-flowering Shrubs 223

Bibliography 224

US Department of Agriculture Hardiness Zone Map 226

Index 227

Preface

The casual observer may find little of interest in a garden during the long winter months, but upon closer inspection plants reveal their true beauty, and there really are many wonders to see. Winter can be a time to stop and admire the full splendour of a tree, like the golden weeping willow, *Salix* ×*sepulcralis* var. *chrysocoma*, its delicate framework of branches naked against the winter sky, its silhouette perfection itself, and its seemingly sleeping twigs swaying in the cold winds, awaiting the arrival of spring. A solitary bumblebee investigates the intoxicating scent of a wintersweet, *Chimonanthus praecox*, humming away while little else stirs; lingering berries, blood-red, hide in the spiny foliage of the English holly, *Ilex aquifolium*, glistening in the frosty morning sun, a gentle reminder that autumn has finished and winter is upon us. Winter is not a season for explosions of flower and foliage. It is not like spring, when plants awake in an amazing array of shapes and colours; nor is it like summer, when we can turn up the heat in our borders with flowering shrubs, herbaceous perennials, and annuals, or by introducing the exotic foliage of tropical bananas and palms. In the hustle and bustle of these busy gardening seasons, our thoughts are occupied with trying to keep ahead of essential gardening chores like weeding, pruning, planting, and watering, and our plants seem to grow before our very eyes.

Winter is slower, more relaxing but equally precious as our seasons go, and not without its own beauty or plant maintenance requirements. It is a season where the rewards of gardening are high, as through the use of delicately scented winter flowers, dazzling coloured stems, vivid coloured fruits, and ornate foliage plants, exciting winter planting displays can be achieved. Such techniques have long been used by gardeners to create colour in the quiet season.

In 1958, British gardener and designer Margery Fish wrote, "We get as much pleasure from one tiny bloom on a winter's day as we do from a garden full of roses in summer." The single flower becomes significant, summing up the essence and importance of winter-flowering plants.

Winter should be considered in its context. It is not simply a season to shelter away from the harsh elements of snow, frost, wind, and rain while we await the arrival of spring. Winter can be far more than this: it can be a joyous time in the garden, a time of great excitement, and I hope that while and after reading this book, you will see winter in a different light. It is a season that is full of intrigue and surprises, small pleasures and magic. It is not simply dead and cold, and it is much more than just a dormant season!

Even in the heart of an English winter, witch hazels unfurl their spider-like flowers.

To fully enjoy the allure of this season and the amazing winter jewels, you have to appreciate why plants struggle to flower in such harsh conditions, which in my mind is intrinsically linked to the beauty of winter as a season and the developing art of winter gardening. Only then can we truly appreciate the full magnificence of winter-flowering shrubs.

Introduction

Winter in the northern hemisphere differs from all our other seasons, as during its influence many plants are dormant. In one sense, winter is easy to define: it begins with the winter solstice, on or about 21 December, and finishes with the vernal equinox, on or about 20 March. This produces a three-month period, fitting perfectly into the four-season concept of our year. Alternatively we could use the measurement of daylight saving for the start and end of summer: summertime begins in Europe and the UK on the last Sunday in March and ends on the last Sunday in October; in the USA it begins on the first Sunday in April and ends on the last Sunday in October. If we were to assume that wintertime then starts, this would mean that winter is roughly a five-month period. But our plants do not follow calendars, especially if you try to determine, through plant growth, when winter starts and ends.

In gardening terms, we tend to distinguish our seasons by plant growth. The winter season begins as the last leaves of autumn fall, which in the south of England would be around the end of November to the first week of December; spring may coincide with the flowering of forsythias or cherry trees, which if the season is mild could be as early as the last week of February. The feeling of spring's arrival is further strengthened by the emergence of new foliage as plants shake off the dormancy of winter.

For me, there is no distinct day when winter simply "starts" or, for that matter, "ends." I tend to view the seasons as a series of transitional periods, defined by shifting weather patterns, temperatures, and sunlight. If we consider the end of November as winter's start (thus borrowing the last light of the autumn) and likewise take the end of March as winter's end (so stealing the first rays of spring, winter becomes a seamless transition between the seasons of autumn and spring. I prefer this approach to the changing of clocks on a set day. All told, then, the total amount of time available for winter gardening may be over four months, or some fourteen weeks, or ninety-eight days (or 686 gardening hours, taking into account the shorter days of winter in the northern hemisphere). This is too long a period for gardeners to spend indoors. Anyone who has suffered a harsh winter knows what it is like when the sun emerges on a winter's day and the temperature begins to rise—what a joyous feeling it is to escape outside, even if it is for only a few hours. What a great release from that cabin-fever feeling!

In the heart of winter, in our own gardens, plants brave ice storms, blizzards, frozen or snow-covered ground, freezing air temperatures, driving rain, and days where the sun fails to shine; and some do far more than brave these adverse conditions: they adapt and succeed in them. But winter gardening isn't

Frost alights on the foliage of *Bergenia* 'Ballawley'.

just about winter-flowering shrubs. To successfully garden during the "dormant" months, much thought must be given to the plants. Unlike spring, summer, and autumn, winter presents us with fewer "wow" factors to play and design with. Still, with the skillful use of plant combinations and bold associations, and by using the full range of plant material available to us, stark contrasts and beautiful results can be achieved.

So, ask me again—why do I enjoy winter? Relaxation and enjoyment spring to mind, as although I do enjoy all seasons, winter is my favourite. In winter I get the time to enjoy the true beauty of plants as they are touched by frost, snow, or sun. As flowers unfurl and their delicious scent fills the air, as I walk and wander, sunlight touches my face and lifts my spirit, and my mood, along with my garden, awakens.

Should it be assumed that winter is the gardener's "quiet" time? I think not. It is far more than a time of reflection for the season just ended and the anticipation of another. This gardening perception should be buried, as by using the right plants, in the right combinations, you could turn a drab and neglected area of your garden into an exciting winter landscape, one which can exude colour, contrast, and scent but also look exciting and stimulating throughout the remaining seasons. Just by including a few winter-flowering plants into our landscape, it is surprisingly easy to achieve flowers from November to March, regardless of your soil's type or pH. In fact, winter gardening can have many rewards, including tantalising scents from frost-hardy flowers, strange and eerie silhouettes highlighted by winter sun, and the bursting of bulbs through frozen soils.

Snow weighs down the flower heads of *Miscanthus sinensis* 'Malepartus'.

Imagine walking through your garden on a cold and frosty January morning and discovering a Chinese witch hazel (*Hamamelis mollis*) in full bloom, its spidery yellow flowers produced in abundance, and its sweet scent drifting through the air. What a wonderfully humbling experience, as elsewhere in our garden our trees, shrubs, and bulbs "hibernate" for the duration of winter. For those shrubs who have adapted to flower during the winter the rewards are high and the competition for pollinators is low: in winter, many flies are still active and are more than capable of pollinating many of our true winter-blooming plants, like witch hazels, daphnes, and shrubby honeysuckles (*Lonicera*). Add to this a small number of other winged pollinators, like some sleepy bees, and winter-flowering has considerable benefits.

Available winter-flowering shrubs for our winter landscape may be split into two groups: those that flower in response to cold temperatures and those that flower in the winter months by default. This includes both plants that flower over a long period, which may extend into early winter, and those that come from other parts of the world, such as the grevilleas and wattles, which flower during our winter (their summer). True winter-flowering shrubs, however, flower in response to reduced light levels and, more importantly, a period of cold or vernalisation (*vernal* is derived from the Greek word meaning "spring"); it is this exposure to cold that triggers their flowering patterns.

Even in the harshest weather, there is something to see in the winter garden.

Why Do Plants Flower in Winter?

Many processes, including age, circadian rhythms, vernalisation, and photo-periodism, are necessary to induce plants to flower. Many of these complicated cycles and processes are not yet fully understood.

All plants undergo a period of adolescence or juvenility before they become sexually active and flower. In some cases, as is common with many short-lived perennials and shrubs, this may take only a few years; certain trees, however, including some groups of magnolias, may remain in their juvenile stage for twenty to thirty years before they begin to flower. Luckily for us very few winter-flowering plants fall into this group. If we were to raise new plants from seed, they may only take three to five years to flower, but most of the plants we buy from our garden centres or nurseries will have been asexually propagated (cloned) by cuttings or grafting and may therefore have already reached sexual maturity. Reaching sexual maturity does not govern in what season a shrub will flower; it marks only that it is old enough to do so.

It is important for plants to know precisely when to flower during the day, and circadian rhythms are the means by which plants tell the time of day. This is different to photoperiodism, which distinguishes the time of the year, and is covered later. Circadian rhythms ensure that plants flower when their most likely pollinator will be active—during daylight in most cases, although some plants that are bat- or moth-pollinated flower during the evening. Circadian rhythms can work for a limited time even when there is no light at all, but at some point they may rest. In many winter-flowering plants the function of circadian rhythm is linked to vernalisation and photoperiodism.

Certain plants require a period of cold (vernalisation) to initiate flowering. Often seed collected from plants grown in temperate regions require a period of cold or vernalisation, which is normally associated with winter, to enable their germination in spring, when growing conditions are more favourable. In this case, the cold temperatures inhibit germination; this is known as quantitative vernalisation. Many winter-flowering plants flower both in response to vernalisation and in response to short day length. Most winter-flowering plants are classed as obligate vernalisation plants: they will not flower unless they have been exposed to cold temperatures, usually recorded between 0 and 5°C (32 and 40°F), for a period of time.

Many people associate vernalisation with very low temperatures, but this is not the case: the best results are gained when the temperatures are close to freezing, but seldom below them. Although many studies have explored why plants flower in the spring after they have been subjected to lower temperatures, few have addressed why plants flower in winter itself. In such cases vernalisation is linked to short days or long nights, so a secondary trigger must be the length of darkness—that is, the plant's response to photoperiodism. Many winter-flowering plants fall into the category of qualitative short day (long night) plants.

Plants measure night length using a chemical called phytochrome that is present in the leaves and absorbs light energy; when the days become longer, the phytochrome absorbs more light energy, and the plants know what time of year it is and initiate hormones to begin flowering. If a plant also requires a period of cold before flowering, then a flowering "switch gene" controls if a plant will flower or not. A period of cold between 1 and 10°C (34 and 50°F) can "switch off" the gene, and flowering can commence. It is possible that some winter-flowering plants may have alternative pathways to flowering, whereby vernalisation on its own, or photoperiodism on its own, can override other triggers to flowering, but this is not yet proved.

Flowering in wintertime may seem straightforward, but it is not; the relationship between vernalisation and photoperiodism is complicated. For example, many winter-flowering plants are deciduous, and yet day length is measured by the leaves; plants like witch hazels must begin to measure shorter days following the summer solstice, and then once the leaves fall, vernalisation must take over. By contrast, *Viburnum farreri* flowers late in autumn, so it must rely solely on photoperiodism.

The ability for plants to flower during the winter months enables them to reduce the level of competition for pollinators of their flowers. I have spent many a watchful hour trying to identify the pollinators of witch hazels—imagine my surprise when I discovered they were pollinated by small flies with additional help from the occasional sleepy bumble bee; the flies are around in sufficient numbers to justify the amount of ripening fruits that developed the following autumn. It seems to me that flowers pollinated in the heart of our winters face the harshest challenge, especially those that will be damaged by freezing temperatures. Whatever the price, in terms of energy, to produce flowers in the heart of winter (and where scent is involved, the expenditure must be even higher), somehow the benefits must outweigh the cost. So the next time you see a shrub flowering in the middle of winter, spare a thought to what went into producing that flower, and wonder at the marvel of nature.

Winter Gardens

My love of winter-flowering shrubs began as a student, when I purchased a copy of Graham Stuart Thomas's *Colour in the Winter Garden*; it is hard to read such a monumental work and not fall for winter gardening. My research for the Hillier Winter Garden (see the next chapter, "Designing for Winter") took me to many other winter-orientated gardens and plantings in both the UK and USA: Anglesey Abbey and Cambridge Botanic Garden in Cambridgeshire; the Royal Botanic Gardens, Kew, Surrey, and its garden at Wakehurst Place, in West Sussex; the Royal Horticultural Society's Garden at Rosemoor, Devon; and the Mullestein Winter Garden at Cornell Plantations, Ithaca, New York. All these gardens moulded my ideas on planting combinations for my pending project (and strongly influenced my selection of winter-flowering shrubs for the A-to-Z section of this book). Since then I have continued to travel in search of winter-flowering shrubs and winter gardens. All these gardens hold large collections of winter-flowering shrubs, and in each one, I encountered attractive landscape designs, some formal and some informal, but always with an emphasis on plant association to create strong contrasts.

The two that were most instrumental for me are Cambridge Botanic Garden and Wakehurst Place. The Winter Garden at Cambridge Botanic Garden, which opened in 1979, remains in my view the best example of what can be achieved in a relatively small space: its inspirational plantings occupy a mere 0.2 hectare (0.5 acre). The garden is surrounded on three sides by a clipped hedge, which shields the garden, provides a backdrop for the plants, and slows down air movement, thus allowing scent to build; the hedges along the south boundary are cut shorter to allow winter sun to penetrate into the garden. Cambridge is fairly unique as winter gardens go, as the soil there is alkaline, which inhibits the use of rhododendrons, camellias, and many of the heathers. The thoughtfully constructed landscape provides a breathtaking array of plants carefully selected for the winter landscape. Its size makes the garden intimate, and the foliage, stem, and flower contrasts are bold and striking. The planting areas have been sculptured and raised, not only to show off different angles and views but also to inhibit clear views across the garden, and hence create some mystery. It is an easy garden to enjoy, and its scale is such that it can be replicated in one's own garden. A real gem and an inspirational centre for anyone wishing to embark on a winter design, this garden offers one of the best collection of winter plants in the UK and is certainly worthy of a visit.

The second, Wakehurst Place (which is owned by the National Trust but managed by the Royal Botanic Gardens, Kew), is in West Sussex. The Winter Garden was designed in 1986 by Tony Schilling, who was then curator; it is 0.4 hectare (1 acre) in size and is shielded from prevailing winds by the walled garden. The Winter Garden is laid out as five island beds surrounded by lawn. Again, considerable effort has gone into plant associations—a mixture of evergreen winter-flowering heathers and rhododendrons, as the site has an acidic soil. It is more informal than the garden at Cambridge and as such seems less structured, although there are as many good features. Hidden in corners are flowering Himalayan daphnes (*Daphne bholua*) and coloured-stemmed dogwoods (*Cornus alba*), interplanted with Himalayan birch—strong images that teach us the importance of plant association. If you are looking for a more informal, island-bed approach to winter gardening, then this is it.

One of the newest gardens I have visited is the Mullestein Winter Garden at Cornell Plantations, Ithaca, New York, which displays plants that are interesting in all seasons and gives considerable insight as to which can flourish under the harsh realities of a zone 5 winter. The centrepiece of the garden—an open paved area with a series of raised beds made from stone—lends a distinctly formal feel to the garden; the plantings within the raised beds are themselves very formal, with a strong influence from dwarf conifers. Surrounding the formal area is a series of beds containing plants for their colourful winter bark, unusual growth habits, winter fruit, or evergreen foliage. I visited in the heart of an Ithaca winter, December, and nothing was in flower. Here, winter is a long season that rarely loosens its grip until late February; witch hazels and cornelian cherries flower in March. But even in its snow-covered state, the collection of coloured-stemmed dogwoods and maples was exceptional.

Dogwoods at the Mullestein Winter Garden, displayed against a background of snow.

My love of and respect for winter plants has matured from these experiences. For me, winter is a fascinating time in the garden, a time to enjoy the true beauty of our garden plants for their shape and form—and if we get the benefit of flowers and scent, then what a bonus! I like to think of winter as the season of scents and silhouettes.

As with all plantings new or old in our garden, it is essential that we take into account our soil type, pH, and garden habitats, as some flowering plants are limited to neutral or acidic soils, and to a lesser extent different habitats, like sun or shade. The quality and depth of your garden topsoil is important; it is imperative that you test your soil to determine not only its pH, its nutrient requirements and possible deficiencies, and its geology, but also what is required to work or cultivate it: everything you do in the garden relates back to the quality and "growability" of your soil.

Understanding Your Soil

The key item in any garden is its soil. No matter what other problems already exist—poor drainage, frost pockets, too much shade—you can select plants best suited to these conditions. If the plants are not suited to your pH, however, whatever you do, you will be struggling against the odds.

Soil means different things to different people; these differences are reflected in the various words we use to describe it—earth, dirt, or mud, for example. In looking at the component parts of soil and how each of these contributes to plant growth, we must bear in mind that the nature and proportion of soil components varies greatly from one area to another. No two soils are identical!

Generally we are interested in the area where plant roots grow, or the topsoil. The precise nature of our topsoil depends upon the size of rock particles that make up its bulk, which in turn make the soil act in a certain way. These particles range from coarse sand and grits to clay particles that are not visible to the naked eye. The varying proportion of each of these components determines the nature and extent of the spaces between the particles and hence the balance between water and air. Soils are classified into approximate groups on this basis.

Sandy soils

The typical sandy soil contains a high percentage of sand particles. Thus, sandy soils drain freely, which reduces the risk of winter rotting—very important to those plants that require free-draining soils. Root growth begins early in sandy soils as they tend to warm up quickly in the spring; conversely, they cool down quickly in the winter. Sandy soils require constant work; they need more irrigation or water conservation through mulching than other soils. They are also termed "hungry" soils, requiring as they do copious amounts of organic matter to keep them fertile. The major advantage of sandy soils is that they can be cultivated at most times of the year.

Silt soils

Silt-based soils tend to be nutrient-rich, but they also have high water-holding capacity, so drainage can be a problem, especially in winter. Because the particles have a capacity for smearing, they tend to compact easily (especially on the surface of the soil); water tends to run off, eroding the soil in its path. Because of their high water content, they have a more even temperature, warming slowly in spring and cooling slowly in autumn. Silt soils with a high sand content provide some of the most easy-to-work, nutrient-rich, free-draining soils. Adding copious amounts of sand to a silt soil can dramatically improve its drainage capacity.

Clay soils

Typically clay soils are slow to drain when wet and by nature tend to be very sticky and difficult to cultivate. Addressing drainage issues (installing drainage systems, incorporating sand to "open" the soil up) can improve things. Clay soils overlaying chalk soils can drain very quickly. Liming clay soils is still commonly practiced and helps to stop clay particles from binding, by keeping them in a flocculated state. Once clay soils dry they are as hard as concrete, and large cracks can appear. They compact easily, and like silt soils they have a more constant soil temperature. Clay has surprisingly good nutrient levels and is the most fertile soil if it can be cultivated successfully.

Soil pH

The reaction of soil, also called pH, represents its degree of acidity or alkalinity. The pH of the soil will strongly influence the selection of plant material because the pH affects the availability of nutrients for plant growth. Normally our gardens soils are made up of a mixture of minerals (rock, sand, particles of clay or silt). On such mineral soils where the pH is below 4.5, aluminium, iron, and manganese are so soluble in the soil that they become toxic to certain plants, while other mineral elements, such as nitrogen, phosphorus, potassium, sulphur, calcium, and magnesium, can become deficient or even unavailable, limiting plant growth. In addition to this, the important activities undertaken by organisms like earthworms, soil bacteria, and fungi—which help to break down organic mater into a form of nutrients that are soluble to plants—are greatly hampered on such soils. This can be bad news for many of our garden plants. Conversely, if a soil is above pH 7, alkaline deficiencies of iron and manganese are likely to occur.

A pH of 5.5 to 7.5 is optimum for most plants and is definitely the best for a wide range of winter-flowering shrubs. Within this range, essential nutrients are readily available, and earthworms and other beneficial organisms can survive here, so deficiencies rarely occur. Some species of plants, however, such as rhododendrons, camellias, and to some extent witch hazels, grow better under slightly acidic conditions; these plants are termed calcifuges. Plants that are more dependent on alkaline soils are called calcicoles.

Finding plants that grow well on alkaline soils is more difficult than finding those that flourish in acidic soils. If you make up two lists, they never seem to balance: the best plants always seem to end up in the acid list. Plants like

Himalayan daphne (*Daphne bholua*) and winter-flowering honeysuckles (*Lonicera* ×*purpusii*) will thrive even in the shallowest of alkaline soils. The main drawback with shallow soils (which can be alkaline or acidic) is that summer drought is an issue—but happily one that can be addressed with the use of organic mulches, good soil management, and occasional irrigation.

Ways to improve moisture retention in free-draining soils

Soils that are light and friable by nature tend to be quick-draining: water percolates quickly through the shallow depth of topsoil, so it is only available for plant growth for a limited amount of time. Adding organic matter to the soil will improve its water-retaining capabilities—for a time: it is a yearly requirement. Many of the organic, recycled soil conditioners manufactured from garden green waste are excellent for this never-ending task, as is animal manure, leaf or mushroom compost, composted bark, or spent hops.

As water quickly percolates through these soils, it is important to retain whatever moisture you can. In areas where summer temperatures get into the high nineties (F) mulching is essential. Mulching helps to conserve moisture lost through surface evaporation and ensures that moisture is retained around the root zone; it also suppresses weed growth, and (if it's organic) adds nutrients to the soil as it breaks down. Organic mulches can be made out of many different materials; pine needles, coir fibre, and composted bark chippings are the most common. Specially made mulch mats can be organic or synthetic; these will also help reduce weed growth, conserve moisture, and last longer than other types of mulches. Synthetic mulch mats are made from woven polypropylene or polythene; organic mulch mats are made from flax, reeds, or even hemp! These are bonded using organic glues or resins and break down slowly throughout the year.

Hardiness

In the UK we are less fixated on hardiness zones than are our colleagues in the USA. We seem more interested in whether a plant will withstand freezing temperatures or not, and although the climates of the west coast of Scotland and the south coast of England do vary considerably from each other, this variation is not as dramatic as the winter and summer temperature differentials between, say, Alaska and Florida. In the UK our climate is maritime; the surrounding oceans have a strong influence on the climate of our island, and as such, our winters are mild, our springs are wet, and our summers are wet but mild. The climate in the USA, by contrast, is strongly influenced by a continental weather pattern. The larger landmass influences weather patterns, and the difference between summer and winter temperatures is vast. In a nutshell, summers can be unbearably hot, and winters, freezing cold. But in the USA, in such a continental climate, such sweeping statements result in the inevitable exception to the rule. Special mini-climates, restricted to portions of Oregon and small areas Vancouver and Vancouver Island along the western coastline of Canada, mimic the maritime climate of the UK; here, high rainfall and cool ocean breezes help to cool the land and temper the extremes. Where weather patterns are similar, similar plants may be grown.

Hardiness, however, is not just about the minimum winter temperature a certain plant species can withstand. This is only one way to gauge hardiness. Another is to gain as much knowledge as possible about the kind of factors this plant is exposed to in its native "wild" habitat, or to discover whether it has been grown successfully in a climate similar to our own. For example, Hampshire in southern England would appear to be a USDA hardiness zone 8 or (in places) 9; it should therefore be possible to grow anything in Hampshire that flourishes within these zones in the USA. In reality, however, this couldn't be further from the truth as in certain of these zones, for instance in South Carolina, Georgia, and parts of Florida, the summers are far hotter. Plants from these climates require hot summers to allow wood to ripen before the onset of winter; it is this ripening of wood that allows them to harden off, and thus gives them their winter hardiness.

A good example is crape myrtle, *Lagerstroemia indica*, hardy in zones 6 to 9, which flowers amazingly in the southern USA north to Washington, DC, and even in some areas of Canada, where it is widely used in landscapes for its flowers, autumn colour, and attractive bark. Its hardiness is linked to the hardening of its wood during summer. It is this hardening off that gives crape myrtles their overall hardiness, so they fail to perform in the UK, with its cooler summers, even though a comparison between zones puts these plants in UK H2 to H4 zones. Although in the USA they survive much colder temperatures than in the UK, they simply fail here unless planted against a south-facing wall, where their wood is ripened by the additional reflected heat from the wall. Unless sited in such a microclimate, they are easily damaged by winter and spring frosts, taking so long to recover that they perform very poorly.

Likewise we grow many plants in the UK that should be perfectly hardy in similar zones in the USA, but they have no tolerance to blistering heat; and although this may not seem a likely issue in the UK, it is of great importance where a continental climate is involved. Many plants will shrivel and die where summer temperatures are too high. A classic example is that of one of our hardiest winter-flowering shrubs, *Viburnum farreri*, supposedly a zone 5 to 8 plant in the USA: it flowers magnificently in the UK during the cool autumn and early winter temperatures—but place this shrub in a Georgia (zones 7 and 8) climate with high summer temperatures and humidity, and even if planted in the shade, it will suffer and fail to flower, and grow very poorly indeed.

As you can see, several factors must be taken into account to evaluate a plant's ultimate hardiness. Soil types, rainfall, daytime temperatures, day length, wind, humidity, and heat—all play a role and must be considered. A hardiness zone is a good starting point but not a conclusive guide as to what will grow in your area. Only through experimentation and experience will you begin to fully understand the range of possibilities for your location.

The delicate flowers and foliage of the shade-loving *Viburnum farreri* 'Farrer's Pink' will not survive the heat of a Georgia summer.

UK hardiness zones

UK hardiness zones are less clearly defined than the more complex USDA hardiness zones, and are based on the ability of our garden plants, which are native to both temperate and subtropical regions, to withstand low temperatures. In the UK we generally term plants hardy to −15°C (5°F) the equivalent of a USDA zone 7 and 8, and these could be grown throughout all the UK. Frost-hardy plants are able to withstand frost down to −5°C (23°F), depending on the duration of the frost; this range can be equated to a USDA zone 9. Half-hardy plants can withstand temperatures below 0°C (32°F); this translates to zone 10. If direct comparisons between the USDA hardiness zones were overlaid across those for the UK, most of the country would fall into zone

8 with most of the coastal areas falling into zone 9. The coldest areas, like the extreme north of Scotland, would fall into a zone 7, but bear in mind we know from the previous section that hardiness is a much more complicated affair, and as such should serve as a guide only.

Another widely adopted form is the hardiness ratings used by the Royal Horticultural Society; these are based on plant types and where they will survive.

H1 plants require a heated glasshouse environment.

H2 plants require an unheated glasshouse environment.

H3 plants are hardy outside in protected locations of the UK, usually those in sheltered coastal or inland locations or in areas influenced by the Gulf Stream.

H4 plants are hardy throughout most areas of the UK.

H1 to H3 includes both frost tender and half-hardy plants that require winter protection but can be grown out-of-doors from spring to autumn in a frost-free location.

These ratings are used throughout a number of RHS publications. Other publications (*The Hillier Manual of Trees and Shrubs*, for instance) use a simple symbol to denote tender species that require protection in all but the most protected microclimates.

USDA and Canadian hardiness zones

North America has a myriad of different weather patterns and microclimates. The USA has long depended upon the USDA hardiness zone map, the most recent version of which divides North America into eleven hardiness zones, with zone 1 representing the coldest areas (often the furthest north or those where elevation or mountain ranges affect temperature) and zone 11 representing the warmest tropical areas, like Florida and California.

The map is widely used as a guide to hardiness in the USA, for both agricultural and amenity crops; a similar map, issued by the Canadian Agricultural Department, is available for Canada.

The USDA is working on a revision of the map (a draft 2003 version of which, developed by the American Horticultural Society, was briefly—but no longer— available on the AHS's Web site); it will have fifteen zones (to reflect growing regions for tropical and subtropical plants), four more than the current (1990) version (which appears at the end of this book). No release date is set.

USDA hardiness zones	Equivalent UK zones
zone 1: below −46°C (−50°F)	
zone 2: −46 to −40°C (−50 to −40°F)	
zone 3: −40 to −34°C (−40 to −30°F)	
zone 4: −34 to −29°C (−30 to −20°F)	RHS H4c: hardy through all eastern Europe and throughout most of eastern North America.
zone 5: −29 to −23°C (−20 to −10°F)	RHS H4b: hardy throughout most of the UK in areas where winter minimum is −24 to −20°C (−10 to −5°F).
zone 6: −23 to −18°C (−10 to 0°F)	RHS H4a: hardy in most low elevations, provided there is some shelter and winter minimum of −18°C (0°F).
zone 7: −18 to −12°C (0 to 10°F)	RHS H3: hardy in sheltered areas where winter minimum is −15°C (5°F).
zone 8: −12 to −7°C (10 to 20°F)	RHS H2: hardy only in the most sheltered areas of the UK where the winter minimum is −12°C (10°F).
zone 9: −7 to −1°C (20 to 30°F)	RHS H1b: requires cool glasshouse protection if temperature falls below −7°C (20°F).
zone 10: −1 to 4°C (30 to 40°F)	RHS H1a: requires glasshouse conditions.
zone 11: above 4°C (40°F)	

Heat zones

The ferocity of the summer sun can cause many garden plants to fail even if they are hardy to that zone. Whereas in the case of freezing, death and destruction of cells can be produced very quickly and are highly visible, the effects of heat damage are more subtle: overexposure to high temperatures can put a plant under severe water stress and can result in premature wilting, leaf scorch, a loss of vigour, and a reduction in disease resistance.

The AHS's heat-zone map is made up of twelve zones, each of which indicates the average number of days each year the area in question experiences temperatures above 86°F (30°C)—the point at which plants may suffer heat damage. The zones range from zone 1 (with less than one average heat day per year) to zone 12 (with more than 210 average heat days). The AHS's ratings assume that adequate water is supplied to the roots, as the accuracy of the heat-zone coding can be distorted by a lack of irrigation, even for a brief period of time. The heat-zone system is relatively new, and it will take a long time for many of our garden plants to be coded; still, it is slowly making its way into publications—not this one, however, as insufficient heat-zone information was available as I wrote.

Planting and Caring for Your Winter-Garden Plants

A properly planted and maintained shrub will grow faster and live longer than one that is poorly planted. This is especially important if you bear in mind that the most common reason shrubs or trees die in our gardens is that they were planted too deep. In such cases, the plant slowly suffocates from the root system upward—certainly not the way to treat your newly purchased prize possession.

Today we can buy our plants from various outlets—garden centres, mail-order catalogues, DIY (Do It Yourself) centres—but they come to us from these suppliers in one of only three ways. The most common and favoured way is containerised or pot-grown—most common because we can buy and plant at almost any time of the year, the exceptions being when the soil is frozen or waterlogged. Containerised plants allow for great flexibility: we can walk into a garden centre in the morning, collect our plant, and plant it within a matter of hours. Container-grown plants themselves are more flexible; their root systems suffer little damage as they are removed from the container, hence they establish quicker, so the survival rate is higher. The greatest restrictions of this method are the portability of the pots and the size of plant that can be grown in them. Container-grown shrubs range in size from very small plants measured in litres or gallons, which are relatively cheap, to large shrubs in massive pots. These are very expensive; specialised equipment is required to move them. Containerised material, again, is considerably more flexible and can be planted throughout the year; however, some periods are more flexible than others. Planting in late summer or early autumn, when the soil is still warm enough for active root growth, allows plants to establish new roots and settle into their location before winter arrives and the ground freezes. Some plants, however, such as magnolias, are best planted during the spring, as their root growth is only initiated at this time; planting in autumn simply kills large quantities of root area and slows their establishment dramatically.

A second way plants come to us is balled and burlapped (often called B&B). In this case, a shrub or tree has been grown in a nursery field, its roots balled and wrapped in a fabric to hold the soil together. Balled and burlapped plants are grown in a nursery soil and lifted when dormant, so this method tends more to be used for evergreens. These plants are less portable and tend to be larger in size. Generally larger shrubs are sold root-balled as they are cheaper than containerised plants; they grow quickly, but the drawback is that they can only be planted during their dormant season, normally November through March. Root-balled plants can have their planting season extended by burying the root balls in composted bark later in spring; such a practice is common place in the USA and UK.

Last are bare-rooted shrubs, which have a much shorter shelf-life and can only be sold or planted when they are dormant, as all the soil is completely removed from around the root system. This means that larger shrubs can be sold, and these are relatively cheap compared to the same size sold in containers or balled and burlapped. Bare-rooted shrubs are usually deciduous and require much higher aftercare, as they have little root system when planted. Bare-rooted material can only be lifted and planted during its dormant season, usually between December and February.

Root-balled or bare-rooted shrubs can be planted during late winter or early spring. On heavy soils, planting is best left to early winter, when the soil has drained and warmed up; on light soils that cool quickly in the autumn, planting is best done in spring as the soil warms again.

Planting shrubs

The most widely used and successful planting method currently is as follows.

1. Dig a shallow but broad planting hole, three times wider than the diameter of the root ball or container of the plant being planted but only very slightly deeper. Digging the soil in the area around the shrub encourages the roots to expand into the surrounding soil and greatly improves the plant's establishment.

2. Place the shrub in the hole and check to see if it is at the proper height for planting. This is essential: the height should be the same as the height at which it was grown in its nursery field, or to the top of its container. If the soil is free-draining, plant so that the height of the compost at the top of the container is at existing soil level; in poorly draining soils, plant the shrub slightly proud (raised above the surrounding area), to keep the roots out of the poorly drained soil. Doublecheck the height; plants will suffocate if planted too deeply. If you are unsure, it is better to plant the shrub a little high, 5cm (2in) above the base of the existing soil, and then allow the shrub and soil to settle. Just before planting, remove the container or the burlap material.

3. Fill the hole about one-third full with the surrounding soil and gently but firmly pack the soil around the base of the root ball. Continue adding and tamping soil until the shrub is planted.

Applying fertilizer at the time of planting is not recommended, as the root system is dormant and cannot take up any fertiliser. It is far better to apply slow-release fertilisers during the spring after planting. However, incorporating material impregnated with mycorrhizal fungi (naturally occurring, friendly fungi that help plants take up water and nutrients) can greatly enhance the rate at which your shrub will establish. A number of these products are available as soil additives or root dips and can be applied during planting. Studies have shown that shrubs and trees establish more quickly and develop stronger stems and roots if they are not staked; however, protective staking may be required to stop browsing animals or vandals, or in exposed sites. Stake large shrubs only if they fail to stand up on their own or they are at risk of being blown over by the wind. If you are going to stake, use a short stake driven in at a 45° angle, which will stop the root ball from rocking and ease establishment. Flexible rubberised tree and shrub ties are the best as they allow for stem growth without restricting the stems. Any stakes and ties used should be removed after the first year following planting.

Mulching will aid establishment, help retain moisture, and reduce weed competition, while ensuring a more stable soil temperature. The most commonly used form is composted bark, but leaf litter, pine straw, shredded bark, garden compost, or wood chips will also work. A 5 to 10cm (2 to 4in) layer is ideal; place the mulch around the shrub and extend out to the drip line of the shrub (the outer tips of the branches). More than this may cause a problem with oxygen and moisture levels within the soil and thus affect the root system. Mulch should not be piled up around the stems of the shrub as this can cause them to heat up and rot. Inorganic mulch mats can also be used.

Maintenance

For the first season or two, especially after a short period of especially hot or dry weather, watch your shrubs closely for signs of moisture stress. You can identify this by touching the foliage: if the leaves feel warm, then your plant is not transpiring and needs watering. Water the shrubs well and slowly enough to allow the water to soak in; this is best achieved early in the morning or late in the evening. Some species of evergreen trees may need protection against winter sun and wind; in such cases, wind protection can be applied by using a permeable windbreak or by spraying the foliage with an anti-desiccant.

Pruning

Pruning is usually not needed on newly planted shrubs apart from removing crossing branches or those damaged during planting. Lower branches may require pruning to provide ground clearance so that other plants can be planted below them; larger shrubs may need pruning to allow more light to enter the canopy. Small branches can be removed easily with secateurs; larger branches are best removed with a pruning saw. All cuts should be vertical and allow the branch collar to remain intact. Pruning is best done in late winter or early spring; during this time the shrub is less likely to "bleed," as sap is not rising. If this is not possible, then summer is another suitable time.

Regular pruning regimes to encourage flowering, fruit set, and stem colour can be undertaken once plants have established. Individual pruning requirements are discussed in more detail in the A-to-Z section on winter-flowering shrubs.

Variety within a winter planting is important,
as seen here with *Phormium* 'Maori Queen'
and *Mahonia aquifolium* 'Apollo', with *Cornus
sanguinea* 'Winter Beauty' in the background.

Designing for Winter

Many of us may already have winter plants in our gardens, and we may also feel that a good winter-flowering shrub may enliven our winter landscape, but all too often this is the only type of winter plant we focus on. I cannot recall how many times I have been confronted with winter designs that are little more than a coloured-stemmed dogwood, a handful of snowdrops, and a winter-flowering shrub thrown in for good measure. I am not advocating that everyone convert their entire garden area to focus on a single season (not even winter!), but instead suggesting that rather than a token winter-flowering shrub, some thought be given to the overall content and structure of our gardens in winter. Winter plantings must be visually stimulating and highly attractive; and they are relatively easy to create, if you have a strong eye for companion planting. To achieve this, a strong structure is required: when your winter shrubs are flowering, they are the stars, certainly, but they should be supported by a range of other nonflowering plants, including evergreen companion shrubs and groundcovers. Then as flowering treasures fade, other plants can provide interest and take over the mantle. Achieving a cohesive winter planting requires the use of plants for flower, fruit, foliage, and form, and these must provide value for money and work hard for their place, not only in the winter but also for the remainder of the year. Such additional values can include attractive bark or stems, scented flowers, and good autumn colour—and if they have good habit, then what a bonus. Not all our garden plants are such superstars, so they must be used wisely and interplanted with other plants that provide some of the other attributes we are searching for. It is worth remembering that winter gardening is not just about winter-flowering shrubs. They are an important and necessary element, but they are only a small part of the overall equation.

In a winter planting, the transformation between autumn and spring is important, so there should, if possible, be a succession of flowering within these periods. As a guide, a winter display must hold a percentage of different plants selected to highlight flower and scent; this percentage is relatively low, however, and may result in only 10 percent of the overall design. Likewise, attractive fruit-producing plants may hover around the 10 percent mark as well. The remaining 80 percent should then be carved up between plants with attractive stems or bark (30 percent) and evergreen shrubs and groundcovers, ornamental grasses, and winter-flowering bulbs (50 percent). Such a mixture provides the balance between the winter "spectacular" and the remaining seasons.

As with any other garden design project, thought should be given to how we intend to use the space, not only in winter but also for the remainder of the year. This is important as it is highly unlikely that we will sit in the garden in winter for any length of time; we are more likely to wander through the area. Although we will spend some time out-of-doors during the winter, in most climes it will be far less than we would in summer. This inability to spend prolonged periods of time out-of-doors means that we might want to extend a winter planting into an area which we can view from a frequently used room in our house, or site it near a resting place within the garden, like a covered seating area or summerhouse, or some other area where, if the weather permits, we can enjoy the beauty of the garden. With the introduction of gas-fired heaters, it is now possible to heat external areas like patios during late autumn or early winter; such areas are usually in close proximity to our home, so we can escape indoors quickly if the weather turns foul. Whatever the weather, we can quickly pop out-of-doors and snip some branches of our favourite winter-flowering shrub and retire hastily back inside. A wide variety of winter-flowering plants can be cut and forced indoors, filling our homes with their delightful scent. Witch hazels, daphnes, wintersweet, and winter box all last well indoors; winter-flowering viburnums and honeysuckles force well, but individual flowers last only a few days once cut. Quite wonderful winter displays can be achieved using coloured stems and evergreen foliage, with the occasional winter-flowering branch added in.

Dramatic effects can be achieved by illuminating the plants in our gardens at night. Uplighters or spot- or floodlights transform tree shapes, coloured stems, and architectural foliage plants, providing a focal or talking point. Mock-up some outside lights and run weatherproof extension cords around the garden to illuminate individual plants, and see what they look like as viewed from your favorite room in the house. Once you have settled on the best locations, you can consider installing a more permanent array of lighting. Low-voltage lighting systems are now more and more affordable and simple to install. Or even better, solar-powered lights are becoming more efficient and are moveable and easy to install.

Considerations of Design

Before we dive headlong into the garden and start madly selecting winter plants, it is worth considering a few fundamental elements that are essential when designing any garden space. Our gardens should be more than just a collection of individual plants. Regardless of how interesting the specimens are, a collection of the best and most highly attractive plants may not create a beautiful landscape; rather, it is our use of space and the plants we select to fill it that will transform our garden into the paradise we visualize.

I strongly believe that our gardens are an extension of our characters, places of relaxation, enjoyment, and mystery. Our plants mold and unite our garden by blending into and borrowing from the surrounding landscape, creating pleasing planting combinations, framing views, and casting our eye away from unsightly elements, like our neighbour's washing line or garden shed. Hard landscape features like pergolas, patios, seating areas, raised beds, and summerhouses can help us to hide or screen such views, while the plants link the hard landscaping features together, providing harmony in our gardens and highlighting seasonal changes.

Fastigiate trees like *Fagus sylvatica* 'Dawyck Gold' can be used to hide unsightly views and in themselves create focal points in the winter.

Any design should address what is in the realm of possibility for a given location, with consideration for climate and the native soils. We should begin with an analysis of the site, first to establish what already exists and then to decide which elements we are going to retain and which to remove. We should note things that we like, and things that we do not, keeping in mind how the area will be used, by all who will use it—the whole family, if necessary. Critical questions are our planned recreational uses of the space, ease of maintenance, wind and frost protection, views to enhance or hide, sitting areas, how the indoors will relate to the outdoors, sunny and shady locations, and so on. Again, it is not feasible to turn the whole garden into a winter planting, so a full-blown garden masterplan is not required; winter plantings may sometimes involve only a minor adjustment to an existing planting.

By the cunning use of trees, shrubs, herbaceous plants, evergreen groundcovers, climbing plants, and bulbs, a feeling of harmony within the overall scale of our garden can be achieved. Selecting the right plant for the

Strong contrasts are key in a winter garden. Here a groundcover bramble provides a foil for red-stemmed dogwood.

right location is imperative. Mistakes with herbaceous plants or small shrubs are insignificant, but poor selection of trees or large shrubs can be expensive, resulting in unnatural pruning in an attempt to fit a big plant into a small space, or worse, trying to relocate a semi-mature tree. The importance of researching your subject cannot be overemphasised. To truly inform yourself, go beyond the grower, garden centre, or nursery supplier to find a semi-mature specimen in a public or botanic garden. A garden designed for winter should be based on knowledge, not impulse.

Admittedly, the urge to indulge in the fine art of impulse buying is strong. Garden centres and nurseries have at their disposal a truly global and breathtaking array of plants to tempt us. Such a range inevitably fuels experimentation, and this is good—experimentation tests boundaries and brings contrast into our garden spaces. But a word of caution: experimentation requires a certain level of plant knowledge and must be firmly based on such parameters as how the plant grows, where it grows, and what it requires to grow. Above all, is it capable of adapting to our chosen garden landscape? We term this "the right plant in the right place," or "landscape utilisation" of plants. Such knowledge comes in large part with a combination of experience and experimentation, which makes our successes exhilarating and our failures lessons learned.

The Hillier Winter Garden

From 1991 to 2004 I was fortunate to work at the Sir Harold Hillier Gardens (formerly known as the Hillier Arboretum) in Hampshire, England. Working in the heart of this massive collection of more than 12,000 different woody plants, I became aware of how many could flower outdoors in an English winter—hardly surprising in a mild maritime climate, somewhere near the equivalent of a USDA zone 8 or 9—and there I was given the opportunity to lead the design and construction of a winter garden, a garden based on winter-flowering shrubs, with an eye to include architectural foliage, coloured stems, striking barks, and also fruits, and a supporting cast of evergreen groundcovers, ornamental grasses, and flowering bulbs.

The Winter Garden at the Sir Harold Hillier Gardens is one of the newest and largest dedicated winter gardens in the UK (just before my departure in March 2004, to join the National Trust, it was extended by another 0.2 hectare/0.5 acre, an increase in area to over 1.2 hectares/3 acres), and for me it was a dream come true to be involved in such a wonderful project. Chris Carter of the British landscaping firm Colvin and Moggeridge skillfully designed the layout (I say skillfully, because Chris had the additional task of coming up with a design that would have to hide or screen a large electricity pylon close to the garden's western boundary; this he did by bending the main lawn areas away from the pylon, encouraging a sight line along an east-to-west axis directed toward a focal point in the garden's centre). To develop all the planting designs was a real challenge that took well over a year, during which time I visited several gardens to gain inspiration; I also picked up ideas from less likely sources, like petrol station forecourts or people's front gardens. Often I would see a combination I liked and would simply adjust the plants to enhance a winter theme. Work on the garden started in December 1996 and was complete some eighteen months later; in total more than 650 species were used, in well over 750 different permutations of planting combinations.

My aim in creating the Winter Garden was to show visitors how rewarding and effective winter gardening can truly be. The garden, which displays plants for fruit, flower, foliage, form, and texture, is at its best from late October through to March. The carefully chosen site commands some excellent views of the surrounding countryside, and although relatively flat, the lack of mature trees nearby allowed for excellent penetration of winter sunlight as well as a touch of borrowed landscape.

The initial impression of the Winter Garden is striking. At its entrance are areas designed on such a scale that their central ideas can be replicated at home. But I was (and am) keenly aware that few gardeners can ignore large tracts of garden from one season to the next: the winter garden must therefore prove its worth year-round. So I planted for lasting effect; contrasts drove my designs. A typically intimate grouping: black mondo grass, *Ophiopogon planiscapus* 'Nigrescens', drift-planted in front of the wiry, ghostly stems of *Rubus cockburnianus* 'Goldenvale', both of which are hardy throughout the UK (zone 6). In late winter, pure white clusters of grape hyacinth (*Muscari armeniacum* 'Album') flowers appear through the black strap-like foliage, providing a further link to the white stems of the bramble. This white-on-black look is replaced in summer by an even more sizzling display: the palette changes to black-on-yellow, as the starkness of the white stems disappears behind golden yellow leaves, and the hyacinths disappear below ground.

I tried to select plants that displayed a range of features, like the hips or coloured thorns of roses, as well as those commonly associated with winter gardening, like scent and coloured stems. I used the ultra-hardy Himalayan rose, *Rosa sericea* subsp. *omeiensis* f. *pteracantha* (zone 6), in such a way that, when the sun shines through the thorns, they glow a gorgeous scarlet-red. This

Above: Winter sun was an important element in the construction of the Winter Garden at the Sir Harold Hillier Gardens.

Above: *Ophiopogon planiscapus* 'Nigrescens' and *Rubus cockburnianus* 'Goldenvale' provide a stark contrast in winter.

Right: In summer the mood heats up as *Rubus cockburnianus* 'Goldenvale' reveals its golden foliage.

Rosa sericea subsp. *omeiensis* f. *pteracantha* is attractive in flower, as here in June, but the true beauty of its thorns is fully revealed only in winter.

effect is so subtle that only by exploring the garden on a regular basis (not to mention standing exactly in the right spot) would you discover the sight.

A major concern was how to create a sense of unity within the garden. To achieve this I repeated groups of plants, focusing mainly on evergreen ground-covers, like ivy, vinca, and bergenias, interplanted with ornamental grasses, such as selected forms of *Miscanthus sinensis*, *Carex comans* (bronze sedge), and *Molinia caerulea* (purple moor grass), to give a linear or contrasting colour effect. I interspersed these areas with herbaceous plants, like hellebores, mondo grass, and liriope, and to introduce a seasonal display, I planted drifts of early-flowering daffodils (*Narcissus* 'January Gold', *N.* 'February Gold'), crocus, and snowdrops to pop up and then disappear through the patchwork of foliage.

My fondness for ornamental grasses grew, as did my knowledge and appreciation for this wonderful group of plants, and I continued to use them at every opportunity. Throughout the winter months, these plantings of ornamental grasses act like beacons to guide you through the garden, as their dried flower heads glow in the winter sun. At the entrance I used *Miscanthus sinensis* 'Malepartus' (zone 4), a bold group standing tall above the compact *Hebe albicans* 'Red Edge' (zone 8), which requires a protected location in the UK. This was proved highly effective as a bold start to the groups of trees planted for their winter stems.

I used the entire right-hand side of the garden to display birch trees grown for their winter bark. Although I mainly selected tree-like specimens with nice straight trunks (which we kept clear of side branches), I also included multi-stemmed, shrub-like specimens, which are more suitable for smaller gardens.

Long shadows and *Miscanthus sinensis* 'Malepartus', standing tall and lit up by the winter sun.

Throughout this area, I used groups and individual specimens. To achieve this vision of ghostly white stems drifting through the landscape, I used the Himalayan birch (*Betula utilis* var. *jacquemontii*), the Russian rock birch (*B. ermanii*), and the Chinese red birch (*B. albosinensis*). The aim of such a large planting was twofold: firstly to allow visitors to compare both stem colour and habit, but secondly, to create a powerful first image of the Winter Garden—the starkness of the stems, at their most naked in winter, against the different layers of planting. To maintain sightlines through the birches, I primarily used groundcovers. One was my old favourite, the butcher's broom, *Ruscus aculeatus*, with its stark, deep green, spiny foliage and bright red berries growing out of the leaf-like structures (which are in fact the flattened and modified

Striking groups of *Betula utilis* var. *jacquemontii*, drifting through the Birch Grove.

stems); this wonderful hardy British native is suitable for zone 7. Hybrid hellebores, *Helleborus ×hybridus*, provided late-winter flowers, while the Mediterranean spurge, *Euphorbia characias* in its various forms, produced contrasting silvery foliage in winter and yellow-eyed, greeny flower spikes in spring, as well as providing shelter and contrast for the black mondo and other lower-growing grasses. These were then punctuated (in appropriate places, where scent could build) by individual witch hazel shrubs and winter-flowering honeysuckle, *Lonicera fragrantissima* and *L. ×purpusii*; their scent was allowed to drift in areas of low air movement provided by the shelter of hardy bamboos and the stark stems of the coloured-stemmed dogwood *Cornus alba*. The Birch Grove is still developing as a feature, one that will define itself in maturity.

I continued the winter-flowering theme throughout the garden, with displays of both winter-flowering honeysuckles and viburnums, for people to compare. In pockets around the garden, delightful scents fill the air, as planted in a much bolder group is a stand of fifteen winter-flowering honeysuckles, *Lonicera ×purpusii* 'Winter Beauty'. I chose this location as it was in a heavy clay soil and situated in a windy corridor close to a seating area; although I would normally use scented plants only in a windless area, I decided to attempt to "blast" the sweet scent into the seating area by using the natural channeling effect of the corridor and the sheer number of shrubs involved. The gamble paid off, and the scent extends some 100m (330ft) into the shelter of the Winter Garden.

In the more protected southern side of the garden, I used stewartias (*Stewartia pseudocamellia*, zone 5), Himalayan cherries (*Prunus rufa* and *P. serrula*), and a collection of coloured-stemmed maples (*Acer tegmentosum*, *A. ×conspicuum*, and *A. griseum*). The winter-flowering viburnums I placed within 10m (30ft) of each other in three separate areas; again, I went for controlled scent in areas of low wind movement. In the dense shade nearby I used the Christmas box, *Sarcococca confusa*, situated close to a woodland path. I was often amused to see people heading straight for the viburnums (even though many of their flowers were damaged by frost) when they caught the scent of the winter box. I situated the parents of the hybrid viburnums so that comparisons could be made—and with the faint hope that possible improvements in the breeding line would be obvious.

I congregated a winter stem collection using the hardy Nepalese cherry, *Prunus rufa*, and the Tibetan cherry, *P. serrula* (zone 5). Both are ornamental trees grown for their winter bark effect (most certainly not for their flowers or autumn colour, which on both counts is poor). For those of us afflicted with shallow chalk soils, these trees may prove to be the best and only alternative to the Chinese paperbark maple, *Acer griseum*. Both are strongly tactile plants;

Chinese paperbark maple, *Acer griseum*, is one of the most ornamental trees for bark effect.

their fine bark is silky smooth and just begs to be stroked and polished—the best form of therapy for gardeners. The Tibetan cherry, *P. serrula*, is a quality winter-effect tree and has the most wonderful, mahogany-coloured, silk-like bark that shreds and peels in winter and hangs from the branches. Close to it I positioned its Nepalese relative *P. rufa*, which is similar in bark effect but vastly darker, almost a dark chocolate compared to the mahogany of *P. serrula*. The

Trees with shedding bark should be positioned so the bark is illuminated from behind, as here with *Prunus rufa*.

bark is also rougher, and shreds much finer. I trained and planted both single and multi-stemmed specimens and positioned them to be backlit by the winter sun, which transforms the shredding bark into strips of marmalade-coloured tinsel.

As to the display of flowering plants around these majestic trees, I threw caution to the wind and planted groups of the most profusely scented plants I could get my hands on. Nothing comes close to the Himalayan daphnes, *Daphne bholua*, when in full flower. In my view the best of its many forms is *D. bholua* 'Jacqueline Postill', which flowers from Christmas to March. It dominates its location, and easily out competes the nearby Christmas box, *Sarcococca confusa*. Although there are many other flowering shrubs here, this area of the garden is dominated by the brilliant stems of the maples. The most commonly grown maple for winter stem effect must be the Chinese paperbark maple, *Acer griseum* (zone 5). This delightful tree has the most wonderful, cinnamon to copper bark that flakes and curls as stems and branches increase in girth. It is not silky smooth like *Prunus serrula*, but it does have the most vibrant autumn colour. The best colour is produced primarily on acidic soils, although it will grow on deep fertile alkaline soils.

Throughout the winter garden I relied on witch hazels. Their flowers are bullet-hardy in the UK, guaranteeing that from late December until March the collection will have bloom, and so frost-resistant, they survive even the harshest winter weather, as in the cold night they curl down for protection. Many are scented, many are not. The most commonly grown yellow-flowered hybrid witch hazel, *Hamamelis ×intermedia* 'Pallida', reliably produces the largest amount of showy flowers of any witch hazel, and, as a bonus, produces a delightful scent that lingers in the winter air.

Hamamelis ×intermedia 'Pallida' remains the best of the yellow-flowering witch hazels.

Creating the Winter Garden really did open my eyes to the spectrum of plants available for winter planting, and although the numbers used were staggering, I believe I could easily have included more, without destroying the fabric of the garden.

Diversity of planting produced dramatic effects in the Winter Garden at the Sir Harold Hillier Gardens.

The Importance of Winter Sunlight

Winter sun is a critical element of winter gardening. Sunlight, no matter how often it shines, is a precious commodity in winter. Some countries have large quantities, whereas in the south of England it can be elusive, so capturing and utilising it is important. Sunlight focuses the eye on the subtle characters of plants and lights up the foliage caught by an early morning frost, if one is brave enough to venture outdoors to see it. Anyone contemplating a winter garden must consider this key external factor: the level and amount of winter sun that can penetrate unhindered into the landscape. Although winter-flowering plants themselves can easily increase the level of colour in the winter garden, winter sunlight simply transforms a garden and makes our plants look brand-new.

Sunlight illuminates and highlights foliage, adding to the excitement of winter gardening.

Prior to planting in your garden, it is worth familiarising yourself with the position and location of winter sun and how this changes throughout the day. Especially in northerly latitudes, the winter sun is very low on the horizon, making for long shadows and much backlighting when it is out. Evergreen ground-covers such as ivy (*Hedera helix*) and bergenias positively shine at such times, an effect made even more impressive if the foliage is covered in frost. Special consideration should be given to plants with flaking bark, which, when lit up, differs in colour to that of the stem—a subtle but breathtaking effect.

Winter sun emphasises the architectural foliage of ornamental grasses and linear plants like the tender New Zealand flax, *Phormium tenax* (zone 8). The use of ornamental grasses as complementary plantings is, in my view, an essential if somewhat obscure element of winter gardening; although the foliage may be dead, many forms of the Chinese silver grass, *Miscanthus sinensis*, hold their form long into winter. Leaving dead foliage and flowers provides a talking point. Nothing for me is more spectacular than the spent flower heads of ornamental grasses illuminated as the sun fades low on the horizon on a winter's day.

In short, winter-flowering displays are best located where they will capture some sunlight. Positioning a planting along an east-west axis will maximise sun penetration; however, in some situations this may not be possible, especially

The importance of ornamental grasses like *Miscanthus sinensis* 'Flamingo' to the winter landscape cannot be overstated.

when you are trying to establish a display within an existing mature planting. In such cases, it is worth exploring your options. Watch your garden throughout the winter and note the spots where the sunlight enters. Small pockets within the garden that get occasional sunlight for limited parts of the day, a sort of natural spotlighting, are also worth exploring. Areas that attract morning sun will be more prone to a quick thaw after freezing temperatures, which causes flower damage, especially to those with easily damaged petals like camellias, winter-flowering honeysuckles (*Lonicera fragrantissima*), winter-flowering viburnums (*Viburnum ×bodnantense*), and wintersweet (*Chimonanthus praecox*). In such places, use plants with more hardy flowers: witch hazels (*Hamamelis*), winter box, *Sarcococca*, or the cornelian cherry (*Cornus mas*), whose flowers are very rarely damaged by a quick thaw.

If sunlight is not a regular occurrence, then it may be worth using shrubs with larger flowers, as these will show up more, especially if an evergreen plant serves as a backdrop. Flowers that are highly scented also indicate their presence. Colour too is a consideration. For example, in a shady location, white-flowering *Camellia oleifera* would stand out far more than a red-flowering form like *C. sasanqua* 'Crimson King'. And in a shady location, with its slower temperature fluctuations, flowers would thaw more evenly and may not be damaged by frost. Likewise a yellow-flowering witch hazel like *Hamamelis ×intermedia* 'Pallida' will stand out more in the landscape than a red-flowering form such as *H. ×intermedia* 'Diane'—and if the yellow flowers are caught by sunlight, so much the better.

In shady borders, try using brighter flowering plants, like the elusive *Camellia oleifera*.

In very shady areas, where no sun ever shines, any attempt to use vivid flowering shrubs like the witch hazel will fail. In such conditions, use a more adaptable plant, like the oriental winter box, *Sarcococca orientalis*, whose small white flowers, obscured by the glossy green leaves, fill the air with scent in late December and early January.

Stem and Bark Effects

From a design aspect, the winter bleakness which most of us dread has an advantage. A feature unique to winter and often unappreciated is the lack of foliage on deciduous plants. Their naked silhouettes can be used as points of architectural impact, especially if one selects a plant with unusual branch configurations, colourful fruits—or patterned, peeling, or coloured stems and bark. Winter is clearly the best time to enjoy the great variety of hues and textures to be found among stems and barks.

Coloured winter stems and bark are wonderful assets in the winter landscape and can be used in many different ways: as a central focus to a planting scheme, as a contrasting colour for other plants, or—when planted in drifts—as a feature in their own right.

Only a handful of winter-flowering plants have the added benefit of attractive bark, with probably the most noticeable being the ultra-hardy Persian ironwood, *Parrotia persica*, whose flaking bark resembles a London plane (*Platanus ×hispanica*). The Persian ironwood also has exceptional autumn colour, but its downfall is its size, as it is a widely branching shrub to small tree, often wider than taller. Another good but again large shrub that flowers in the winter is the cornelian cherry, *Cornus mas*, which has interesting flaking yellowish brown stems. *Arbutus unedo*, again quite a large shrub or small tree, offers cinnamon-coloured flaking bark.

A number of medium-sized trees provide shade and privacy for our garden throughout the spring, summer, and autumn—and winter interest in the form of bark or stem colour. Probably the most commonly planted tree for this purpose

Arbutus unedo is noted for its attractive bark, which is silky smooth on younger branches.

is the birch. In the UK, and in areas of the USA where birch bark borers and sapsuckers are not a problem, few trees can rival the Himalayan birch, *Betula utilis*, for its outstanding beauty and grace. Hardy in the USA to zones 7 and 8, the Himalayan birch comes in many different variations of bark colour, ranging from ghostly white to copper-brown and dusky salmon-pink. Many forms have been named, and although they are relatively short-lived as a tree, seldom surviving over 150 years, they are quick to establish and grow.

Betula utilis var. *jacquemontii* can be used to create an eerie, ghost-like presence in the winter and spring landscape. Although these birches will tolerate alkaline soils, they are short-lived on very shallow soils and do far better on neutral to acidic soils, especially those that retain moisture during summer. I have many favourites for use in the UK and Europe, for example *B. utilis* var. *jacquemontii* 'Doorenbos', which has been sold on the Dutch market for a number of years. It is quite common in our landscape; it doesn't have the whitest bark of this group, but nevertheless it is a very pretty tree. 'Grayswood Ghost', a form with fantastic white bark, was selected from a tree growing at Grayswood Hill, Surrey, England. 'Jermyns' is the most vigorous of this group and will quickly make quite a large tree; it was selected by Sir Harold Hillier, of Hillier Nurseries, Hampshire, England, from plants he had received from Belgium. 'Silver Shadow' is the cream of this crop; it is smaller than all the other var. *jacquemontii* cultivars and has the whitest bark of any birch. It was introduced by Hillier Nurseries, from a selection grown at one of their nurseries.

Betula utilis var. *occidentalis* 'Kashmir White' is another exceptional form collected by Roy Lancaster in 1978 and selected for its striking white bark. Kenneth Ashburner, the National Plant Collection holder of *Betula*, selected *B. utilis* 'Ramdana River' for the same feature in 1991.

Betula ermanii, Russian rock birch, is one of my favourite birches for its graceful habit; it never quite reaches the stature of the Himalayan birch but is much more tolerant of heat and may survive in zone 5. It seems hardier than its Himalayan cousin, and its creamy white bark is a cinnamon-pink colour when first exposed. 'Grayswood Hill' originated from Grayswood Hill, Surrey, England, and has attractive white bark. 'Hakkoda Orange', with orange-white bark, was selected by Kenneth Ashburner from seed collected in Japan.

Betula nigra is among the best birches for damp soils and the very best for the USA where bark borers and sapsuckers are a problem, especially where other birches are overstressed by summer temperatures. A zone 5 tree, it is hardy throughout the UK. *Betula nigra* 'Heritage', the most widely sold river birch in the USA, has corrugated, creamy white bark and deep glossy foliage in the summer. 'Wakehurst', a British selection made from a tree growing at Wakehurst

Many birches with wonderful bark, as here with *Betula utilis* 'Ramdana River', are best grown multi-stemmed in the winter landscape.

Betula nigra Dura-Heat is a river birch selection with good stem colour and heat tolerance.

Place, West Sussex, UK, has orangey to creamy white bark. Dura-Heat, a form with exceptional white bark, was selected from a tree growing in the southern USA and seems to have the best heat tolerance of this group. 'Summer Cascade' is a new form with attractive white flaking bark and a strongly weeping habit, similar to *B. pendula* 'Tristis'—although in my view this American selection is far superior and of better constitution. It will be interesting to see how it performs in Britain and Europe.

Betula papyrifera is more widely seen in the northern USA, where it is their native canoe birch or paper birch. It is a large vigorous tree with white flaking bark. 'St George', a particularly fine selection made by Kenneth Ashburner, has white and tan bark colouration. 'Vancouver' is another Ashburner selection with multicoloured bark of brown, pink, and white and breathtaking orange autumn colour. All grow well in the UK and are hardy to zone 2.

Several smaller trees also have wonderful bark. These can be used either as intermediate trees, or, if grown and trained as multi-stemmed specimens, large shrubs. *Acer griseum* (Chinese paperbark maple) is the real gem of this group, and although it prefers acidic soils, it will thrive on all but the shallowest of chalk or alkaline soils. With flaking cinnamon bark and fabulous autumn colour, this is a tree for all seasons. Gingerbread, a hybrid between *A. griseum* and *A. maximowiczianum*, is intermediate between both parents; it is faster-growing than the paperbark maple and has good autumn colour, and although the bark is not as good, it will make a fine substitute where *A. griseum* cannot be grown. I believe this tree was selected from a plant raised from seed from E. H. Wilson's original introduction of *A. griseum* at the Harvard University's Arnold Arboretum, Massachusetts, USA. Seedlings resembled the Chinese paperbark maple but had different leaves, and it became obvious that this was a hybrid with *A. maximowiczianum* (*A. nikoense*). An interesting hybrid that grows well in the UK and seems as hardy as the Chinese paperbark maple, Gingerbread will thrive in zone 4.

The Chinese paperbark maple, *Acer griseum*, remains a favourite with garden designers for its winter appeal.

Acer pensylvanicum 'Erythrocladum' is another outstanding small maple with fantastic candy-pink new growth that gets more intense as winter approaches. Although it will only grow on acidic soils, it is a real showstopper and among the most attractive of the snake-bark maples (white striations mark the stem and smooth bark in such a way that they resemble snakes). This tree can be pruned in late summer to create a wonderful multi-stemmed effect. It is a woodland tree found throughout the Appalachian mountain range and is hardy to zone 3, but has little heat tolerance. *Acer ×conspicuum* is a group of maples with *A. pensylvanicum* and *A. davidii* as parents; the two most notable forms are 'Silver Vein' with white striations up the smooth green stem, and 'Phoenix', which has bright red winter shoots similar to *A. pensylvanicum* 'Erythrocladum'. *Acer rufinerve* 'Erythrocladum' is similar in all respects to the red-stemmed form of the Pennsylvanian maple and requires the same growing conditions. The so-called snake-bark maples are hardy in most areas of the UK and have little heat tolerance, but will thrive in light shade in zone 6.

The best Japanese maple for winter stem colour and a particular favourite of mine is *Acer palmatum* 'Sango-kaku' or the coral-bark maple (zone 5). The leaves, among the finest of any maple, turn a rich orange in autumn, and they fall to reveal crimson-red stems. This vigorous Japanese maple will grow in alkaline conditions but will not thrive on shallow chalk soils. One maple that will is the box elder, *A. negundo*. A recent introduction of this species, made by Pat McCracken, of McCracken Nurseries, North Carolina, USA, has pale yellow stems that are tinted white; it is aptly named 'Winter Lightning' and can be pruned into a multi-stemmed tree to produce the best stem colour. It may prove to be a spectacular winter tree, ultra-hardy, to zone 3.

Stewartia pseudocamellia Koreana Group is the best of this group of camellia relatives. In July, numerous pure white, yellow-centred camellia-like flowers are produced, and these are followed by orange, purple, and yellow autumn colour. The winter bark effect is exquisite, a camouflage pattern of orange and browns. Stewartias are restricted to zones 5 to 7 and thrive in many areas of the UK, but are best in woodland situations, where they have a cool, acidic soil.

Again, *Prunus serrula* (Tibetan cherry) and *P. rufa* (Nepalese cherry) offer spectacular bark. One of my favourites of the several clones of *P. rufa* is the form collected in 1973 by Roy Lancaster, under a Beer, Lancaster, and Morris (BL&M) expedition, in Nepal. Sadly, the Nepalese cherry is infrequently seen in our gardens, which is a shame, as it makes an excellent garden tree, albeit considerably less vigorous than its Tibetan relative. In areas where the Himalayan cherries will not grow, the Manchurian cherry, *P. maackii*, is much hardier. Instead of deep glossy bark, its bark is golden brown, and flakes. 'Amber Beauty' is a Dutch selection with amber-coloured bark and a more conical habit. All these cherries will thrive in any soil conditions, alkaline or acidic, sands or clays, and all make superb substitutes where many of the aforementioned maples will not grow.

If space is a premium and you are looking for something to complement your flowering shrubs while adding to your winter interest, then look no further than the coloured-stemmed dogwoods. *Cornus alba*, among the most widely planted

Cornus alba 'Sibirica' remains one of the better red-stemmed dogwoods.

of the coloured-stemmed dogwoods, is hardy throughout the UK and to zone 3 in the USA. It comes in a number of forms. 'Sibirica' has almost iridescent crimson-red stems; 'Sibirica Variegata' has similar stems but white and green variegated foliage that exhibits wonderful autumn colour. 'Ivory Halo' is a smaller variegated form from the USA, while 'Red Gnome' is even more compact, positively miniature in stature, but has green leaves. 'Aurea' carries the most charming yellow foliage throughout the growing season.

Cornus sericea (*C. stolonifera*) offers a different colour variation and includes two forms with green-yellow stems, 'Bud's Yellow' and 'Flaviramea'. 'Bud's Yellow' is said to have better resistance to canker in the USA. 'Hedgerow Gold', 'Silver and Gold', and 'White Gold' are forms with variegated foliage and yellow shoots. 'Cardinal' has orange-yellow shoots and green leaves, and 'Issanti', a more compact plant, has deep red shoots. *Cornus sericea* is native to eastern North America; all forms are hardy throughout the UK and can be widely planted in the USA to zone 2, although forms with yellow foliage may require protection from strong sunlight.

Cornus sanguinea is a common hedgerow plant in the UK, especially in the south of England. Although it usually has reddish purple stems, some forms have highly striking orange and red shoots along with exceptional autumn colour and good tolerance to chalk soils. Hardy throughout the UK and highly tolerant of alkaline soils, it is proving to be popular in the USA, where it is hardy to zone 5. Winter Flame, a selected seedling raised from open-pollinated plants of *C. sanguinea* 'Winter Beauty', has bright orange tips and red-based shoots. 'Magic Fire' has stem colour similar to 'Winter Beauty', which in turn seems the same as 'Midwinter Flame' but tends to have a suckering habit; their stems are

Cornus sanguinea 'Winter Beauty' is the best coloured-stemmed dogwood for alkaline soils.

yellow-orange throughout the year, then, in winter, the reddish tints intensify, producing almost a two-tone effect: yellow-orange at the base and red at the tips. All coloured-stemmed dogwoods look fabulous if planted in mixed groups—that is to say, incorporating forms with red, orange-red, and yellow stems.

A wide variety of ornamental brambles have a whitish bloom covering their purple stems, and these can look stunning in winter. *Rubus cockburnianus*, *R. biflorus*, and *R. thibetanus* have such eerie white stems, slender and arching and covered in aggressive thorns. Like all brambles, they will root from the tips, and new plants develop from them, so it is important to trim the tips during the summer to prevent their touching the ground. All these brambles are extremely rampant and quite large, exceeding 2m (6ft) in height. A real treasure is *R. cockburnianus* 'Goldenvale'; it is similar in many respects to the green-leaved type but less vigorous and much shorter, only 1m (3ft) tall, although it will still run. Its foliage seldom scorches in sunlight, and the colour intensifies during the summer months. *Rubus peltatus*, a compact Japanese species with white-over-purple stems, seldom exceeds 1m (3ft) tall; it is by no means as vigorous as those already mentioned. All the white-stemmed brambles are hardy in the UK,

Fantastic combinations can be created by using coloured-stemmed dogwoods and brambles, as seen here with *Cornus sanguinea* 'Winter Beauty' and *Rubus biflorus*.

Some brambles can be rampant, but *Rubus peltatus* is very well behaved.

but be warned: most will layer and cover large areas quickly. They are less widely used in the USA, to zone 6.

Coppiced willows (their colourful stems are cut down to the ground every year in late winter, unless otherwise stated) are grown in the USA, Europe, and the UK, where they are an especially popular winter-garden plant. All willows thrive in alkaline or acidic conditions but do best in moisture-retentive soils, and are best grown in full sun; too much competition from other plants causes stress, which can result in disease and a loss of vigour. *Salix alba* 'Britzensis', among the most widely grown of the white willows for its bright scarlet-orange winter shoots, is a vigorous form but does suffer from canker and anthracnose. *Salix alba* var *vitellina* has the most delightful bright yellow shoots, but it should be pruned every other year, as it is less vigorous. The violet willow, *S. daphnoides* 'Aglaia', is also worthy of note; it has silvery foliage throughout the year, crimson-red stems in winter, and is very vigorous. *Salix ×rubens* 'Basfordiana', a hybrid between the white willow (*S. alba*) and the crack willow (*S. fragilis*), has long been cultivated for its bright orange-red twigs and slender yellow catkins.

The most curious of the willows are the contorted or twisted hybrids of the white willow and the weeping willow, *Salix babylonica*. Most commonly used are the contorted forms of the weeping willow, mixed with the best stem variants from the white willow. *Salix ×sepulcralis* var. *chrysocoma* is a beautiful, often medium to large tree, with very long, twisted branches that are golden yellow in winter; it can be coppiced but is best grown as a standard tree. The vigorous 'Dart's Snake' is ideal for growing as a coppiced stem form, as the twisted dark green corkscrew-like stems make quite a feature. 'Erythroflexuosa' is the most widely planted of the coloured-stemmed twisted willows in the UK; its vigorous and highly twisted yellow-orange shoots are very eye-catching. The coxcomb willow has to be the weirdest of them all: *S. udensis* 'Sekka' exhibits fasciation, a disease that causes plant stems to be produced in such a way that the shoots elongate sideways to produce wide purple-coloured fan-like growth. In this willow some shoots become flattened and curl, and can be encouraged by hard pruning. All the willows mentioned are widely adaptable throughout the UK, especially where there is sufficient moisture in the soil during the growing season. In the USA experimentation is required; growing below zone 5 may be possible.

Evergreen Companion Plants

Winter is when coniferous or broad-leaved evergreens truly come into their own, as counterpoints and complements to the season's stark deciduous skeletons. Not only does their foliage bring colour, visual depth, and texture to the landscape, they also make useful windbreaks—sheltering our winter-flowering plants, slowing air movement, and allowing scent to build—and provide shelter and food to the birds and small animals they will attract to your garden.

Evergreens can simply be a presence in their own right; many imposing evergreens like the Japanese mahonia (*Mahonia japonica*, zone 6) are essential shrubs for any winter planting, as they not only produce scented flowers during November but also have strongly architectural foliage. As hedging, evergreens may be the interesting and necessary dark backdrop against which your other plantings will shine. English yew, *Taxus baccata* (zone 6), is ultimately the best for this purpose, although it is slow-growing and expensive to buy as large plants. Similar effects can be achieved with other hedging plants; privet (*Ligustrum ovalifolium*), western hemlock (*Tsuga heterophylla*, zone 6), common holly (*Ilex aquifolium*), and cherry laurel (*Prunus laurocerasus*, zone 7) are just a few of the many options available to us for this purpose.

Coniferous material is all too infrequently used in today's gardens. It is very much out of vogue—unless you happen to be a nursery producing thousands of Leyland cypress (×*Cupressocyparis leylandii*), now thankfully outlawed in the British Isles for use as a boundary hedge. Many people have a perception that all conifers are too big for their gardens and simply give them a stiff ignoring; on the contrary, many conifers are compact enough to take the place of a large shrub, right down to groundcover plants in size, and many of them have attractive foliage colour, which intensifies during the winter months or in response to cold.

The mountain pine, *Pinus mugo* is one such shrub. Its selections 'Ophir' and 'Winter Gold' are just two examples of dwarf conifers that could easily take the place of a hebe or small bun-shaped holly—with the added benefit of having foliage that turns a golden yellow in winter (zone 3). There is also an unparalleled supply of blue-foliaged conifers at our disposal. Forms of the Colorado white fir have been selected for their intense blue foliage; *Abies concolor* 'Compacta', if given a sunny spot, can attain shrub-like stature (2m, 6ft tall) and produces the most intense greyish blue foliage; a form of the Spanish fir, *A. pinsapo* 'Horstmann', is another blue form even smaller in stature than

Heathers make great companions for dwarf conifers, as seen here with *Pinus mugo* 'Ophir' and *Calluna vulgaris* 'Alexandra'.

'Compacta' (zone 6). And 'Golden Spreader', a compact form of *A. nordman-niana* (Caucasian fir) offering the most beautiful golden yellow foliage, may attain a height of over 2m (6ft) but is very slow-growing, retaining a conical habit (zone 4).

A wide number of evergreen shrubs can be used to create year-round interest in our gardens, or to screen out unwanted views or utilitarian areas. The Japanese spindleberry, *Euonymus japonicus*, is widely planted as it will tolerate a wide range of soils; its cultivar 'Chollipo', a particular favourite of mine selected by the Chollipo Arboretum in South Korea for its dark green leaves, which are banded yellow along the edge, is proving to be quite a strong-growing form that has good heat tolerance. *Daphniphyllum himalaense* subsp. *macropodum* (*D. macropodum*) is a wonderful foliage plant similar in appearance to rhododendron but without the showy flowers. The deep green leaves have a purple leaf stalk, and the foliage is arranged in a very attractive way; the mulberry-like flowers are fairly well obscured by the leaves and are followed by showy fruits. This surprising hardy evergreen shrub will tolerate a wide range of soils as well as high summer temperatures—so much so that it is becoming an increasingly popular landscape plant in the southern USA (zones 6 and 7), as well as being perfectly hardy throughout most of the UK.

One of the most valuable groups of evergreen plants in the UK, especially in the south of England, are the pittosporums. They are native to Australia and Southeast Asia and if subjected to high summer temperatures are surprisingly hardy (zone 9). Many pittosporums produce unusual-looking chocolate-coloured scented flowers, but they are mainly grown for their attractive foliage, which, if cut, will last a long time in floral arrangements. *Pittosporum crassifolium* and *P. dallii* are two of the hardiest of this group. *Pittosporum crassifolium* is a small to medium-sized shrub with long thick leathery leaves and deep purple flowers that are masked by the foliage. *Pittosporum dallii* by contrast is a much bigger shrub and may, if given the space, attain small-tree stature; it has long, toothed leaves and fragrant creamy yellow flowers during mid summer. For foliage the best of the pittosporums is *P. tenuifolium*, cultivars of which vary in size from medium to large shrubs, to compact bun-shaped shrubs. 'Garnettii', a hybrid between *P. ralphii* and *P. tenuifolium*, is the most widely grown foliage plant for the cut flower industry; it will attain large-shrub stature, and its leaves sport irregularly creamy white variegation over a green base that is flecked pink and red during winter. 'Tom Thumb' is a hardy, compact form with a height and spread of about 1 × 2m (3 × 6ft); each spring, its green new growth contrasts with its mature purple leaves, and slowly throughout the summer, the new foliage turns to purple. 'Purpurea' too has foliage that starts out green and then

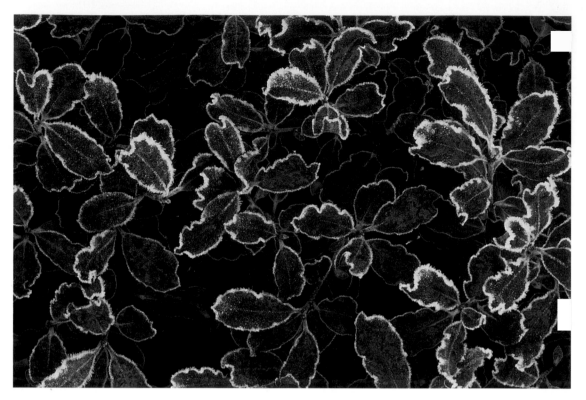

The intricate foliage of *Pittosporum tenuifolium* 'Tom Thumb' is highlighted by frost.

turns a deep rich purple; it is seemingly not as hardy as the green forms and reaches over 4m (12ft) tall. 'Warnham Gold', originated at Warnham Court, Sussex, England, is the best for winter colour: the young leaves emerge greenish yellow and then intensify to golden yellow.

Pittosporum patulum and *P. undulatum* are two species that should be more widely grown. *Pittosporum patulum* is a delightfully slender shrub, reaching 4m (12ft) tall, with dark crimson flowers in May; *P. undulatum* is similar in size and has very long, slender leaves with a markedly wavy edge. It too produces fragrant creamy white flowers in May but is less hardy than many covered here.

Aucuba japonica (spotted laurel) is a versatile evergreen that will tolerate quite dense shade and has seemingly disease-free foliage, and female forms produce large, bright red berries. 'Crotonifolia', a female selection, produces boldly spotted evergreen leaves and plenty of bright red berries during the winter; 'Golden King', a male version of 'Crotonifolia', seems to thrive better in deeper shade; 'Longifolia' has luxuriously long leaves that are bright green and again produces lots of berries; 'Hillieri', a very heavy-fruiting variety with long, deep green foliage, is worthy of consideration. Aucubas were widely used during the Victorian era as landscape plants; they are hardy throughout the UK but are restricted to zone 7 in the USA.

Several evergreen viburnums provide both interesting foliage and, throughout other seasons of the year, attractive and often scented flowers. *Viburnum calvum* is similar in many respects to laurustinus (*V. tinus*) and has hairy and wavy green leaves and white flowers during summer (zone 8). *Viburnum cinnamomifolium* is a fabulous foliage and flowering form native to China and resembling *V. davidii*, although it is much bigger in stature and will not take the same level of exposure. Its leaves are large and long but attractively narrow; in summer, quite large panicles of ivory-white flowers are followed by clusters of small black fruits (zone 7). A large and imposing evergreen—but unfortunately susceptible to deer damage. *Viburnum cylindricum* (zone 6) is another imposing evergreen that has the potential to grow quite large, almost to tree stature. The foliage is a silver-green and has a waxy surface, which, when drawn on with a stick or pencil, turns white; it is, in fact, possible to write your name carefully on the leaf. Its large clusters of white flowers are borne for most of the summer. Occasionally, new growth will be damaged by frost.

A more compact and incredibly hardy species is *Viburnum davidii*, probably the most widely planted of the evergreen viburnums (zone 7), a compact, well-behaved shrub whose attractive deep green foliage is characterized by three distinct veins running through the centre of the leaf. The small clusters of flowers that are borne during the summer are not the plant's best attributes, but the metallic blue fruits which follow are incredibly attractive. These plants often tend to be dioecious (unusually, it seems that some flowers have strongly male tendencies, others, female, making stripping out sexes difficult), so both sexes

Viburnum davidii is an attractive and versatile evergreen grown for its flowers, foliage, and fruits.

are required to produce a fruit set. Although a ratio of one male to three females is recommended, I have always got a much better fruit set by pushing the ratio of males higher. With its compact and bushy habit, this is one of the best viburnums for landscape planting. In 1964 Hillier Nurseries introduced an accidental hybrid between *V. calvum* and *V. davidii* from seed collected from a plant of *V. davidii*; this new hybrid, *V. ×globosum* (zone 7), originated at their West Hill Nursery, Near Winchester, England. It is almost intermediate between both parents, retaining the height of *V. calvum*. The original plant still exists at the Sir Harold Hillier Gardens and is now well over 2.5m (8ft) tall, forming a very symmetrical dome as wide as it is tall. In leaf it is vaguely reminiscent of *V. davidii* but smaller and having the curious habit of twisted foliage. Small off-white flowers are produced in distinctly flat-topped clusters in spring but often at other times of the year. Small blue-black fruits follow in autumn, but these are in no way as showy as those of *V. davidii*.

I have always had a soft spot for *Viburnum propinquum*. Although it is not one of the hardiest of this group (zones 7 and 8), its habit always reminds me of an evergreen and compact version of *Cornus alternifolia*, and I imagine that with a bit of judicial pruning it would be quite easy to accentuate the layered habit of its branch structure. A delightful species, similar in many ways to *V. davidii*, it has glossy green, three-veined leaves, greenish white flowers, and blue-black fruits in the autumn, and requires a semi-woodland habit, as the foliage is susceptible to wind and frost damage.

Viburnum rhytidophyllum (leatherleaf viburnum) is my least favourite: I have searched my soul for reasons to like this popular shrub, with no success. Though it is often listed as a wonderful, even distinguished landscape plant, I just can't see it. To me, it is a scruffy large-growing shrub with horrid-smelling flowers during summer; if you plant the opposite sex nearby, it will produce oval red fruits, which finally fade to black. I can think of another twenty viburnums I would rather use. The pink-flowering 'Roseum' is slightly more interesting, but 'Variegatum' is just hideous—its variegation looks like bird droppings! I would have to be paid a lot of money to include this plant in my winter garden, but if you are looking for a large, bold viburnum with corrugated foliage, then this is for you.

Plant shapes can look different in different conditions, as seen here with *Mahonia ×media*, its bold foliage highlighted by snow.

Plants with Presence and Attitude

I have always enjoyed using plants as living sculpture, and in the winter setting—where strong shapes are a bonus in the landscape—a plethora of plants can be used for this purpose. The main criterium to be filled: they must have a strongly architectural shape or form. This strong form can be put down to much-defined linear lines or habit, as with weeping or strongly fastigiate growth, and winning plants may even have, in addition to strong shape or form, very bold foliage, or massive leaves. They differ from plants covered in the previous sections in that they are used predominantly to punctuate the landscape. Large ornamental grasses are a very good example of this: during spring their new, strongly linear foliage develops; in summer and autumn dramatic plume-like flowers appear and, over time, fade and change colour; and finally in winter they have sufficient strength to hold dead foliage intact until early spring.

The most commonly grown of these grasses, Chinese silver grass (*Miscanthus sinensis*), is a startling punctuation point in any winter landscape. Plants are especially attractive once the foliage and flower heads have died, and they are caught by a winter frost. It is important that you control the urge to cut down the foliage in late autumn, while you are tidying up the garden in preparation for winter. Leaving the dead foliage intact until spring maximises this effect.

Most cultivars of and hybrids involving *Miscanthus sinensis* are incredibly gardenworthy. Each year as I check through the *RHS Plant Finder*, I find that a long list of new forms has been added to what was already a massive list. Many of the most commonly grown forms were raised in northern Germany during the 1970s by Ernst Pagels, a former pupil of the great grass-gardening pioneer, Karl Foerster. Pagels used *M. sinensis* 'Gracillimus' as the basis of his hybridization program; his aim was to raise new forms that would flower profusely, hold their form and flowers over a long period, and have attractive foliage, and his success can be seen throughout our gardens. Ornamental grasses are increasingly popular; new hybrids are still being introduced from Germany, North America, and the UK, which just goes to show the impact ornamental grasses have had as worthy landscape plants. Now widely incorporated in landscape designs, they are ultra-hardy in the UK and thrive in zone 4, although hardiness will vary from cultivar to cultivar.

Miscanthus foliage is various, from deep luscious green, to white variegation in the centre of the leaf or on its edge, to yellow-banded and even some red-tinted blades. Height too can vary, from 0.5 to 4m (1.5 to 12ft), and both autumn colour and flower colour are important considerations. The following is a small selection of those grasses I have enjoyed growing over the years.

Though it is not the tallest, *Miscanthus sinensis* 'Morning Light' should not be left off of anyone's list, and if space is a premium, then this is for you. It is a small-growing, incredibly slender-leaved form, seldom reaching more than 1.5m (5ft) in height; the foliage, with its very narrow variegated band, gives it an almost silhouette-like appearance in the landscape. *Miscanthus sinensis* var. *condensatus* 'Cabaret', an impressive plant growing up to 2m (6ft) tall with arching foliage, is a vastly different beast, with bold variegated stripes up the centre of its quite wide leaves. Taller yet at more than 3m (9ft) and with exceptional variegated foliage, *M. sinensis* var. *condensatus* 'Cosmopolitan' is a good doer in the UK climate. If these are too tall, then search out *M. sinensis* 'Rigoletto', which at 1.2m (4ft) is a much more manageable affair. There are also an increasing number of banded forms, similar to *M. sinensis* 'Zebrinus', which are called the zebra grasses. *Miscanthus sinensis* 'Zebrinus' itself is a very bold grass, long cultivated for its yellow-banded foliage and good flowers during the autumn; it is tall, 2.5m (8ft) in height, and with age can spread to make quite an imposing plant. *Miscanthus sinensis* 'Hinjo' is smaller, seldom growing to more

Miscanthus sinensis 'Morning Light' is a great Chinese silver grass for general planting.

Miscanthus sinensis 'Sarabande' dominates the winter landscape.

than 1.2m (4ft) and having the widest zebra banding of this group. *Miscanthus sinensis* 'Kirk Alexander', a form I came across in Georgia but hadn't seen in the UK, seems the best suited for the US market; it is 1.5m (5ft) tall with delightful foliage, but how it will do in the cooler climate of the UK is unknown.

The flowering forms are my favourite, as it is the dried flower heads that give them the edge in the winter. *Miscanthus sinensis* 'Sarabande' is one of my all-time favourites with its dense foliage, columnar growth habit, and open-plumed flowers, which are less dense than many other forms. It flowers during early summer, often partnering *M. sinensis* 'Malepartus'; both flower for a long period and are of similar height, around 1.5m (5ft) but with flowers to around 2m (6ft). The flowers then persist long into winter, and both give an excellent account of themselves with their foliage beginning to break up in late winter. Slightly taller is *M. sinensis* 'Grosse Fontäne' ("big fountain") with its silver-streaked central-veined foliage and its broadly open, silvery flower heads—a dramatic sight in the winter and a real eye-catcher the rest of the year.

For my final selection, I have chosen a couple of Chinese silver grasses that simply by their presence make some of the largest and most dramatic statements within the winter landscape. In the UK, the aptly named *Miscanthus* 'Giganteus' grows to what can only be described as an obscene height (3.5m, 11ft) with a robust habit that occasionally requires some human intervention to stop it from blowing over. Amazingly, during a heavy rain it will flop almost flat, but correct itself once dried. An imposing grass and a sight to see in the garden, especially during winter. *Miscanthus sacchariflorus* is a slightly shorter (3m, 9ft) monster and is more common than its taller relative. It flowers reliably, and the arching blooms are a delight. Grasses of this nature are not for the fainthearted, however, and in a normal suburban garden would look grossly out-of-scale.

As a group of ornamental grasses, Chinese silver grasses are unrivalled, but a word of caution here: I have been growing them for more than ten years, and up until recently seedlings were few and far between. But with the influx of new forms, I have noticed seedlings springing up everywhere—I am not sure why. Maybe it has something to do with warmer temperatures in the south of England, or possibly someone has inadvertently introduced a particularly fertile male form. One thing I know for sure is that these grasses are now seeding aggressively into parts of the garden. I was even more alarmed, when travelling through the Blue Ridge Mountains in North Carolina, USA, to see seedling miscanthus grasses appearing everywhere—not by the hundreds, but in the millions—and I am informed that this grass is on invasive weed lists in many states, particularly in the Mid-Atlantic and Southeast.

Pampas grass, *Cortaderia*, is a much coarser presence in the landscape, and lately it is less frequently seen (reminds me somewhat of dated park plantings or once-in-vogue mix-planted island beds). New Zealand pampas grass, *C. fulvida*, is among the most awe-inspiring of this group. It also happens to be the largest, with strongly arching leaves reaching up 1.5m (5ft) tall, and unlike the typical pampas blooms, these are heavily weeping, giving a more shaggy effect. The colour of the flower heads, which can persist long into winter, varies from rich flamingo-pink to white. One peculiar habit is that large swaths of foliage die for no apparent reason during summer, which may be an indication that the soil is too dry, as this species thrives near water. The more traditionally grown pampas grass, *C. selloana*, is all too familiar to us, and its effect in the winter landscape—its massive plumes swaying in a winter's breeze or being weighed down by a heavy frost—cannot be overstated. Planted en masse they are breathtaking, but how many of us have the space to do this? Fortunately they look equally dramatic planted singly, as accents. Foliage-wise they are not the most attractive of the ornamental grasses, but their plumes are certainly among the most spectacular. Most are very hardy in the UK but are considerably less hardy in the USA, where they struggle in zone 7 or lower. Plants of the pampas grasses are either male or female; most of the best-flowering forms are female, and where both sexes are present seedlings will start to appear. It is from such encounters that new forms have been raised. *Cortaderia selloana* 'Monstrosa' is an imposing plant, and although its lax foliage reaches 1.5m (5ft) its massive flowering plumes stand bolt upright, to an impressive 3m (9ft). If this seems somewhat scary then there is a more compact form to hand: *C. selloana* 'Pumila'—with pure white featherduster-like flower heads that seldom go beyond 2m (6ft) in height and mounded foliage to 1m (3ft)—is for those of us with less space. There are also a number of white and gold variegated leaf forms. *Cortaderia selloana* 'Gold Band' produces an attractive mound of golden hues throughout the year, and American introduction *C. selloana* 'Sunstripe' has a distinctive golden band down the middle of the leaf. Both develop mounds of 2.5m (7.5ft) tall foliage and 3m (9ft) flowers and would make attractive companions for purple- or bronze-foliaged plants. The variegated and golden-leaved forms are less hardy than other pampas grasses but worth trying where heat may improve their hardiness.

Spanish oat grass, *Stipa gigantea*, is another favourite that I have enjoyed growing on the shallow chalk soil of my home garden, where it flowers in early April. The foliage stands to 75cm (30in), and from it rise open-headed plumes, with golden yellow seed heads, to 2m (6ft). This display is seldom rivalled by

Molinia caerulea subsp. *caerulea* 'Variegata' with *Calluna vulgaris* 'Con Brio'.

any grass, much less by any other herbaceous plant. It is not only a useful garden plant when in flower, but the flower heads dry naturally and persist long into winter. As its common name suggests, this oat grass will thrive in very dry locations and is among the best grasses for chalk soil. Hardy throughout the UK and to zone 8 in the USA.

One stunning grass combination that I use for late autumn, early winter colour is variegated moor grass, *Molinia caerulea* subsp. *caerulea* 'Variegata', in the company of *Calluna vulgaris* 'Con Brio'; the two complement each other perfectly, the golden yellow foliage of the grass providing a foil for the maroon flowers of the heather.

Several other ornamental grasses can be used in the winter landscape. The switch grasses, *Panicum virgatum*, have been widely used in the USA for many years; they are a native prairie species grown for foliage and flower, to 1m (3ft) tall, and they are increasingly available in the UK. Some of the best for blue-grey foliage are *P. virgatum* 'Heavy Metal', 'Cloud Nine', and 'Blue Tower', to 2m (6ft) tall, while 'Squaw', 'Strictum', and 'Warrior' grow to around 1.5m (5ft) tall and have beautiful purple-tinted open flower heads and yellow foliage in autumn. All switch grasses are hardy in the UK and are a zone 5 plant in the USA.

Bamboos represent excellent value for money in our gardens, and if you select the right species, especially those that are clump-forming and do not run, you will be rewarded with wonderful cane colour and attractive foliage. Many people have the misconception that all bamboos are highly invasive plants that can tear your house down and rip through concrete. On the contrary, a number of more well-behaved members of this group are hardy and will tolerate a wide variety of conditions, including quite shallow chalk soils, and will not tear up your yard.

Phyllostachys is one such bamboo. Some species in the genus are invasive, but the ones listed here are tried and tested both in the UK and USA; given sufficient wind protection in winter, most should be hardy in the UK, and in the USA, experimentation in zones 6 to 8 should provide the best results. All are best viewed if the lower foliage is removed to a height of 1m (3ft), so that the culms (canes) can be easily seen, and all have easy-to-sever culms. The black bamboo, *P. nigra*, has deep black stems that may reach 4m (12ft); it is a widely arching species that is very well-behaved in the garden. Where I have encountered it in North Carolina and Georgia, *P. aureosulcata* 'Spectabilis' has wandered around, but in the UK the tendency is minimal. To avoid competition, this and other bamboo species produce underground shoots that grow through the soil and allow new canes to develop away from the main plant; their spreading habit can be curtailed by cutting off the farflung shoots as soon as they emerge above ground, cutting close to the parent plant with a garden spade. The spreading of

Phyllostachys aureosulcata
'Spectabilis' fronted by
Cornus alba 'Sibirica
Variegata'.

Phyllostachys vivax f.
aureocaulis has wonderful
golden yellow culms.

P. aureosulcata 'Spectabilis' is slow and easy to control, and it is also one of the easiest of the golden-caned bamboos to grow. It will thrive on even the shallowest of chalk soils, as long as its root system is kept moist throughout the year, especially during the summer—easy enough to achieve if the plants are well mulched during spring and summer. Organic matter will allow for the production of thicker culms, especially if farmyard manure is used. The canes of *P. aureosulcata* 'Spectabilis' are bright yellow, with a green stripe running up the culm; in spring, the emerging shoots are flushed candy-pink.

Phyllostachys bambusoides is aptly called the timber bamboo for its size in Japan and the USA, where canes over 20cm (8in) in diameter can grow over 25m (75ft) tall—extraordinary growth when you consider that they do this in just one season. The canes are harvested for fences and other ornamental features, and although while living the timber bamboo is useful for screening out unsightly buildings or views, it is not overly attractive as far as the colour of its canes goes. Still, some of its forms are truly beautiful. 'Allgold' is a compact form with the most delightful golden yellow culms; like most bamboos in this section, the foliage is quite fine and so casts little shade. 'Allgold' is more vigorous than *P. aureosulcata* 'Spectabilis', and the canes are thicker and more yellow. *Phyllostachys bambusoides* 'Castillonis' is a much more graceful affair, with slightly arching stems and airy variegated foliage; the cane is golden yellow and has a green stripe up the nodes on the stems.

Phyllostachys vivax f. *aureocaulis*, a compact but strong-growing form with erect golden yellow canes that are striped yellow, is similar in many respects to *P. bambusoides* 'Allgold', although 'Allgold' only occasionally has green stripes up the stem. All bamboos with ornamental canes should have the canes thinned each year; simply remove the thinnest canes once all the new canes have fully extended in late spring.

Not all plants with bold foliage are grasses or bamboos. Numerous shrubs are available for this purpose, some evergreen and some deciduous. The strongly architectural foliage of the mahonias is unsurpassed in the winter garden, and many announce the season's arrival by flowering in early winter, their bright yellow, sometimes scented flowers dangling down from the centre of the foliage like golden jewels (see the A-to-Z section for more on these versatile landscape plants). The sacred bamboo (*Nandina domestica*), a close relative of mahonias, is much more delicate, both in overall appearance and also in leaf and flower. It is very much like a compact bamboo but with much prettier, feathery foliage that produces purple-red flushes in autumn and spring, and showy panicles of white flowers in summer; very decorative red berries are produced regularly in warmer climates but only occasionally in the UK. Sacred bamboo requires protection in our climate, but it is an important landscape plant in the USA, where numerous forms are grown for habit, foliage, and fruit. Driving around the southern USA, I've encountered these plants in all kinds of situations. The dwarf form is a key element in every McDonald's landscape and is present at seemingly every shopping mall; the larger forms are ever present as garden shrubs, growing in full sun or shade, and I have seen many with "car stopping" ability when in fruit, their crimson-red berries dripping from the foliage like some kind of blowsy Christmas decoration. It is a far more impressive plant in the USA, where they will thrive in zones 6 to 9 or 10; but in the UK it is usually restricted to southern gardens, and it is often only here that they flower well.

In the UK a few pretty, dwarf forms are grown; they seldom flower but have purple foliage throughout the year. *Nandina domestica* 'Fire Power' is the better plant: it retains it purple foliage better than the similar 'Nana Purpurea'. 'Wood's Dwarf' has been around in the USA for a long time but is seldom seen here, which is a tragedy as it is very compact and has fantastic winter colour of a rich purple-red; selected by Ed Wood, of Oregon State University. In the USA *N. domestica* Gulf Stream is one of the most widely grown of the compact forms, reaching 1m (3ft); its foliage is occasionally tinted red but intensifies as autumn and winter approaches into a rich scarlet-red. 'Harbour Dwarf', a close second to Gulf Stream in the marketplace, is another compact form with rich blue-green foliage throughout the spring and summer, lots of flowers and fruits, and red-tinted foliage in winter. 'Alba' is an interesting form with off-whitish, creamy yellow berries; it is similar in all respects to the straight species and is often listed as 'Aurea' or *N. domestica* f. *leucocarpa*. Until a hardy form is trialed for the UK market, these will never make their way into our gardens as bread-and-butter plants, alas, but will remain novelty plants for expensive landscapes made up of metal and decking.

Aralia elata (Japanese angelica tree) and *A. spinosa* (devil's walking stick, Hercules' club) might seem odd introductions to this "presence and attitude" section, but for me this is winter gardening at the extreme. Both species are highly adaptable to a wide variety of soils, and both have massive but deciduous tree fern–like leaves and large, bold clusters of terminal white flowers in late summer. *Aralia elata* flowers in the autumn and has almost spineless stems, while *A. spinosa* flowers in summer and is in berry in autumn, and has spiny stems. Both will produce suckering stems up to 4m (12ft) tall and are hardy throughout the UK, suitable for zones 4 and 5, although the champion Japanese angelica tree in the UK is over 8.5m (25ft) tall. Their winter impact is their naked, spiny, branch-like stems that look like they have been stabbed into the ground randomly by an angry giant, creating a fascinating talking point.

Aralia elata, its giant stems standing naked against the winter sky.

Fatsia japonica, by contrast, is a bold-foliage evergreen shrub native to Japan that is often found inhabiting north-facing courtyards, where protection from winter wind and freezing temperatures is at the highest. Thriving in such areas in the southern half of the UK and hardy in zones 8 to 10 in the USA, this plant will illuminate any dark courtyard with its glossy green palm-like foliage and creamy white flowers during late autumn. These are followed by small black fruits similar to that of ivy, its close relative. *Fatsia japonica* 'Variegata', with white-streaked and -edged foliage, is a much more appealing plant, although both are often at the top of a deer's menu. If uneaten they can grow to almost tree-like proportions, 4m (12ft) tall and equally wide, and will develop quite thick stems.

This covers only a small number of the grasses, bamboos, and shrubs that I like to use for presence and attitude; others, of course, can punctuate the winter garden, but alas, space limits their inclusion here.

Plants with Fruits

Berries, nuts, and fruits are often associated with autumn, the season of mellow fruitfulness, a time when a breathtaking array of fruits ripen, providing a feast for wildlife. Although many fruits are gobbled up quickly, some remain deep into the winter and will remain for our pleasure occasionally into the spring. Fruits come in a spectrum of colours, many of them vivid and most unusual in the plant world, from acrid yellow to metallic blue, from porcelain to the more traditional reds, yellows, and oranges. Some fruits are edible, others are not, and they are borne variously on trees, shrubs, and herbaceous plants and climbing vines.

All-time favourites of mine and an excellent value for the money are the beautyberries or beautybushes, *Callicarpa*. Most forms grown in the UK are native to China, Japan, Korea, and North America, excepting the American native *C. americana*, which is not widely planted here—a shame, as I first saw this wonderful shrub in full yellow autumn colour, its bright violet, tinted purple berries borne in dense clusters along the stems and weighing down the branches. I can only assume that they are not widely used in the UK because they are not widely known, or possibly because they do not fruit well. In the USA they are hardy in zones 7 to 9 and fruit very well indeed, although the birds strip the fruits in early winter. A white-flowering form is also grown, and I have seen some poor specimens in botanic gardens in the UK that do not do it any justice: the marble-white berries of the forms I've seen in the US are almost iridescent in the landscape. Like most beautyberries, they are best grown in groups to ensure a strong fruit set.

Callicarpa americana fruits heavily in the USA but, alas, not in the UK.

Callicarpa bodinieri var. *giraldii* 'Profusion' is a much safer option for the British climate.

Widely cultivated in the UK is the prolifically fruiting *Callicarpa bodinieri* var. *giraldii* 'Profusion', which many people suggest is self-fertile as it will produce large quantities of berries even if planted singly. Hardy to zone 6, it will thrive in a variety of locations and soils, including chalk, and will reach over 2m (6ft) tall. It is somewhat of a straggly-looking shrub unless pruned regularly to maintain a more compact habit. Undertake pruning after flowering. Shoots can, if required, be cut to within 30cm (12in) from the floor; if this is too aggressive, remove the oldest stems regularly to maintain a more balanced shrub. In July the flowers of the beautyberry are also a talking point. The largest are found on the Japanese form, which also has the largest leaves: *C. japonica* var. *luxurians* initially shows lots of promise, but big flowers does not mean big fruit, unfortunately; and although fruits are numerous, they are quite small and also very pale (but nevertheless still violet). These small, unusual-looking fruits, with their obscure colour, are not recognised by migrant birds as food; they therefore persist long past the rose-flushed, yellow autumn leaves and will remain attached until dislodged by several frosts. Both the violet- and white-berried (*C. japonica* 'Leucocarpa') forms are quite compact, seldom exceeding 2m (6ft) tall, and do, if interplanted with each other, look quite wonderful.

Staying with the theme of unusually coloured berries, one of my favourites is *Cornus amomum* not only because of its metallic blue berries but also for its deep purple-red stems. This North American native can reach quite a large size, 4m (12ft) in height, and is so widely arching, it is often wider than tall. Although less planted than the other coloured-stemmed dogwoods (*C. alba*, *C. sanguinea*, and *C. sericea*) and not often seen coppiced, it can be equally attractive if it is pruned hard. Its stem colour is darker and purpler than *C. alba* but nevertheless appealing; its white flowers, like those of its close relatives, are unattractive, but its berries make a fine display and contrast well against the stems and the yellow autumn leaves, particularly in the UK. A hardy dogwood suitable for growing throughout the UK, and hardy in zones 4 to 8 in the USA. Many other dogwoods have attractive berries, although they do not persist into the winter; *C. alba* 'Sibirica Variegata', for instance, produces delightful purple autumn tints that contrast with its white berries.

The spindleberries (*Euonymus*) are a very useful group of shrubs for those of us who are not fortunate enough to have acidic soils. They are hardy throughout the UK (zones 6 to 8) and represent good value for your berry money as they often have good foliage colour and interesting seed capsules to boot. *Euonymus grandiflorus* is an absolutely delightful shrub from the Himalayas and China; its semi-evergreen foliage, which turns a rich wine colour during the autumn, is complemented by pink capsules which split to reveal bright scarlet fruits. A large-growing shrub, to about 3m (9ft) tall and wide, and suited for alkaline or chalk soils, it is one of the best spindleberries I have ever encountered and, in my opinion, is far too infrequently seen in our gardens. A close second must be *E. europaeus* 'Red Cascade' (zone 3) with its masses of rosy-red fruits that, considering their small size, are produced in such abundance that they seem to weigh down the foliage, which in autumn turns a rich scarlet-red. A delightful sight even after the foliage has fallen, and the fruits remain long into winter.

If vivid fruits are your calling, then why not try the blue-fruiting elderberry? *Sambucus cerulea* is native to North America, where it grows as a large, wide shrub with long, arching branches. If this habit is not to your taste, then it can be pruned on a three-year cycle down to a smaller framework. The massive heads of blue-black fruits, dusted with a white bloom, follow the large heads of off-white flowers in autumn. Like our native elderberry, *S. nigra*, the fruits of this species can also be used for jelly and jam making, and for a very distinctive wine or cordial. This useful and adaptable medium-sized shrub will grow in a variety of locations and soil types and is hardy throughout the UK and in zones 5 to 7 in the USA.

The genus *Cotoneaster* also contains some amazing fruiting gems, both trees and shrubs of all shapes and sizes. Some have been tarnished with the fireblight brush, but many will give hours of hassle-free pleasure. The first batch I've selected can be grown on a single stem, and although this effect does take some maintaining, it is worth the effort; these can be used as substitutes for trees in a small suburban garden, if their foliage is lifted to such a level that it allows for underplanting. These imposing shrubs reach over 4m (12ft) tall and often as wide, and in autumn and winter the branches are heavy with the masses of fruits. *Cotoneaster* 'Cornubia' can reach up to 6m (20ft) tall and has semi-evergreen foliage, which during autumn is weighed down by polished, blood-red fruits that adorn the branches like clusters of rowan berries, forcing the branches to arch even more. A wonderful introduction in 1930 by Exbury Gardens, Hampshire, England, and of unknown parentage, *C.* 'Rothschildianus' is another Exbury hybrid that is slightly smaller in stature but with the distinction of having fruits that start off creamy yellow and ripen to a deeper yellow. *Cotoneaster frigidus* remains one of my all-time favourites. Many of the plants grown in our gardens as this species are in fact hybrids and not the real thing. The genuine article is limited to botanical collections: I shamelessly used my favourite specimen, collected by plantsman Roy Lancaster under a BL&M expedition, from Nepal, to help hide the electricity pole at the Sir Harold Hillier Gardens. There it made quite a large shrub, plastered in scarlet-red berries during the autumn and winter, when most of the foliage was lost. *Cotoneaster frigidus* f. *fructuluteo* has all the charm and grace of the species and distinctive yellow fruits. *Cotoneaster ×watereri* 'John Waterer', a semi-evergreen shrub with long, arching branches laden with bright red fruits in autumn and winter, is the best of this batch for smaller gardens, as it will thrive in a variety of soils and is hardy throughout the UK. In the USA, all of this group will thrive in zones 6 to 9.

Ground-hugging evergreen cotoneasters are great in the winter landscape, both for their attractive berries and for their dark green foliage, which provides a wonderful foil for more ephemeral plants, like dwarf daffodils, which may pop up through them. *Cotoneaster dammeri* must be the most useful of this group; it is a beautiful groundcover shrub that will quickly form dense mats of deep rich evergreen foliage with wonderful pure white flowers during summer and masses of shiny, bright red berries in the autumn, which persist long into winter. The Himalayan species *C. microphyllus* will produce a similar effect, although its leaves are smaller and the foliage and branches, sparser. Tiny white flowers are produced abundantly during summer, and these are followed by pinkish white fruits; it is altogether a more compact affair, and much slower growing. *Cotoneaster salicifolius* 'Gnom' is similar to *C. dammeri* in that it is a quick-growing, but it tends to form hummocks rather than being completely prostrate. It flowers profusely during summer, but its bright red fruits, which contrast with the purple-tinted foliage, do not tend to be as abundant as those of *C. dammeri*, but they do persist longer. All the cotoneasters mentioned in this group will thrive in neutral soil and are best grown in full sun and allowed to creep into shady areas, where they will flower and fruit less. All are hardy throughout the UK, and in the USA in zones 5 to 9, although *C. microphyllus* may require more sun protection.

Berberis ×*carminea* 'Pirate King' is a compact barberry suitable for general planting.

The barberries are also worthy of inclusion here, as besides masses of colourful fruits they can provide beautiful flowers and create impenetrable barriers, thanks to their hidden thorns. Many of the deciduous forms have fantastic autumn colours, and some of the evergreen species produce tints reminiscent of *Mahonia japonica*, their close relative. The following barberries are, in my view, the cream of the crop. Nothing is more breathtaking than coming across a group planting of *Berberis* ×*carminea* in the heart of autumn— unless of course you try to cut through the middle of it, and that *would* be breathtaking! *Berberis* ×*carminea* (zone 6) is a group of hybrids between two Chinese species introduced by E. H. Wilson between 1903 and 1904; *B. aggregata* and *B. wilsoniae* (named for his wife) are two exceptional plants in their own right, but mix the two together and fireworks are produced. *Berberis* ×*carminea* 'Bountiful' is a real sight in autumn: its bright tints contrast with outrageously fleshy, bright coral-red berries that weigh down its branches, giving an arching appearance to this 1 to 2m (3 to 6ft) tall shrub. *Berberis* ×*carminea* 'Buccaneer' is similar but can grow slightly taller and has large clusters of deep red berries,

The wonderful berries of
Berberis 'Georgei'.

which last long into December—far surpassing any other in this group (I've seen fruits as late as early February). *Berberis ×carminea* 'Pirate King', a smaller affair seldom reaching 1m (3ft) tall, is the best in this group when space is at a premium. All these barberries are extremely hardy and tolerant shrubs that will survive in sun or shade, and light or heavy soils.

Berberis dictyophylla (zone 6), a native of western China, remains my favourite for the winter garden, as not only are its red berries attractive (although I wish there were more of them—plant in groups for a much higher fruit set) but its stems, leaves, and berries are covered in a whitish bloom similar to that of *Rubus cockburnianus*. Regular pruning results in a vase-shaped, more compact specimen, around 1.5m (5ft) tall, and also maintains the stem colour, which is ghostly white and by far the best attribute of this shrub, although the berries bring a subtle character change during winter. *Berberis* 'Georgei' is another delightful autumn-colouring and -fruiting variety whose origin is somewhat of a mystery. In May it produces exceptional pendent racemes of yellow flowers with pink-tinted stems. The foliage colours well in autumn, when the heavy crops of green-orange change to bright red as the fruits ripen—at this time, it is stunning and one of the most brightly coloured plants in the garden. I first fell in love with *B. koreana* (zone 4) when I came across it in beautiful autumn colour at the Royal Botanic Gardens, Kew, Surrey, England, its branches weighted down by large clusters of bright red fruits. This Korean species has quite large leaves and is reasonably compact, seldom reaching more than 2m (6ft) tall but suckering into a wide bush. The fruit production is spectacular for a berberis. Even more impressive is *B. koreana* 'Red Tears', which has purple autumn tints and large, bright red fruits that persist long into winter. If you don't have sufficient room for such widely growing or suckering shrubs, then try the "ankle biter" *B. wilsoniae* (zone 6), commonly known as Mrs Wilson's barberry. It reaches only around 1m (3ft) with arching thorny stems (hence, ankle biter) and small, light green leaves that turn to pale tones of orange and red in autumn and blend with the coral-coloured fruits, which are borne in small clusters. The fruits become more visible as the leaves fall in late autumn.

All the barberries mentioned in this section should thrive in most locations in the UK and will grow in a wide variety of soils; in the USA, they should all be hardy in and around zone 6 and should be fairly tolerant of heat. That said, it is worth experimenting, as those with thorns will certainly stop people shortcutting across areas in your garden.

If size is an issue then *Gaultheria procumbens* (wintergreen) may be the answer to your prayers, as this very tidy little groundcover shrub will produce masses of fruits in late autumn. If favoured with a moist, acidic soil, it will flourish and quickly spread, its foliage, smelling of wintergreen, providing a foil for the bright red berries into winter. A close relative of the wintergreen is *G. mucronata*

The blood-red fruits of *Gaultheria procumbens*—especially as here, in a large-berried form—are highly attractive during winter.

(*Pernettya mucronata*). Surprisingly hardy considering its South American origin, it is one of the most highly ornamental of the dwarf evergreen shrubs for acidic soils, especially when its large fruits, 2.5cm (1in) in diameter, are produced during autumn and winter. Hardy throughout the UK, it is a very adaptable winter-garden shrub, reaching 1m (3ft) tall but suckering and associating well with heathers, dwarf conifers, and even rhododendrons. Selections of *G. mucronata* have been made for their fruit colour: 'Bell's Seedling' is a self-fertile form with dark red berries; 'Sneeuwwitje' (Snow White), 'White Pearl', and 'Wintertime' have large, pure white berries; 'Lilacina', 'Lilian', and 'Pink Pearl' have lilac berries; 'Cherry Ripe', 'Crimsonia', and 'Mulberry Wine' have deep purple berries. Most forms seem to be male or female, and planting in groups seems to produce the best fruit set. They have proven hardy throughout the UK and in the USA in zones 5 and 6.

The weird fruits of *Decaisnea fargesii* are sure to attract comment.

Once you have seen the metallic-blue pods of *Decaisnea fargesii* you will never forget them. They are bean-like but fleshy to the touch and somewhat pulpy inside, and have relatively small seeds considering the size of the fruits, which are plump and round, around 10cm (4in) across, sometimes more. Fruits are borne in late autumn, following the even weirder yellow-green flowers, produced on racemes over 50cm (20in) long in late spring. This medium-sized Himalayan shrub will grow to around 2m (6ft) tall in sun or shade, in a fertile soil that retains some moisture during the summer. It has an attractive habit, with long, arching branches, and its highly architectural, bold pinnate foliage adds a tropical note to the garden. Hardy in the UK, and a zone 6 to 7 plant in the USA.

From small shrubs to medium-sized trees, hollies provide a plethora of fruit colour and shape. The females bear the fruits; it is advisable, therefore, to have a male nearby so that fruit is produced. Both male and female forms also exhibit wonderful foliage, which is another welcome sight in the winter garden. I have always been envious of the fantastic displays of berries on the American hollies, which flounder in the UK due to lack of heat or, possibly, poor pollinators.

The English holly (*Ilex aquifolium*) is a bread-and-butter plant in the UK but has some heat-tolerance problems in the USA, especially in the southern states, and suffers frost damage further north. Recommended for zones 6 and 7, zone 10 on the West Coast (where far better specimens exist). In the UK, without the heat of summer and the freezing temperatures of winter, they form stately trees or shrubs, depending on how they have been treated; they are among the best evergreen shade trees or shrubs for our climate, growing in coastal and wooded areas, preferring deep, fertile, often heavy soils but not restricted to acid or alkaline soils. *Ilex aquifolium* 'Amber' and 'Bacciflava' have always been two of my favourite English hollies, not so much for their foliage, which is just deep green, but for their bronzy orange-yellow and bright yellow fruits, respectively. Both crop very heavily as long as there is a male within "flying" distance, and both can be kept shorter by clipping or regular pruning. Pruning can dramatically enhance the strongly conical look of 'Green Pillar', the best holly for architectural effect in the garden. Its deep red berries provide considerable winter interest, and its shape is exquisite; with age, however, they broaden, and plants must be clipped to maintain their conical shape. 'Pyramidalis' is very similar in shape and, again, with age it broadens in habit; but it is self-fertile and doesn't require the intervention of the opposite sex. 'J. C. van Tol' and 'Madame Briot' are the "best of the best" for their bright red fruits. 'J. C. van Tol' has green foliage and is self-fertile; 'Madame Briot' has spiny green foliage with a distinct dark yellow mottled edge to the leaf.

If the overall scale of the English holly is off-putting, then why not try the shorter-growing Chinese holly? *Ilex cornuta* 'Burfordii' is not afflicted by the USA climate and performs admirably in both countries. Slightly large for a Chinese holly, it will reach over 3m (9ft) in height, forming a tight ball shape, and heavy fruit production occurs without the need for a male pollinator. It is one of the most widely grown of this group and is hardy in zones 6 to 9, with some frost damage to the foliage if not grown in a sheltered location in zone 6. In the UK I have seen occasional damage to the foliage, but this is unusual and occurs only after a late spring frost, once new growth is initiated. Apart from this, it seems reasonably hardy throughout the UK. Pale orange-red fruits persist into late winter and look wonderful against the shiny, deep green foliage.

Ilex opaca, the American holly, is an impressive tree similar in stature to the English holly, but like most things American it is far bigger than its British counterpart. In the USA it is an excellent replacement for the English holly, with matt green but equally spiny foliage and a distinct network of veins through the leaf; I have witnessed some pretty amazing specimens in North Carolina, close to 14m (40ft) tall but much narrower in width. It is proven hardy in zones 5 to 9 and can be widely used. In the UK, where I have encountered it, it grows but somewhat slowly and dislikes our wet winters. In the USA a number of forms are grown for their berries. 'Crooneburg' is hermaphrodite, with male and female flowers, and so does not require a pollinator. It fruits incredibly well; fruits are red, measuring 20mm (0.5in) in diameter, and are borne over a long period on this compact pyramidal form. 'Jersey Princess' has bold green foliage and bright red berries, which it holds through into early March; it should be planted with its pollinator, 'Jersey Knight', which is a male with deep glossy green leaves. 'Merry Christmas' and 'Old Heavy Berry' are both heavy croppers; their bright red fruits are quite a sight nestled against the pale green foliage.

Ilex ×attenuata 'Longwood Gold' is a choice yellow-fruiting holly.

Ilex ×attenuata, commonly known as Foster's hollies, are hybrids between *I. cassine* and *I. opaca*. Among the most popular hollies for the southern USA, the first were raised and selected by Mr E. E. Foster of Bessemer, Alabama, although several have since been introduced from elsewhere. They are of great beauty in the landscape, their narrow evergreen foliage providing an excellent foil for their red or yellow berries. I was fortunate enough to visit the University of Georgia's Tifton Campus, where John Ruter has amassed quite a remarkable holly collection, and the following have stuck in my memory. 'East Palatka', discovered growing in the wild in East Palatka, Florida, has small foliage and an abundance of small, bright red berries. 'Longwood Gold' nearly blew my socks off—masses and masses of small, bright yellow fruits nestled among the narrow green foliage, producing a wonderful effect. Link this to its attractive shape and habit, and this is arguably the best yellow-fruiting holly I have ever seen. 'Savannah' produces the most fruit of this group; masses of small, bright red fruits adorn its branches. 'Sunny Foster' is also a favourite; its foliage is a delightful golden yellow that fades to pale green with maturity, and its masses of bright red fruits persist long into winter. Foster's hollies are hardy to zone 6 and have little trouble with summer heat. I have seen one or two specimens in the UK, but they seldom perform. I brought back cuttings of 'Longwood Gold', but they have been painfully slow to establish themselves.

Ilex decidua, native to the southern USA, will grow in full sun or in dense shade; it prefers heavier soils and is among the most alkaline tolerant of the American hollies. The evergreen *I. opaca* seems to provide an adequate pollinator for this deciduous species, as does its widely used selection *I. decidua*

Ilex decidua thrives in the USA but simply does not perform in the UK.

'Red Escort', which has exceptional foliage and habit. I wish we could really grow this amazing holly well in the UK, as to see one in full glory in a USA winter—its blood-red berries at their starkest against virgin-white snow in Ithaca, New York, or against blue skies in Athens, Georgia—is to die happy. They really are winter showstoppers. But alas, in the UK they just do not perform. Whether it is lack of a good pollinator or lack of summer heat to ripen the wood, I am not sure, but in the UK climate, they do not look like the same shrub. *Ilex decidua* 'Council Fire' (Hartline), 'Pocahontas', and 'Red Cascade' are very heavy red-fruiting varieties; 'Council Fire' has the most persistent fruits, hanging on into March in some cases, although the bright red fruits are small, 10mm (0.25in) in diameter. 'Byers Golden' (Byers) and 'Finch's Golden' ('Gold Finch') are the two most widely grown yellow fruiters (although I am not as taken by this colour variant—it's all a matter of taste); fruits of both persist long into winter. All forms are large shrubs, reaching 5m (15ft), sometimes taller, and often as wide as tall.

Ilex verticillata 'Winter Red' is one of my all-time favourites.

Ilex verticillata (common winterberry) is another deciduous holly, and one with extreme cold hardiness, thriving in zones 3 to 9, and reaching around 3m (9ft) tall with a similar spread. It grows throughout the USA in a wide variety of conditions and habitats; notably, it is among the best American deciduous hollies for tolerance to waterlogging. Both male and female forms have been selected, males as pollinators. *Ilex verticillata* 'Alfred Anderson', 'Jim Dandy', 'Jackson', 'Southern Gentleman', and 'Johnny Come Lately' serve this purpose well. Females are very sensitive to their pollinators as flowering times must coincide, so it is often best to ask locally which "services" which. *Ilex verticillata* Berry Nice is a real showstopper: I saw a plant in North Carolina during a winter trip, and I nearly crashed the car—the berries were produced in such abundance on the naked branches that it stood out in the landscape like a beacon (best fruit set is achieved using 'Southern Gentleman'). 'Christmas Cheer', smaller and more compact than Berry Nice, somehow doesn't produce quite the impact. 'Chrysocarpa' is a form with orange-yellow berries. Birds don't seem to recognise its fruits as food until all the red and orange berries are gone, so its fruits (and those of many yellow-fruiting plants) persist long into winter; fruit set on 'Chrysocarpa', however, is not as good as the red-fruiting forms. 'Fairfax' and 'Jolly Red' are more compact forms that may eventually reach 3m (9ft) tall but are somewhat dome-shaped in habit; both fruit well, with rich red berries. 'Winter Gold', with orange-yellow fruits, was selected as a branch sport of 'Winter Red', which is one of my all-time favourites: it bears a profusion of bright red berries that can be cut for winter arrangements and seem to last forever.

Ilex verticillata has been used in a number of hybrids; very popular and widely planted are the results of its cross with *I. serrata*, the Japanese winterberry. 'Apollo', a male form, is widely used as a pollinator for the most widely grown forms, and like most such hybrids, its emerging foliage is tinged purple; it's a large-growing shrub reaching small-tree stature at 3m (9ft) but with an upright habit. 'Sparkleberry' has been grown in the UK and does fruit reasonably well, although this is probably by accident rather than by design. Still, it was a sight in early winter, when the small, bright red fruits glisten on the naked branches. 'Autumn Glow' is slightly more compact (a mere 3m, 9ft tall upon maturity) and produces loads of small, bright red fruits that contrast nicely with its vivid yellow and purple autumn colour, but this is only evident in northerly locations. 'Bonfire', one of the best in the USA, has masses of bright red berries that weigh the branches, creating a widely arching effect; it's slightly taller and wider in stature, ultimately making a rounded shrub 4m (12ft) tall by 3m (9ft) wide.

The various sections of this design chapter were meant to function as a taster, to whet your appetite to the range of plants that are available for the winter garden—for their fruits, their sculptural quality, their value as evergreen backdrops, their stem and bark effects. Obviously there are far more than are presented here, but with this chapter I hope I have guided you toward a selection of those that would make fine supporting players to your winter-flowering shrubs. The rewards of a thoughtfully planted winter garden are great, and the final decision as to its cast of characters is yours to make.

Winter-flowering shrubs come in many
different guises, as seen here with
Rhododendron 'Christmas Cheer'.

A-to-Z of Winter-flowering Shrubs

Abeliophyllum Oleaceae

Abeliophyllum distichum

Common Names: White winter forsythia, Korean abelialeaf.

Flowering Period: Late winter to early spring.

Flowers: Scented. Pure white, occasionally flushed pink. A pink-flowered form is also grown.

Height and Spread: 1.5 × 1.5m (5 × 5ft).

Abeliophyllum distichum, a slow-growing and somewhat unruly-looking shrub, is vastly underrated and underused as a late-flowering shrub for the winter garden, producing its delicate flowers just before the true forsythias bloom. Its lack of popularity has always been a mystery to me; it may have something to do with its rather unsightly appearance in garden centres, where its long, whippy shoots are often tied to bamboo canes. First impressions aside, this wonderful Korean shrub will thrive and perform admirably if situated in any fertile soil where it can bask in the sun. To get the maximum flower set, plant at or near the base of a south-facing wall, where its shoots and branches can fully ripen before the onset of winter. Given such a location, it produces its fragrant blooms well before the first flowers of any forsythia, which is its nearest relative. In the UK it is completely hardy, although its flowers, which appear in late February, may occasionally be damaged by a late freeze.

Abeliophyllum distichum Roseum Group (pink winter forsythia) now covers all the variants with pink flowers. Several different clones are wandering around in the nursery trade, varying in flower colour from those with a delicate tint of rosy pink to those with no pink whatsoever. My advice to anyone wishing to buy a pink form is to buy it when in flower. The pink-flowered forms tend to be less

The delicate flowers of *Abeliophyllum distichum* are easily damaged by frost.

With regular pruning, the scruffy habit of *Abeliophyllum distichum* can be tamed into an attractive shape.

vigorous and slightly less hardy than the more commonly grown white-flowering forms; they are, however, as beautiful when in full flower.

Cultivation Tips

In the USA it is hardy in zones 5 to 8, occasionally 4 if given protection; in the South it flowers in late February, but further north, up into zones 4 and 5, flowers don't appear until late March or early April—but still ahead of the forsythias. There are simply so few, compact, white or pink-flushed flowering shrubs in bloom during this winter period, that to simply overlook it because of its unsightly growth habit is sacrilege. I have seen it used in a number of different ways; mass planting produces a very beautiful display, as does fan-training it against a wall. Regular pruning can address its scruffy habit and should be undertaken immediately after flowering, by reducing the shoots by half their length. Additional thinning by a third, taking out the weakest shoots, is a must to maintain a less straggly habit, and this can be undertaken throughout the year.

Acacia　　**Mimosaceae**

Common Name: Wattle.

Flowering Period: Late winter and early spring.

Flowers: Bright yellow, scented, borne in clusters.

Height and Spread: If left unpruned, most will attain tree stature, but they can be coppiced and grown as large multi-stemmed shrubs.

Far too few wattles are hardy in the UK, and even fewer are hardy in the majority of the USA. In our climate, most are restricted to the south of England, and even here require the protection of specialised microclimates in our gardens where, packed close to sunny walls or protected by other taller shrubs, they will thrive. The following are worth persevering with, their unusual flowers and light scent making a welcome addition to the winter landscape.

Acacia baileyana (Cootamundra wattle, golden mimosa) is native to New South Wales and Tasmania, where it will grow into a small tree. In the UK, however, it is often grown as a medium-sized shrub with attractive, evergreen, fern-like foliage and large clusters of bright yellow, scented flowers emerging during February and continuing well into March. A gorgeous but less hardy purple-leaved form, *A. baileyana* 'Purpurea', provides one of the most dramatic contrasts between bronze foliage and yellow flowers that I have ever seen; its mature foliage changes from bronze-purple to a delightful blue-green with age. I have seen both the green and purple forms grown as large trees in the south of England and in France, although both can be grown as multi-stemmed shrubs (and with the purple-leaved form, this habit seems to produce a more intense leaf colour).

Acacia dealbata (mimosa, silver wattle) is the least hardy of the wattles grown in the UK. It seems very particular about its location and requires the protection of a south-facing wall, unless cultivated in areas lucky enough to be affected by the Gulf Stream. In these locations it will survive frost damage but is occasionally subject to drought damage; even more critical is its intolerance of wet soils during the winter. I have inadvertently murdered a number of these majestic trees by planting them in unfavourable locations. In the right spot with sufficient sun and good drainage, it can be grown either as a fast-growing evergreen tree or a multi-stemmed shrub. I am a fan of the shrub option, as the tree form seldom retains its lower branches and flowers disappear high into the canopy. Its fern-like foliage has a silvery sheen, and in late winter and early spring is complemented by clusters of yellow, scented flowers. Late autumn frost may occasionally kill the flower buds, meaning there will be no flowers in the winter.

Acacia pravissima (Oven's wattle) is purportedly the hardiest for our climate but, alas, the least attractive of the three, and a difficult plant to train into some kind of acceptable shape. It has a lax habit, with unusual-looking triangular leaves borne on pendulous branches; in February and early March, small clusters of bright yellow flowers are produced along the branches. In my interactions with this so-called hardy form I have never got it past two winters.

Cultivation Tips

All the wattles mentioned here require a fertile but free-draining soil, and are best sited in sunny locations. They also make excellent wall shrubs if fan-trained, but be warned: training to this shape is an arduous task. Most may require winter protection in the form of wrapping with fleece, hessian (burlap), or some other product until they reach sufficient size and establish successfully. They will thrive best in the southern counties of the UK, and do especially well against a south-facing wall. In the USA I would suggest they will thrive in a warm, sunny location in zones 8 to 10, possibly 11.

Most wattles dislike annual pruning regimes that are associated with restricting the size of a tree to form a multi-stemmed shrub. With this in mind, undertake coppicing when the plant is relatively young; your aim should be to create a basic branching network that originates close to the base of the specimen. Once this is complete, the only annual pruning that is required is to reduce the number of newly produced and competing branches. A word of caution: when a wet but mild autumn is followed by a cold winter, large branches or even the entire plant can die. This is often the norm for wattles, as although the climate is suitable for them here, it is far from ideal; and when summers are mild, the branches do not ripen sufficiently before the onset of winter. It is not uncommon for wattles to appear established, surviving for several winters unaffected, and then suddenly to die during a mild spring. If no problems occur, however, the sight of a wattle's crisp, yellow flowers in late winter brings a gentle reminder that spring—whatever its temperament—is on its way.

Arbutus   **Ericaceae**

Common Name: Strawberry tree.

Flowering Period: Late autumn and early winter.

Flowers: Pure white, bell-shaped, often accompanied by strawberry-like fruits.

Height and Spread: Most strawberry trees, as their name suggests, are trees in their own right; however, a number of compact forms fall into the category of medium to large shrubs, and hence their inclusion in this book.

The all-round attributes of this group of plants cannot be overstated to the winter gardener, whose chief aim should be to seek out plants that perform through many seasons but peak in winter. The evergreen strawberry trees are a classic example of this, as they not only flower in winter but also produce large, hard (nonedible) strawberry-like fruits. Add to this attractive, flaking, cinnamon-coloured bark, which although it would not rival *Acer griseum* or *Prunus serrula* is nevertheless a desirable addition, and the following make very worthy plants for winter interest.

Arbutus unedo, the Killarney strawberry tree, will thrive in exposed locations.

Arbutus ×*andrachnoides* is a natural hybrid between *A. andrachne* and *A. unedo* that occurs in Greece where both parents meet; a charming, spreading evergreen tree or shrub, 8 × 8m (25 × 25ft), it has the most attractive flaking bark of any selection, although its flowers are not as showy and not accompanied by fruit. *Arbutus unedo*, the famous Killarney strawberry tree, is delightful—with such a low number of trees truly native to the UK, it is wonderful that we actually possess a small tree of some garden merit in our native flora. I have now seen this species in the wild, clinging to exposed rocks on the windblown and barren Dingle Peninsula; here, they seemed one step away from death, and I wonder that they were ever introduced into our gardens. Fortunately *A. unedo* performs nothing like its wild relatives in cultivation and remains possibly the hardiest of the strawberry trees and the most tolerant of a wide variety of atmospheric conditions. It grows into an open-headed tree or shrub, 8 × 8m (25 × 25ft), and is available in a variety of forms. The following are the most compact, and thus most suitable for general garden use.

Arbutus unedo 'Atlantic' is a free-flowering and -fruiting form, reaching a height and width of 4m (12ft). *Arbutus unedo* 'Elfin King', the best of all, forms a compact shrub, 2.5m (8ft) high and wide, and produces from late autumn to early spring masses of white flowers and numerous orange fruit, which turn red with age. *Arbutus unedo* 'Rubra' is a delightful form with pinkish tinged flowers and masses of fruit, but it is not as compact as 'Elfin King'.

Cultivation Tips

Strawberry trees thrive in both alkaline conditions and acidic, free-draining soils, and they require little attention with regard to annual pruning. It is advisable, however, to lightly thin some of the interior branchlets so that the bark can be easily seen. Deer enjoy the foliage of young plants, and newly planted specimens may require some protection. More recently, several species have been identified as possible hosts of sudden oak death, *Phytophthora ramorum*. Most strawberry trees mentioned here will grow in protected locations throughout the UK as long as they are not grown in soils prone to waterlogging. In the USA, *Arbutus unedo* and *A. ×andrachnoides* will thrive in zones 7 to 10.

Berberis   **Berberidaceae**

Common Name: Barberry.
Flowering Period: As early as February and continuing into spring.
Flowers: Orange, red, scarlet, or yellow.
Height and Spread: 2 × 1m (6 × 3ft) widely arching shrub.

Although most barberries flower in spring, a small minority unfurl their flowers in late winter, injecting the winter landscape with vivid colour. *Berberis trigona* (*B. linearifolia*) is like a welcome breath of fresh air in winter. If left unpruned it is somewhat of a gangly shrub, but it is without doubt among the best of all the barberries when in flower. This native to Chile and Argentina was introduced in 1927 by Harold Comber for its large orange-red flowers, which dangle pleasantly from erect but arching branches; it will occasionally flower a second time in autumn. The leaves are quite small, resembling those of *B. darwinii* but with only a single spine at the tip of the leaf. Several named forms exist, including the impressive *B. trigona* 'Jewel' which is, in my view, the best of this bunch, with scarlet buds that open to reveal a rich and very large orange flower. *Berberis trigona* 'Orange King' also has large flowers of a rich orange but is not quite the match of 'Jewel'.

Berberis ×*lologensis*, a naturally occurring hybrid between *B. darwinii* and *B. trigona*, was discovered by Comber where both species meet in Argentina. It is somewhat taller in appearance than either parent, developing into an erect but arching shrub often exceeding 2 × 2m (6 × 6ft), and exhibits intermediate leaf shapes. Flowers are spectacular, and produced in abundance. Arguably the best form from this hybrid group is *B.* ×*lologensis* 'Apricot Queen', which exhibits the best features of both parents. Slightly more relaxed in habit than any of the other forms, with large brightly coloured orange flowers. *Berberis* ×*lologensis* 'Mystery Fire' (more commonly seen as it is the easiest of the three to propagate) is similar in habit to 'Stapehill' but not quite as erect, with masses of orange-yellow flowers that are deep orange when in bud. *Berberis* ×*lologensis* 'Stapehill', an erect form that produces multitudes of bright orange flowers, is my least favourite.

Cultivation Tips

All these barberries will, if left unpruned, develop to monstrous proportion and swamp any border; they may exceed 4 × 4m (12 × 12ft), a scary sight in any garden. It is worth, therefore, investing some time in pruning to develop a framework from a young age. This is easily achieved by cutting back tall, vigorous shoots to within a few nodes from the base of the shrub, forcing them to shoot again lower down. If this is done on a two- to three-year cycle— removing the most vigorous shoots first and never more than one-third of the total number of stems—then flowering will never be interrupted.

All this group will grow in both alkaline and acidic soils, and in the UK should prove hardy in any location, but thriving best in a sunny location. They may, however, prove short-lived if grown in soils that flood during the winter and spring. In the USA they will thrive in zones 7 and 8.

Calluna   Ericaceae

Calluna vulgaris

Common Names: Heather, common Scots heather, Scotch heather, Scotch ling.
Flowering Period: Early winter, from October, and occasionally long into December.
Flowers: Small, bell-shaped, with colour varying from white to magenta.
Height and Spread: Small, hummock-forming shrubs, usually 30cm (12in) high with a 40cm (16in) spread; if left unpruned, seldom reaching over or spreading wider than 50cm (20in).

Calluna vulgaris, a hardy evergreen British native, is an extremely useful groundcover in sunny locations on acidic soils. Many are grown for their attractive needle-like coloured foliage as well as their flowers. Due to the sheer variety of both flower and foliage colour it is possible to create intricate patterns that provide a long period of interest, far beyond the winter period. For the UK market I strongly recommend the so-called bud bloomers, whose flowers never fully open and whose colour presence, therefore, outlasts those whose blooms fully open.

Calluna vulgaris 'Alexandra' is among the best of the bud-blooming heathers.

Calluna vulgaris 'Melanie' bears its dazzling white flowers over a long period.

Calluna vulgaris 'Alexandra' is a spectacular bud bloomer, a striking form with crimson-red flower spikes that contrast with mid green foliage from August until December. *Calluna vulgaris* 'Alicia' has white flower spikes against bright green foliage from August long into December. *Calluna vulgaris* 'Amethyst' produces vivid purple and crimson flowers over deep, lush green foliage from August until January. *Calluna vulgaris* 'Anette' has delightful crisp-pink flower spikes against deep green foliage throughout August until late November. *Calluna vulgaris* 'Melanie' is the tallest form, growing to 40cm (16in) compared to the normal 30cm (12in) of the others mentioned in this section; it carries its pure white flowers boldly atop green foliage from August until late November. *Calluna vulgaris* 'Marleen', one of the tallest of the bud bloomers, may reach 50cm (20in) tall with striking white, flushed purple flower spikes from August to late December. *Calluna vulgaris* 'Romina' offers intensely dense and clustered flower spikes of purple-red against dark green foliage from late August until December. *Calluna vulgaris* 'Underwoodii', among the first bud bloomers to be introduced, has pale mauve flowers that fade slowly to a ghostly silver-white; blooms last from August until late November.

Cultivation Tips

Heathers are relatively low-maintenance, as long as they are sited in moist, acidic soils. In the USA they are hardy in zones 4 to 6, possibly higher. Bear in mind that this moorland species is probably prone to struggle in high summer temperatures, especially if accompanied by drying winds, so site carefully. The pruning of heathers could not be simpler: remove spent flowers and tip back the new growth with shears or hedge trimmers immediately after flowering.

Camellia — Theaceae

Camellia japonica and *C. saluenensis*

Common Names: Japanese camellia (*Camellia japonica*); Yunnan camellia (*C. saluenensis*).
Flowering Period: Early to late winter.

Camellia japonica requires little introduction as it is the most common and most widely grown camellia in our gardens. The Japanese camellia is listed as having thousands of raised forms, many almost indistinguishable from each other, and some highly unstable and tending to revert to their original flower colour. There are far too many to mention here, so I will restrict my selections to those I feel will perform well in most climates. All will flower from early January, occasionally earlier in the UK, depending on the season. In the USA they are hardy to zone 6, requiring some protection in colder areas. Particularly cold hardy *C. japonica* cultivars have been developed by William L. Ackerman at the US National Arboretum, and at Camellia Forest Nursery, Chapel Hill, North Carolina; these forms, which perform well in both the USA and UK, are indicated with an asterisk (*).

In the UK *Camellia japonica* 'Nobilissima' is the first Japanese camellia to flower; although its blooms are invariably damaged by late frosts, it is worth growing for its ivory-white peony-like flowers, which appear as early as November. *Camellia japonica* 'Debutante'* is a fast-growing, vigorous form with quite large, pale pink, peony-like flowers. *Camellia japonica* 'Adolphe Audusson'*, an old but reliable, tried-and-tested selection, is still one of the best deep reds you'll find. *Camellia japonica* 'Apollo' is among the best for general planting, a semi-double rose-red with petals occasionally blotched white. *Camellia japonica* 'Fire Falls'* is a very early and long-flowering lapsed double with hot-red flowers. *Camellia japonica* 'Jupiter'*, a bright scarlet very occasionally blotched white, is intermittent between single and double flowers. *Camellia japonica* 'Lovelight' is a particularly fine, large-flowering, semi-double white with bright yellow stamens and a good upright habit.

Camellia japonica 'Jupiter', introduced in 1950s, is very reliable for the UK climate.

Camellia 'Inspiration' is an amazing hybrid with large, flamboyant flowers.

In the USA, the following are worthy of note. *Camellia japonica* 'Autumn Mist', an autumn- and winter-blooming camellia from Camellia Forest, is a large white single initially, but as the flowering season progresses, pink flowers develop. *Camellia japonica* 'Pink Perfection'* ('Otome'), a highly attractive double with shell-pink flowers and an upright habit, will certainly turn heads when it is in flower. *Camellia japonica* 'Berenice Bobby'* is a widely used parent of hybrids for its semi-double mid pink flowers. *Camellia japonica* 'Blood of China'* has very large double flowers of a rich salmon-red and a compact growth habit. Also worthy of consideration are members of the April series, which were bred at Camellia Forest by crossing various *C. japonica* cultivars ('Berenice Bobby', 'Tiphosa', 'Reg Ragland', and 'Betty Sheffield Supreme', among others) to create April-flowering forms for zone 6—but in zone 7, they will bloom in winter. They include *C. japonica* 'April Blush' (shell-pink semi-double), *C. japonica* 'April Dawn' (pink double with a white variegation), *C. japonica* 'April Kiss' (reddish pink double), *C. japonica* 'April Rose' (rose-red double, and probably the hardiest of the group). Two Ackerman hybrids are particularly worthy of note and worthy of planting: *C.* 'Frost Queen', a very hardy form with semi-white flowers and probably the best for general landscape use (it may just be a hardy selection of *C. japonica*), and *C.* 'Jerry Hill', a hybrid of 'Frost Queen' with rose-pink flowers.

Camellia saluenensis, more widely known as one of the parents of the *C.* ×*williamsii* hybrids, is not commonly seen in our gardens as it can grow into an imposing (5m, 15ft), wide-spreading, multi-stemmed shrub with masses of delightful soft pink, white, pink and white, and occasionally red single flowers that never quite open fully. They flower from late winter into spring. In the UK they are as hardy as *C. japonica* and in the USA hardy to zone 7. Although widely hybridised with the Japanese camellia, it has a few selected forms, among them *C. saluenensis* 'Exbury Trumpet', from the de Rothschild Estate, Exbury Gardens, Hampshire, England, and *C. saluenensis* 'Trewithen Red', a delightful seedling selection with deep red flowers from Trewithen Gardens, Truro, Cornwall, England. *Camellia* 'Inspiration', an outstanding hybrid between *C. saluenensis* and *C. reticulata*, was raised at Borde Hill, the garden of Cornel Stephenson Clarke, in Sussex, England; its very large (13cm, 5in) semi-double flowers, a soft salmon-pink, appear in February and continue late into spring.

Cultivation Tips

These camellias vary, as noted, in hardiness. Those that flower over a long period, with buds opening during cool, cloudy, damp weather at temperatures of between 10 and 18°C (50 and 64°F), may succumb to camellia flower blight (*Ciborinia camelliae*), one of the most serious diseases of camellias in the USA and very problematic in Canada, New Zealand, Europe, and the UK. The disease, which was first isolated in Japan (where it is believed to have originated), causes the flowers to fall early; it begins as brown specks on the petals and develops into a brown rot, spreading up from the base of the flower. The rot continues until the flower is dead. Camellia flower blight affects only camellias and has been isolated in the UK on *Camellia japonica*, *C. saluenensis*, *C. cuspidata*, *C. reticulata*, and *C.* ×*williamsii* and hybrids of these that flower in late winter and early spring. As yet, only a few reports have been received for early winter–flowering species like *C. sasanqua*, but these are not resistant: I believe it is just a matter of the conditions not being suitable for the fungus to spread when they flower. As there seems to be no chemical control, the only way to reduce the spread of the disease is to collect and "deep compost" or burn infected flowers and remove the leaf litter around the base of the plant until roots are exposed; dispose of this soil and replace with fresh mulch. This is particularly important as the hardened fungal mass can remain viable in the soil for up to three years.

Camellia oleifera flowering at the Sir Harold Hillier Gardens, Hampshire, England, in November.

Camellia oleifera

Common Name: Tea oil camellia.

Flowering Period: Late autumn and early winter.

Flowers: Pure white, yellow-centred, 5cm (2in) across, lightly scented.

Height and Spread: 2 × 2m (6 × 6ft).

Camellia oleifera is difficult to track down and fairly rare in gardens. Much of what I have seen in cultivation is of probable hybrid origin, with flowers closer to *C. sasanqua* 'Narumigata'; in its true form the tea oil camellia has small, fragrant, pure (not off-) white flowers with clear yellow stamens in the centre. The bark of established specimens is a striking cinnamon, and the leaves are serrated. This species is not only the first camellia to flower in winter (a specimen at the Sir Harold Hillier Gardens, with an unusual weeping habit, flowers in late October and on into November), it is much hardier than *C. sasanqua*, both in the UK and USA (but may not be as hardy as hybrid camellias).

Camellia oleifera is an important species in the USA, as it was *C. oleifera* 'Lushan Snow', a selection hardy to −23°C (−10°F) introduced by the US National Arboretum, that was the cornerstone for hardiness in the Ackerman hybrids. This form has the typical flowers of the species and is hardy possibly as far north as Philadelphia (zone 6), more generally in zones 7 to 9.

Cultivation Tips

Camellia oleifera is somewhat easier to grow and establish than the sasanqua camellias—if you can find it. Still, I would recommend protecting newly planted shrubs with agricultural fleece or hessian (burlap) until they are established. The fundamental difference between the two is that the tea oil camellia is less sun tolerant and thus requires more shade, where sasanqua will stand in full sun without any problem. In the UK and USA it flowers well regardless of the previous season's conditions, indicating that wood ripening is not as critical as in sasanquas. The tea oil camellia gets its name from its commercial use in China, where its seeds are harvested for tea oil. Reported outbreaks of camellia flower blight on this species are few.

Camellia sasanqua

Common Names: Sasanqua camellia, sasanqua tea bush.

Flowering Period: Early winter in the UK, early and late winter in the USA.

Flowers: Small, slightly scented, single, occasionally double, in shades of pink, red, and white.

Height and Spread: Varies considerably, depending on conditions and cultivar. In the UK sasanquas range from open, often straggly-looking shrubs to quite compact, well-behaved shrubs. In the southern USA, they perform and flower more prolifically than in the UK, as summer heat and high light levels are a must for this species.

Although this group of camellias is considerably more difficult to site and grow in the UK than other camellias, consider this a challenge: they are worth growing because they are the earliest to flower and the least susceptible to camellia flower blight (although the disease has been found on this group). That said, their early, lightly fragrant flowers, 4 to 9cm (1.5 to 3.5in) wide, provide a welcome respite in the heart of winter, but only if you can tolerate the fact that the blooms may be obliterated by winter frost. Then again, isn't this one of the many challenges of winter gardening?

In the UK—if sited in a free-draining acidic to neutral soil in a protected location exposed to direct sunlight—the sasanquas produce their flowers from early November right through January, often in conjunction with *Mahonia japonica* and *M. ×media*. In fact, these two shrubs complement and partner each other perfectly.

Unfortunately, until established, sasanquas are the least hardy of the commonly grown camellias. In the UK they are really suited only to sheltered sites along the southern coast, the special climates of Devon and Cornwall, and the west coast of Wales, Ireland, and Scotland. They can exist away from such areas if sited in microclimates such as along south-facing walls or in hot, sunny borders. In the continental climate of the USA they perform exceptionally well, especially in the southern and western states, where they appear more sun tolerant than any other camellia but not as hardy. Grown in such warm climates, their habit and overall performance improves; they become well-branched, informally shaped shrubs to 3m (9ft) tall. They thrive in zones 7 (with protection during harsh winters) to 9. At the southern points they will flower as early as September; further north, toward the outer limits of zone 7, they follow a more traditional line, flowering in November and December.

Camellia sasanqua 'Crimson King' is the best of this group for general planting.

Camellia sasanqua 'Duff Allan' is a delicate single white.

I would strongly recommend the following forms for growing in the UK. *Camellia sasanqua* 'Crimson King' is arguably the best for general planting and my favourite blood-red-flowering form. A rather large and somewhat sprawling shrub with small dark green foliage, it may reach around 3m (9ft) in height and spreads much wider. From mid November, a single row of crimson-red petals are produced, surrounding the bright yellow stamens that form the centre of the flower. *Camellia sasanqua* 'Duff Allan' is more compact, with single flowers larger than 'Crimson King', this time white, occasionally flushed pink. *Camellia sasanqua* 'Hugh Evans' is an interesting form with a very distinctive upright habit and quite large salmon-pink, single flowers that are profusely borne from mid November. *Camellia sasanqua* 'Jean May' is a reasonably slow-growing, compact form with almost double flowers of almost salmon-pink, tipped white at the edges. A really distinct form, more suitable for smaller gardens.

Camellia sasanqua 'Narumigata' is one of my favourites for its scent and reliability. It produces wonderfully large, off-white flowers that are touched with pink in early November. An imposing sight when in full flower. *Camellia sasanqua* 'Tricolor' is the complete opposite—compact, almost hedge-like in habit, and early flowering. It is often in flower with 'Narumigata' and a good few weeks before 'Crimson King', but its delicate white-, pink-, and red-flushed flowers are often killed by frost.

Far more varieties are available in the USA, where this group really grows well, and for zones 8 to 9, I would recommend the following. *Camellia sasanqua* 'Angel Kiss' is probably the most unusual-looking of the sasanquas: its pom-pom-like pink peony flowers are borne in profusion on an upright and vigorous shrub. This fine form was introduced by Camellia Forest Nursery, North Carolina, USA. *Camellia sasanqua* 'Bonanza' is one of the deepest pinks of this group, with quite large, almost double flowers, although like 'Crimson King' it has an unruly habit; I suspect it might be a hybrid between *C. sasanqua* and *C. japonica*, making it *C.* ×*hiemalis*. *Camellia sasanqua* 'Daydream' is a fine upright form with delicate salmon-coloured single flowers borne in profusion. *Camellia sasanqua* 'Martha's Dream' is a real showstopper introduced by Cecil Hill, of Homer, Georgia, USA, and named after his wife, Martha; I first saw this in Georgia in late fall (November), when I was taken by the sheer number of delightful pink tipped white flowers weighing down the branches. *Camellia sasanqua* 'Midnight Lover' is a seedling selection from *C. sasanqua* 'Crimson King' made at Camellia Forest Nursery, and if you are a fan of 'Crimson King', then you will be swept away by this improvement upon it, with its deep crimson-red flowers: 'Midnight Lover', which seems to have a better constitution than 'Crimson King', being more upright and less straggly in habit, is the "best red" in a world that has far too few, good red-flowering winter camellias. *Camellia sasanqua* 'Shikoku Stars', one of the hardiest forms yet introduced, was collected by Camellia Forest Nursery from the northern end of the species' range on Shikoku Island, Japan; the flowers are quite small and white and are produced in profusion on this spreading shrub, which has considerable breeding potential.

Camellia sasanqua 'Narumigata' is a wonderful sight when in full flower before Christmas.

Camellia sasanqua 'Daydream' is widely grown in the USA, especially in the South.

For zone 7 and 8 planting I would suggest the Ackerman hybrids raised by William L. Ackerman of the US National Arboretum. The forms in the Winter series, which have hardy selections of *Camellia oleifera* as one parent, were bred for cold hardiness, but in my view, they have lost some of the beauty of *C. sasanqua* in the mix. They will, however, provide sufficient cold hardiness and flower in November (occasionally October) in the more northerly locations, where they have been recorded to survive temperatures between −12 and −9°C (10 and 15°F). The three favourites mentioned here are hardy throughout most of the UK and in the USA seem to be hardy to zone 7, although only through much wider cultivation will their true hardiness be established. *Camellia* 'Snow Flurry' is early to flower, often blooming abundantly in October with pure white flowers. *Camellia* 'Winter's Cupid' (a multiple hybrid between *C. oleifera*, *C. sasanqua* 'Narumigata', and *C. ×hiemalis* 'Shishi-gashira') is a wonderful garden plant with compact habit and single white flowers tipped and flecked with pink. *Camellia* 'Winter's Waterlily' is reportedly the hardiest of this group, having survived temperatures to −26°C (−15°F); its white flowers are intermediate between peony and full double types.

Other hybrids involving *Camellia sasanqua* have been bred in an attempt to increase cold hardiness and to improve flower size and colour. The following are worthy of note. *Camellia* 'China Girl', a hybrid with the impeccable parentage of *C. sasanqua* 'Narumigata' and *C. reticulata* 'Cornelian', was introduced by Camellia Forest Nursery. Its growth is intermediate between both parents with large, deep pink, semi-double blooms being produced from early November; however, the blooms are susceptible to frost damage. *Camellia* 'Carolina Moonmist' (*C. sasanqua* × *C. oleifera*) originated at the North Carolina State University and was introduced by the JC Raulston Arboretum. This relatively cold hardy form has big pink and rose-coloured flowers, and—unusually for hybrids of *C. sasanqua* and *C. oleifera*—it seems to have retained its sun tolerance. *Camellia* 'Christmas Rose' (*C. ×williamsii* × *C. ×hiemalis*), another pedigree plant from the Camellia Forest stable, flowers slightly later than others of this group, and is often in full flower between December and January (early November to January in zone 7). Its semi-double rose-pink to light red flowers resemble roses when first open. *Camellia* 'Survivor' is a very floriferous hybrid between *C. sasanqua* 'Narumigata' and *C. oleifera* raised at Camellia Forest; although its true hardiness is not yet known, it is reported to have survived in Ontario, Canada (zone 1). Regardless of its breeding potential, it is a wonderful, well-behaved shrub which produces its pure white, single flowers from late autumn, and it may yet yield considerable new hybrids from its gene pool.

Cultivation Tips

Sasanqua camellias require a neutral to acidic soil that is rich in humus and a sheltered location, preferably with protection from chilling winds afforded by nearby shrubs. Once established they will flower best after long, hot summers where sufficient irrigation has been applied. Unruly camellias can be tip-pruned from a young age to ensure that they develop a bushy habit; this should be accomplished immediately after flowering. Long periods of drought cause many developing buds to prematurely fall; flower set for the following few years may be lower than usual but will gradually return to full complement. Young, newly planted shrubs should be given the protection of agricultural fleece or a similar product for the first few years. As far as I am aware, there have been a few reported outbreaks of camellia flower blight on sasanquas, but nowhere as bad as on spring-flowering camellias. For more information on camellia flower blight, see under *C. japonica* and *C. saluenensis*.

Camellia sinensis

Common Names: Tea bush, tea bush camellia.

Flowering Period: Late autumn and early winter.

Flowers: Small, fragrant, nodding, single, white, 3cm (1.5in) wide, blooming at
   internodes and often obscured by the foliage.

Height and Spread: 2 × 2m (6 × 6ft).

This rarely grown camellia is more widely known as the source of tea rather than for its quaint value as an early autumn or winter-flowering shrub. It was introduced into the UK as an ornamental in 1768, but its leaves in the form of tea were imported as early as 1652, from China, where it had been grown for thousands of years for tea production.

Considering the variety of tea bush forms, estimated at between 2500 and 3000, it is surprising that so few gardenworthy forms have been named. Those that have include the pink-flowered *Camellia sinensis* 'Rosea' ('Rubra'), which is cited in various publications; I have never seen it myself, but it sounds delightful, with pale pink flowers and burgundy new growth. Camellia Forest Nursery lists eight different forms, many of them grown for their traditional tea use, i.e., for the leaves. I have seen firsthand their interesting, small-leaf form of *C. sinensis* var. *sinensis*, which seems the best for general landscape planting in the USA for zones 6 (with slight protection) to 9. It is a compact shrub, seldom exceeding 2m (6ft), with a bushy habit and masses of small, white, nodding flowers from October through to December. Like most tea bushes, it tolerates a wide variety of soils and will flourish in both full sun and shade.

In the UK the tea bush is seldom seen, as it is difficult to cultivate it in our climate successfully. A seemingly hardy form has flourished for over forty years at the Sir Harold Hillier Gardens in Hampshire, England, in a group protected overhead by large tree canopies and sheltered by surrounding evergreens. This group, which has proven to be quite slow-growing, seems to represent two different forms, a large- and small-leafed variety, which flower every year during November and into late December.

Although it can be grown in the UK in sheltered locations, *Camellia sinensis* (tea bush camellia) is far better suited to the American climate.

Camellia ×vernalis is not widely planted in our gardens—a shame, as there are some wonderful forms available.

Cultivation Tips

If you can successfully grow *Camellia sasanqua* then you should have no difficulty growing this species; in fact, it is in many cases a far easier shrub to cultivate, although some of the varieties grown for tea production vary dramatically in hardiness. It is widely planted in the southern USA for its heat and drought tolerance. Like *C. sasanqua*, *C. sinensis* requires summer heat to ripen the wood before winter. In the UK it prefers a sheltered but sunny location with protection from late spring frosts, which will desiccate emerging leaves and flowers. This compact shrub will require little pruning; any necessary pruning should be undertaken immediately after flowering. Reported outbreaks of camellia flower blight on this species are few.

Camellia ×*vernalis* and *C.* ×*williamsii*

Common Names: Hybrid camellia, vernal camellia (*Camellia* ×*vernalis*).

Flowering Period: Late autumn to late winter.

Flowers: Single and double, in varying shades of pink, white, and pale yellow.

Height and Spread: Medium to large shrubs up to 5m (15ft) with a 3m (9ft) spread.

Camellia ×*vernalis* is a little-known group of hybrids between *C. japonica* and *C. sasanqua* with traits intermediate between both parents. These nicely rounded bushes with a slightly upright habit will slowly reach up to 5m (15ft) tall; they will often flower from autumn and continue spasmodically into spring. Their blooms are not produced in abundance, as with the *C.* ×*williamsii* hybrids, but there is undoubtedly a certain charm attached to this group; the typical garden form has exquisite, pure white, slightly scented flowers, with petals arranged neatly in three rows. *Camellia* ×*vernalis* 'Egao', a rich pink semi-double with contrasting yellow stamens, is a wonderful sight when in flower. *Camellia* ×*vernalis* 'Ginryû' ('Dawn') is a true gem of this group with double, pink tinged white flowers that are produced from winter almost to spring. *Camellia* ×*vernalis* 'Star Above Star' has a mixture of salmon-pink and pale pink, almost white petals that are relaxed, giving a somewhat symmetrical appearance to the flower. *Camellia* ×*vernalis* 'Yuletide', with small but brilliant red single flowers, blooms in late autumn and early winter.

The very diverse *Camellia* ×*williamsii* hybrids between the Japanese camellia (*C. japonica*) and Yunnan camellia (*C. saluenensis*) are considerably hardier and much showier than the straight Japanese species and produce an impressive range of flower colour, type, and growth habit. Originally raised at Caerhays Castle, Cornwall, England, in 1925, by J. C. Williams, these hybrids resemble *C. japonica* in foliage and *C. saluenensis* in flower. Today they are widely grown in several countries and form the backbone of the camellia flowering season. They are among the most adaptable camellias for general planting: they are tolerant of a wide range of soils, will grow in sun and shade, and will take heat. In the USA they are adaptable to zone 7.

Camellia ×*williamsii* 'Anticipation' is an upright form with very large, deep rose, peony-like flowers that are produced in such profusion, they weigh the branches down. *Camellia* ×*williamsii* 'Bow Bells' is not for the fainthearted: it's a big shrub, up to 5m (15ft) with a similar spread (judicial pruning maintains a smaller specimen), but its pink flowers are 100 percent reliable, covering the entire shrub from early February through late April. *Camellia* ×*williamsii* 'Donation' is arguably the best of this group and a real showstopper when, in full

Camellia ×williamsii 'Anticipation' is among the better-known large-flowering forms of this group of hybrids.

bloom, its semi-double pink flowers cover and hide the foliage; it originated at Borde Hill, Sussex, England. *Camellia ×williamsii* 'Jury's Yellow', raised in New Zealand, is most unusual-looking: its yellowish white centre gives its anemone-like flowers a yellow appearance. *Camellia ×williamsii* 'November Pink' is the earliest of this group to flower; its single, rose-pink flowers appear in late October in mild seasons.

Cultivation Tips

In the UK *Camellia ×vernalis* is proving to be hardier than the sasanquas but not as hardy as *C. japonica*; I have seen vernal camellias exposed to quite harsh conditions, where they seem to thrive. In the USA it is probably a zone 7 plant with slight protection. Plants seem to flourish in semi-shady spots, with their foliage in full sun.

Camellia ×williamsii is far more widely grown than the vernal camellia, but alas, it is also proving to be the most susceptible to camellia flower blight in the UK and in the USA. This may have something to do with the closeness of the petals and their ability to trap moisture, thus allowing the disease to spread quickly. It is widely planted throughout the UK where soil conditions allow, and it seems to be quite tolerant of wind as well. In the USA several have survived quite remarkable conditions, and although hardiness does vary from form to form, they are generally recommended for zones 6 to 9.

As with many camellias, limited pruning is required for these hybrids, although the removal of weak and crossing branches may be necessary from

Camellia 'Winton', raised by Hillier Nurseries, UK, has masses of nodding, pale pink flowers.

time to time, and should be undertaken immediately after flowering. Mulching and occasional irrigation may limit the effects of bud fall, which is a response to drought conditions.

Other winter-flowering camellias

Camellia cuspidata is a delightful and dainty camellia with a slightly drooping habit and small, pure white flowers with golden yellow stamens; it flowers in late January, early February, continuing on into spring. New foliage is an attractive bronzy colour. It requires a sheltered location but seems relatively hardy and well suited for the climate in the south of England. In the USA it is hardy to zone 7, possibly 6, and seems to have reasonable cold hardiness. In the UK (and less so in the USA), it has been widely hybridised with *C. saluenensis* to create arching, well-tempered shrubs with small pink or white flowers. *Camellia* 'Cornish Snow' is one such, a late winter–blooming shrub with a lax habit and masses of small, pure white flowers. *Camellia* 'Cornish Spring' is similar in all respects to 'Cornish Snow' but with pink flowers (*C. japonica* 'Rosea', not *C. saluenensis*, was a parent). *Camellia* 'Michael' is similar in habit to and, in my view, the best of the others named here, for its large white flowers. *Camellia* 'Winton' has nodding, soft pink flowers; it originated at Hillier Nurseries, Hampshire, England, and is named after Winton, the old name for Winchester, which was once the capital of the kingdom of Wessex.

I have encountered *Camellia brevistyla* only in the southern USA, but I was smitten with its wonderful, single white flower upon seeing it. It is seemingly hardy to zone 7 and will thrive in the same conditions as *C. sasanqua*. I wait to see how it performs in the UK, once it is introduced.

Camellia taliensis is an interesting species, closely allied to the tea bush (*C. sinensis*) but less hardy, and requiring a protected, frost-free location, where the small, nodding, white flowers (with distinct yellow stamens) develop during January. In ideal growing conditions it is ultimately a large spreading shrub or small tree to 7m (22ft); in less than ideal conditions, it is likely to be considerably smaller (2m, 6ft). It requires frost protection in the UK and is reportedly hardy to zone 7.

Camellia tsaii is a delightful species from warm climates of China, Burma, and Vietnam, where it flourishes in high rainfall. It bears masses of small, white flowers during the heart of winter and early spring, and the new foliage emerges a wonderful bronze colour, on a shrub that, given time, will reach 10m (30ft). It is unfortunately a tender species that is probably only suitable for glasshouse or conservatory cultivation in the UK. It might perform better out-of-doors in the USA, where summer temperatures are higher and wood ripens quicker; I would expect this to survive in zone 8. Slightly hardier than *C. tsaii* is *C. granthamiana*, a wonderful species native to Hong Kong; it is a medium-sized (3m, 9ft tall) shrub with the most amazing deeply veined foliage and large, pure white single flowers produced during December and continuing into winter. Suited only for protected climates in the UK and even there requiring some winter protection.

Chimonanthus   Calycanthaceae

Chimonanthus praecox

Common Names: Wintersweet, fragrant wintersweet.

Flowering Period: January, February, occasionally as late as March.

Flowers: Pale to bright yellow, occasionally stained reddish purple in the centre; double-flowering forms exist, and all are highly scented.

Height and Spread: Medium to large suckering shrub with long, arching branches and a symmetrical shape, if allowed to attain a mature stature.

Chimonanthus praecox (wintersweet) rivals the witch hazel (*Hamamelis*) for its scent and flowering characteristics and remains one of my favourite winter-flowering shrubs for its ease of growth and tolerance of alkaline soils. Three distinct forms of the wintersweet grow in our gardens, although they are commonly confused, being very similar in flower and habit. Further confusion arises from the fact that the superior forms are propagated by grafting; the use

Above left: The highly scented flowers of wintersweets are jewels in the winter landscape.

Above: *Chimonanthus praecox* 'Grandiflorus' is a large-flowering form with golden yellow petals stained red.

Left: A particularly fine form, the double-flowering *Chimonanthus praecox* var. *luteus* sold by Duncan and Davies, New Zealand.

of seed-raised understocks is quite common, as is death of the top stock. Much of what is grown in our gardens is undoubtedly *C. praecox*, which has very pale, waxy yellow flowers that are conspicuously stained and streaked red in the centre. Native to China and in cultivation in the UK and USA since 1766, it is the most widely available and hence commonly grown form.

Chimonanthus praecox 'Grandiflorus' has the largest and deepest yellow flowers of all, which again are stained and streaked red in the centre; it is the best of the commonly grown forms, simply for the size and number of its flowers. *Chimonanthus praecox* var. *luteus* is probably the easiest to distinguish: its pale yellow, often almost yellow-white flowers lack any staining in their centre, and it is often the latest to flower. I have not noticed any difference in scent among the wintersweets. I have, however, seen double-flowering forms with very pale flowers; these were purchased from Duncan and Davies of New Zealand as grafted plants of 'Grandiflorus'. Their top stock had failed, and one can only speculate that the understock was a seed-raised double-flowering form of var. luteus that had grown on. Whatever this plant is, it should be more widely grown. There is also a red-flowering form; I have not yet seen this, but by all accounts it is quite remarkable. *Chimonanthus praecox* 'Trenython' is similar to var. *luteus*, complete to the pale yellow flowers.

Cultivation Tips

In the UK the wintersweet is often grown as a fan-trained shrub against a south-facing wall, where the additional heat ripens the wood during summer and autumn and produces a spectacular display of winter flowers. In the north of England I would recommend this as the best way to grow this shrub, but in the south I would suggest growing it without protection, as it flowers equally well in a sunny location, where—if allowed to attain its full height—it is among the most wonderful of winter spectacles. Although remarkably hardy, the flowers will succumb to frost damage, especially during the sunny days and clear nights of late January, when day and night time temperatures can fluctuate greatly. That said, if summer has been kind, there will be such an abundance of flowers that this hiccup won't make much difference. In the USA *Chimonanthus praecox* is hardy in zones 6 to 9, with the flowers seemingly more frost tolerant; one can only surmise that this is due to the increase in summer temperatures.

The wintersweet is fairly easy to manage and seems to have few pest and disease problems, although honey fungus and phytophthora root rot have been reported, especially where waterlogged winter soils are a problem. Pruning is a breeze and involves removing the older branches to allow new shoots to develop from the base. It is advisable to remove about one-third of the oldest branches on a two-year cycle. Fan-trained, wall-grown specimens must have their long, whippy shoots pruned back to flowering wood immediately after flowering.

Choisya   **Rutaceae**

Choisya ternata

Common Names: Mexican orange, Mexican orange blossom.

Flowering Period: Main flowering period is during late spring and early summer, but it will also flower again in late autumn and continue into early winter.

Flowers: Pure white, highly scented, borne in clusters in profusion.

Height and Spread: A dome-headed shrub, symmetrical in shape and seldom reaching 2 × 2m (6 × 6ft).

Choisya ternata in its various guises is technically not a winter-flowering shrub: its main and most spectacular flower display is in the spring and summer. That said, its late autumn repeat bloom is worthy of note as there is little else in flower during this period; add to this its aromatic, deep evergreen foliage, and its inclusion here seems warranted. The Mexican orange blossom was first introduced into the UK in 1825 from southwest Mexico (and to the USA in 1866). It is a small to medium-sized shrub, attractive both for its aromatic trifoliate leaves and dazzling flower display. *Choisya ternata* Sundance was raised from a golden sport of *C. ternata* by Peter Catt of Liss Forest Nurseries, Hampshire, England, and with its neat habit and bright golden young foliage remains one of the best-selling small shrubs in the UK market. *Choisya ternata* Moonshine, introduced in 1992, is much larger in stature and has larger, bolder foliage and flowers.

In 1982 the first hybrid in the genus appeared, when Peter Moore of Hillier Nurseries crossed *Choisya ternata* with its southern USA relative *C. dumosa* var. *arizonica*, creating *C.* 'Aztec Pearl'. The resulting hybrid is intermediate between both parents with three to five slender, finger-like, bright green, aromatic leaflets. Like *C. ternata* it flowers profusely both in the spring and then again in late autumn, early winter; but unlike the Mexican orange the flowers are pink in bud and open pure white, and it has the added advantage of being more compact, with a more desirable habit. A more recent Peter Moore introduction is *C.* Goldfingers, a yellow form of *C.* 'Aztec Pearl', this time with *C. ternata* Sundance and *C. dumosa* var. *arizonica* as parents. The foliage is much smaller than that of *C. ternata* Sundance, more akin to that of *C. dumosa* var. *arizonica*, and its overall habit is more lax. Again, it flowers both in the spring and in the autumn.

Cultivation Tips

In the UK Mexican oranges are fairly easy to grow and thrive best in sunny locations, although those with golden foliage are not suited for alkaline soils in sunny locations—here, their foliage burns. This is also the case in the USA, where the green forms only are suitable for zones 7 to 9. I have seen *Choisya ternata* Sundance turn to a crisp in North Carolina but survive perfectly well if placed in the shade. *Choisya* 'Aztec Pearl' may offer the best option both for its habit and sun tolerance; I saw a fine-looking plant thriving in the mountains of North Carolina, near Asheville. I have also witnessed severe frost damage on plants in exposed locations; plants may require frost protection for the first few winters after planting to help them establish in the USA.

Pruning is fairly easy: tip new growth when young and continue this practice as plants mature, to develop a symmetrical habit. Overgrown shrubs may be cut back hard to allow growth to regenerate. The best time to hard prune is after spring flowering, although this will result in the loss of autumn flowers.

The flowers of the cornelian cherry, *Cornus mas*, are exceptionally hardy.

Cornus officinalis, a close relative of the cornelian cherry (*C. mas*), is coarser in appearance and has flaking bark.

Cornus   Cornaceae

Cornus mas

Common Names: Cornelian cherry, winter-flowering dogwood.

Flowering Period: January to March (March in colder climates)—the heart of winter.

Flowers: Masses of bright yellow flowers borne in clusters on naked stems.

Height and Spread: Deciduous shrub or small tree to about 6m (20ft) in height and 5m (15ft) in width, although upright forms do exist.

Cornus mas is an ultra-hardy shrub that will flower in early February in the UK but not until late February, early March in the USA in zone 4. The flowers are bombproof, and although they are only slightly scented, the overall effect against a blue sky is pretty special. The many forms are grown for their flowers, habit, foliage, and bright red, cherry-like fruits, which make exceptionally good jam!

Cornus mas 'Aurea' has bright yellow leaves during the summer; these fade to green before turning a purple-pink in the autumn. *Cornus mas* 'Aureo-elegantissima' ('Tricolor'), a painfully slow-growing form with variegated yellow foliage tinged with pink margins, is best situated in full sun. Both *C. mas* 'Golden Glory' and *C. mas* 'Hillier's Upright' have an upright habit. 'Hillier's Upright', now seldom sold, originated at Hillier Nurseries, Hampshire, England, before 1974. 'Golden Glory' is probably the best cornelian cherry for general planting as it is quick-growing and has very large flowers, attractive habit, and large, bright red fruits, produced in abundance. If you have the room, a small group of 'Golden Glory' is a wonderful winter spectacle, rivalling any winter-flowering shrub. I must rank *C. mas* 'Variegata' as one of the best variegated plants currently available and an extremely good cornelian cherry; it flowers and fruits well, and its variegation is very clean.

Cornus mas 'Flava' has yellow fruits; *C. mas* 'Jolico', *C. mas* 'Macrocarpa', and *C. mas* 'Redstone' are all grown for their fruits, which they produce in large quantities, although they are equally good in flower.

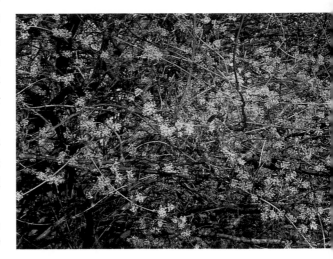

The winter effect of *Cornus officinalis* is quite spectacular.

Cornus officinalis, native to Japan and Korea, is a closely allied species; some botanists consider it to be a subspecies of *C. mas*, which is native to Europe. To the untrained eye the two appear identical, but *C. officinalis* is more coarse-looking with rougher-furrowed bark and flowers slightly larger and about two weeks earlier than *C. mas*, often in flower in late January. Fruits are bright red, and autumn tints are a rich purple.

Cultivation Tips

Cornus mas and *C. officinalis* have been in cultivation since the late 1800s. Both are very hardy and will grow throughout the UK without any problems. In the USA they are hardy in zones 4 to 8, although the variegated and golden forms may prove less so. They will thrive in both acidic and alkaline soils but will produce a more attractive shrub or small tree if grown in full sun, and are better grown in a moisture-retentive soil. Both are a pruner's nightmare as they produce crossing branches with alarming regularity, and although training from an early stage is relatively easy, tackling a mature plant is another question. Mature shrubs are probably best left unpruned, as once you start it is difficult to finish, and no matter when you leave off, you will have rendered the shrub into a hideous spectacle. That said, any pruning—even that by the bravehearted—should be undertaken after flowering.

Correa 'Dusky Bells' is one of my favourite Australian fuchsias.

Correa backhouseana is the interesting species used to create *C.* 'Ivory Bells' and many other hybrids.

Correa   **Rutaceae**

Common Name: Australian fuchsia.

Flowering Period: In the mildest climates from November to late March.

Flowers: Pale pink, red, greenish white, or green, bell-shaped, tipped with yellow-green or occasionally pink.

Height and Spread: Low-growing evergreen shrub seldom reaching 2.5m (8ft) tall and wide, more commonly 1m (3ft) or even more compact.

Correa alba 'Pinkie' is an attractive white-flowering form with pink-tipped petals. *Correa* 'Dusky Bells', a probable hybrid between *C. pulchella* and *C. reflexa*, is a compact, dwarf shrub with pinkish red flowers. Arguably of the same parentage is *C.* 'Mannii' (*C.* ×*harrisii*, *C.* 'Harrisii') with yellow stamens protruding from the long (2.5cm, 1in) scarlet-red flower; it is the most compact and probably the best of the Australian fuchsias.

Correa 'Ivory Bells' is a *C. alba* and *C. backhouseana* hybrid with creamy white flowers that are 2.5cm (1in) long, while *C.* 'Marian's Marvel' is an upright form with pendulous flowers pink at the base and then fading to yellow-green at the tip. *Correa reflexa* is the most widely seen in botanic or public gardens as it makes an excellent winter-flowering shrub for the glasshouse (and is a special sight indeed if grown in a mild enough climate); flowers 2.5cm (1in) long are produced in abundance right through winter and can be either red tipped with green (commonest form) or simply pale green.

Cultivation Tips

Correas can be cultivated only in the mildest areas of the UK and are suitable for the extreme south or other areas affected by the Gulf Stream; in the USA they are zone 8 plants. They thrive best in locations where sun and free-draining soils are available, but prefer acidic soils that do not waterlog during the winter months, as overly wet conditions in winter cause plants to fail quickly. In the UK they can be grown against south-facing walls; in the USA, with the increase in light levels, reflected light from walls can be problematic. Pruning is seldom necessary apart from helping the shrubs to develop a "tidy" habit; such trimming should be undertaken after flowering has finished.

In essence Australian fuchsias do not flower in response to cold periods but rather because they are southern hemisphere plants flowering toward the end of their spring, which happens to be our winter. They add variety to the winter garden, bringing with them unusual—and welcome—flower shapes and hues.

Corylopsis   **Hamamelidaceae**

Corylopsis coreana

Common Names: Korean winter hazel, buttercup winter hazel.

Flowering Period: Late February, early March.

Flowers: Fragrant, yellow, cupped, borne in hanging tassels, appearing before the foliage in early spring.

Height and Spread: Painfully slow-growing but eventually reaching 2 × 2m (6 × 6ft).

It is unfortunate that *Corylopsis coreana* is seldom seen or offered by nurseries as it is the first of the winter hazels to flower—often weeks in advance of *C. pauciflora*, *C. sinensis* var. *calvescens*, *C. spicata*, and other more widely grown forms. Its flowers are typical of the winter hazels; its foliage is quite large and produces a blue-green colouration that, prior to its turning a radiant butter-yellow in autumn,

Corylopsis coreana, the Korean winter hazel, is too infrequently seen in our gardens.

The Korean winter hazel should also be considered for its attractive blue-green foliage and autumn colour.

displays a purplish tint. Although somewhat more compact than most of its relatives (possibly excepting *C. spicata*), this species is a real gem and will often flower toward the tail end of some of the late-flowering witch hazels (*Hamamelis japonica* or *H. vernalis*). But don't be mistaken: even against such competition, this is a class act. I have sometimes seen this species offered as *C. gotoana* var. *coreana*.

Cultivation Tips

Finding this plant for sale is actually more difficult than growing it. The best location is that of light-dappled shade, interplanted with other winter-flowering shrubs, although it can grace a sunny location as well. It thrives in moist, acidic, humus-rich soils that does not become waterlogged in late winter or early spring. As with the witch hazels, summer drought can cause serious problems: summer irrigation is a must. If you are looking for a companion plant, then look no further than *Rhododendron dauricum*. Pruning couldn't be simpler: remove old shoots every three years. In the UK this form should survive and thrive in most locations, as long as you remember the summer irrigation. In the USA it should be hardy in zones 6 to 9; in the southern states more shade during summer would be advantageous. In my view, all the winter hazels should be more widely planted, as they are remarkably hardy and tolerant of a wide range of soils.

Daboecia   **Ericaceae**

Daboecia cantabrica
Flowering Period: November.

Flowers: Bell-shaped, carried in long racemes, similar to those of heather but larger, in shades of white, red, and purple.

Height and Spread: Low-growing evergreen shrubs seldom reaching 50cm (20in) tall, more commonly 30 to 35cm (12 to 14in), with a 30cm (12in) spread.

A useful group of late summer-flowering evergreen shrubs, similar to heathers in their lime-hating proclivities, but whose flowering period extends into early winter, making them useful evergreen groundcovers in the winter garden. There are numerous flowering forms.

Daboecia cantabrica 'Bicolor' has white and rose-purple individual flowers that are often mixed together on a single flower spike—very attractive when seen as a mass planting. In contrast *D. cantabrica* 'David Moss' reads as masses of pure white, while *D. cantabrica* subsp. *scotica* 'Jack Drake' has ruby-red flowers and is somewhat shorter than the norm at 20cm (8in), but makes an excellent companion plant for any white-flowering forms. *Daboecia cantabrica* subsp. *scotica* 'Waley's Red' has deep magenta flowers and is reasonably tall at 35cm (14in); it makes a stunning companion for the best of the whites, *D. cantabrica* subsp. *scotica* 'White Blum', with its upright habit and tall, straight flower spikes.

Cultivation Tips

Daboecias prefer moist, acid conditions with a cool root run. They are easy to prune using hedge trimmers (whether electric, gas/petrol, or manual) or even a Strimmer (Weed Whacker) immediately after flowering, removing the old flower spikes and surrounding growth. It is possible to sculpt some interesting shapes using this method, which seems to mimic the natural action of sheep grazing and keeps plants compact and dense but does not interfere with flowering.

Daphne   **Thymelaeaceae**

Daphne bholua

Common Names: Himalayan daphne, paper daphne.

Flowering Period: Early January through to March, although there have been
   reports of it flowering as early as November in mild years.

Flowers: Very highly scented, mauve in bud, opening white or reddish mauve.

Height and Spread: Can reach over 2m (6ft) high with a 1.5m (5ft) spread.

Daphne bholua is a variable species with a wide distribution throughout the eastern Himalaya, where the unbreakable bark is stripped from plants and used to make paper pulp and rope (hence, paper daphne), and where it flowers from February to March and then produces black fruits in April. In cultivation, fruits are seldom produced, unless flowers are hand-pollinated. The wonderful valley of *D. bholua* planted by Tony Schilling (then curator) at RBG Kew, Wakehurst Place, West Sussex, is one of the most breathtaking and sensual sights I have ever seen in a garden in winter. The various white, pink, and mauve flowers fill the air with strong but sweet scent, which can be experienced some considerable distance away. *Daphne bholua* 'Alba' is the name given to the several forms with pale pink or pure white buds that open to reveal almost pure white flowers; this group is probably better cited as *D. bholua* f. *alba* (and perhaps the best forms could then be given cultivar names). All the white forms have narrow evergreen or semi-evergreen foliage; plants available on the UK and European markets tend to be fairly variable but distinctive, especially if you're lucky enough to buy the pure white form. *Daphne bholua* 'Darjeeling', an evergreen to semi-evergreen high-altitude form originally distributed by an Indian nurseryman called Ghose of Darjeeling in 1961, flourished against a wall at RHS Garden Wisley, in Surrey, England, where it reached over 3m (9ft) high; although generally produced by grafting it is one of the easiest of this group to be produced by cuttings and is among the first daphnes to flower, with its pale pink-budded, opening white, highly scented flowers.

    Daphne bholua var. *glacialis* 'Gurkha', collected by Major Tom Spring Smyth (T.S.S. 132B) at 3200m (10,500ft) in eastern Nepal in 1962, is probably the hardiest Himalayan daphne currently available. Unfortunately there is confusion over the true identity of this wonderful form; it may be that the original plant has been over-propagated, or perhaps many of the plants in cultivation were collected from open-pollinated plants and grown as seedlings. In its true form, it is fully deciduous and may reach 2m (6ft) tall and 1.5m (5ft) wide, and produces masses of tight clusters of very highly scented white flowers, which are mauve-

Daphne bholua 'Jacqueline Postill' produces masses of intoxicatingly fragrant flowers from December to March.

Daphne bholua 'Peter Smithers', like many Himalayan daphnes, produces flowers on wood of all ages.

purple on the outside, from Christmas until late February. *Daphne bholua* 'Jacqueline Postill', another of the great introductions made by Hillier Nurseries, England, was raised by Hillier's propagator Alan Postill from seed collected from 'Gurkha'. Himalayan daphnes seldom produce seed in gardens, and it was therefore quite an event when Alan noticed seed developing on 'Gurkha' in 1982. He collected the seed and germinated it, and the resulting seedling he named after his wife, Jacqueline. *Daphne bholua* 'Jacqueline Postill' differs from 'Gurkha' in its semi-evergreen habit; it flowers in profusion when in leaf, the white-centred interior of the flower contrasting well against the pale mauve of the petal's exterior, with a perfume superior to that of 'Gurkha'—in fact, it will dominate a garden to such an extreme that it excludes the scent of witch hazels and Christmas box, *Sarcococca*.

Daphne bholua 'Peter Smithers' was named in 1990 from a plant grown at Wakehurst Place, UK, from seed collected from Peter Smithers's garden in Switzerland, from a group of seedlings he collected from Daman Ridge in 1970. They are very quick-growing, reaching over 2m (6ft) in four years, semi- to evergreen and producing masses of highly scented flowers, purple in bud, with the inner petals purple-pink, fading to white in the centre. Other plants from this collection, circulated as *D. bholua* 'Daman Ridge' and *D. bholua* 'Peter Smithers Seedlings' (both invalid names), are seedlings raised and distributed to various people from the plants growing in his Swiss garden. *Daphne bholua* 'Glendoick' is a quick-growing selection from a plant collected by Peter Cox of

Glendoick Nurseries in Scotland (it was originally going to be distributed as 'Heaven Scent'); I have not seen the original plant, but it is reportedly a hardier, bigger-flowering, and richer flower colour form than *D. bholua* 'Jacqueline Postill'. If this is true, it must be a spectacular sight when in flower. *Daphne bholua* 'Sheopuri'—alas, no longer in cultivation—was a named form from seedlings collected in Sheopuri, Nepal, by G. Herklots in 1962. It grew for many years at Windsor Great Park, England, a very compact, white-flowering form with semi-evergreen foliage; it is possible that some of the various forms of *D. bholua* f. *alba* originated from this plant. *Daphne bholua* 'Rupina La' is a strange form with very thick stems named from a plant growing at Wakehurst Place from seed collected in Nepal in 1983 by Tony Schilling, under the collector's number Schilling 2611; many people suggest that this form is best grown in a cool or temperate greenhouse.

Cultivation Tips

Himalayan daphnes from lower-elevation collections tend to be evergreen and not as hardy as the deciduous but hardier higher-elevation forms. The evergreen forms are best grown against a south-facing wall, or in a cool glasshouse, although they will thrive out-of-doors remarkably well in the south of England. The deciduous *Daphne bholua* var. *glacialis* 'Gurkha' is best for widespread planting, while *D. bholua* 'Jacqueline Postill' and 'Peter Smithers' are the preferred evergreen to semi-evergreen forms. In my view *D. bholua* 'Jacqueline Postill' is the very best and will take some beating. All Himalayan daphnes will thrive in both acidic and alkaline conditions as long as they receive sufficient moisture during the growing season. To achieve this, I mulch the plants with leaf litter or composted bark. 'Gurkha' and 'Jacqueline Postill' seem hardy across most of the UK, and I have seen both flourishing in Edinburgh, Scotland; however, neither will tolerate extreme wind exposure. In the USA, they seem to be a complete unknown, and I can only suggest that they may be tried where *D. odora* will flourish, so I am nervously going to recommend zones 7 to 9 for most evergreen forms and, maybe, a zone 5 for *D. bholua* var. *glacialis* 'Gurkha'.

Daphne bholua var. *glacialis* 'Gurkha' can be distinguished by its deciduous habit.

One of their main drawbacks is that many Himalayan daphnes are still propagated by grafting. I have experience with plants of *Daphne bholua* 'Jacqueline Postill' grafted onto *D. longilobata* (used because it readily produces seed); they grow vigorously for eight to ten years and then die suddenly the next, as the root system has collapsed. I have also easily propagated *D. bholua* f. *alba* and *D. bholua* 'Darjeeling' from cuttings (the plants grew quickly) and rooted 'Gurkha' and 'Jacqueline Postill' (the plants took a long time to root, and those that did were very slow to establish). Of the original propagules, all the 'Gurkha' eventually died, but a few of the 'Jacqueline Postill' are still alive and flourishing, some eleven years after they were propagated.

In the end, both 'Gurkha' and 'Jacqueline Postill' may prove to be the best two daphnes of this group for general planting, especially now that micropropagated plants of 'Jacqueline Postill', courtesy of Hillier Nurseries of Hampshire, England, are making their way onto the marketplace. Microprogated plants, which produce suckers like those in the wild, are more long-lived than grafted plants. According to Major Tom Spring Smyth, 'Gurkha' grows for a very long time in the wild as a suckering shrub (he had great difficulty in finding seedlings as most of the young-looking plants were in fact suckers). This suckering habit may lead to longevity in our gardens as, according to reports, the centre of the shrub dies and the suckers grow on (and remember, 'Jacqueline Postill' was raised from seed collected from 'Gurkha' and as such may retain its suckering habits). Recently planted micropropagated plants are now suckering, which will allow these Himalayan daphnes to live for thirty to forty years in our gardens.

Other winter-flowering daphnes

Common Names: Spurge laurel (*Daphne laureola*); mezereon, February daphne (*D. mezereum*); winter daphne, fragrant daphne (*D. odora*).

Flowering Period: *Daphne jezoensis* flowers as early as November through to March; *D. laureola* and *D. laureola* subsp. *philippi* flower during February and March; *D. mezereum* and its various forms flower during January and February, occasionally March; *D. odora* flowers in February and March.

Flowers: *Daphne jezoensis* is a real star with brilliant yellow, sweetly scented flowers; *D. laureola* has curious yellow-green fragrant flowers that are obscured by the foliage; *D. laureola* subsp. *philippi* is a less vigorous form with smaller flowers; *D. mezereum* has white, red-purple, or rose-pink scented flowers; *D. odora* has very fragrant purple or white flowers.

Height and Spread: Most will not exceed 1.5m (5ft) with an equal spread; these daphnes are all classed as small shrubs.

The brilliant yellow flowers of *Daphne jezoensis* are distinct among winter-flowering daphnes.

Daphne jezoensis, a deciduous Japanese treasure introduced around 1960, made quite a stir as the list of winter-flowering daphnes was at that time very small. It is somewhat odd: its new leaves are produced in autumn and are pale green, ripening to blue-green if you get the conditions right. Highly scented clusters of sweetly scented yellow flowers are produced in January, but I have seen it flowering as early as November. In the summer it drops all it leaves completely; I was scared to death the first time I witnessed this, thinking I had killed another daphne.

Daphne laureola is not the most spectacular of the winter-flowering daphnes, but it does have its use. Its unusual clusters of scented yellow-green flowers are hidden beneath its large evergreen leaves in such a way that it is difficult to work out whence in the garden the scent emanates. The effect becomes more obvious through the day, as the scent builds, and is strongest at night. It is a useful, small shrub for planting in quite dense shade beneath other, taller shrubs, and will thrive in locations otherwise suitable only for *Sarcococca*, the Christmas box. *Daphne laureola* is native to south and western Europe, including the UK, where it thrives in shady locations, on alkaline soils that are very dry during the summer. *Daphne laureola* subsp. *philippi* is an even more compact form found in the Pyrenees, and although more commonly seen in the rock garden, it is perfectly happy if planted elsewhere in the landscape. Both forms are long lived, and plants over twenty years old have been reported.

No winter-orientated planting or winter garden should be without *Daphne mezereum* and its purple-red flowers—no plant looks quite like it in the landscape in February. It has been popular for its sweetly scented flowers for hundreds of years and is considered by many to be one of our best native shrubs, inhabiting chalk woodland in a few locations in England. A number of forms appear in commerce, with flowers varying from purple-red to white. *Daphne mezereum* f. *alba*, a quick-growing white-flowered form with yellow translucent fruits, was probably selected from a wild population. Although many of the white-flowering forms come true from seed, they do exhibit slight variation in flower size and colour, from white to cream; and the berries too vary, from white to pale amber. *Daphne mezereum* 'Bowles' White' ('Bowles' Variety') is a superior white-flowering form with pearl-white berries and exceedingly good habit, up to 2m (6ft) tall; again, as it is commonly seed-raised, it will exhibit slight variation. *Daphne mezereum* var. *autumnalis*, a strange form with large purple-red flowers from September right through to February, is now reduced to a few specimens tucked away in botanical or specialised collections. *Daphne mezereum* 'Alba Plena' is a magnificent double white that, unfortunately, seems to have dropped out of commerce; I have tried for years to track down this plant without success, and I am almost convinced that it no longer exists, but I will keep trying. *Daphne mezereum* 'Rosea' is a seedling selection with pale rose-pink flowers rather than the more traditional and vibrant purple-red blooms; *D. mezereum* var. *rubra* is a selected form with flowers more reddish than purple. Both these forms appear from time to time in seedling populations. There is also a report of a double red form which, like the double white, I have not seen. Reports of a variegated mezereon have been around since 1856, when *D. mezereum* 'Variegata' arose in a batch of seedlings raised in a garden in Leeds, England. A single form is still available, although I doubt it is the same form from all those years ago; it is more likely to be another seedling variation. The variegation is a green and yellow mottling—very different from the unsightly virus speckling that plagues this species.

The fragrant or winter daphne, *Daphne odora*, is a useful evergreen species native to China and Japan and cultivated in the UK since 1771. A slow-growing shrub, it may reach only 2m (6ft) high with a dome habit and masses of highly scented pale purple flowers. Several forms are available in the UK, considerably more in the USA; I have encountered the following, many of which, in my view, should not have been named.

Daphne odora f. *alba*, a long-established selection with off-white to pure white flowers and rich green foliage, is not the hardiest of available forms. *Daphne odora* 'Aureamarginata Alba' is a fairly recent introduction with white flowers and yellow margins to the leaf. *Daphne odora* 'Sakiwaka', which originated in Japan, is another pure white form. *Daphne odora* 'Aureomarginata', the hardiest of this group, has a yellow margin on emerging leaves that fades and narrows to a creamy white and contrasts against the reddish purple flowers; it is hoped its reverse variegated form, *D. odora* 'Geisha Girl', with a creamy white centre to the leaf and green margin, will be as hardy. *Daphne odora* 'Walberton', originated at Walberton Nursery, West Sussex, England, looks very similar to *D. odora* 'Aureomarginata'; although I have not seen this form in flower, I wait to be impressed! *Daphne odora* 'Clotted Cream', named by Karan Junker of PMA Nurseries, Somerset, England, is another variegated selection with a very wide white band around the leaf; it has recently been replaced by *D. odora* 'Double Cream', which retains the attractive white margin but is more vigorous. *Daphne odora* var. *rubra* is a fairly compact form with deep red flower buds that open to reveal reddish pink flowers. Similar is *D. odora* 'Rose Queen', which has rich green foliage and dark, deep red flowers.

Cultivation Tips

A major drawback to *Daphne mezereum* and *D. odora* is that they are affected by a virus that causes lack of vigour; leaves curl in an unsightly manner, and in some cases the plant dies. That said, virus-free micropropagated material is resetting the balance, and daphnes are now making a comeback.

Daphne jezoensis is best suited to a moist but free-draining soil, preferably in a slightly acidic soil in a slightly shady location that gets late morning sun. It is a compact species, requiring little pruning at all. In the UK it should be hardy in most areas; in the USA it is hardy in zones 6 to 8. *Daphne laureola* and its subsp. *philippi* are ideal for dry, shady areas and will grow happily in both alkaline and acidic soils. They grow extensively throughout the UK, and in the USA they should prove equally adaptable and thrive in zones 5 to 8. *Daphne mezereum* is undoubtedly the hardiest of this group and will thrive in heavy alkaline soils as long as they do not bake hard in the summer months. Hardy throughout the UK and zones 4 to 8 in the USA. *Daphne odora* 'Aureomarginata', the most commonly grown of the odora group, has survived considerable frost damage in the UK; that said, it is better suited for the south of England or areas with less winter rainfall, as this last will see this small, compact evergreen daphne off more quickly than anything else. Suitable in the USA for zones 7 to 9. Note: these daphnes fruit very well in favourable conditions, and the fruits—along with other parts of the plant—are poisonous.

Dirca   Thymelaeaceae

Common Names: Wicopy, leatherwood.

Flowering Period: As early as February but normally March.

Flowers: Yellow, daphne-like, usually borne in clusters of three on naked branches and differing from *Daphne* in that the stamens and style protrude beyond the flower.

Height and Spread: 2m (6ft) tall by 4m (12ft) wide.

Dirca occidentalis (western leatherwood) is somewhat rare in its native habitat of California. *Dirca palustris* is more widely spread and more commonly seen in the USA; there it has some landscape appeal, especially in areas of shade, where its lush foliage can develop and turn butter-yellow in autumn. Native Americans used leatherwood bark for the string in bows, as fishing line, and for basket making; one can assume that the bark is as strong as that of the Himalayan daphnes. The western leatherwood is somewhat larger, both in stature and in flower size; I have seen it only a few times in gardens in the UK. Both are suckering species and in the wild can cover quite a reasonable area.

Cultivation Tips

Both species prefer shady locations, predominantly those that are fertile and moist throughout most of the year. In fact, I have witnessed a large, suckering clump of *Dirca palustris* partially submerged during the winter months, and it still flowered in abundance in March. Both leatherwoods are collectors or curiosity plants, and it is a shame that neither is more widely planted, as anywhere *Daphne laureola* would thrive, I am sure *Dirca palustris* would. I have not seen either leatherwood offered by nurseries in the UK, which is disappointing as either would make a delightful landscape feature, flowering away in winter in a woodland garden. As for hardiness I can only surmise that both species would be perfectly hardy in the UK if given the right conditions. In the USA, *D. palustris* is arguably the hardier of the two, zones 4 to 9, and is more readily available from seed-raised plants. *Dirca occidentalis* is hardy in zones 6 to 8, a trouble-free small shrub with good autumn colour and a useful plant in the winter garden.

Edgeworthia   **Thymelaeaceae**

Common Names: Paperbush, fragrant paper bush, oriental rice paper plant, knot plant.

Flowering Period: February and March, occasionally in April.

Flowers: Pendulous, silky white, fragrant, yellow-centred, borne in large clusters, groups of forty to fifty individual flowers on naked branches.

Height and Spread: 2.5 × 2.5m (8 × 8ft). Plants tend to sucker and may exceed these dimensions; some new cultivars are more compact.

There is something quite romantic and somewhat tropical about seeing a paperbush in full flower during late February, its silky white but yellow-centred pendulous clusters of nodding flowers hanging their heads from the stout branches. Even with its blooms fully closed and protected from the winter air, this delightful shrub still has a photographic appeal. *Edgeworthia chrysantha* (or *E. papyrifera*, as I knew it then) was a particular favourite of mine when I was attending college at Cannington, Somerset, England, where a large plant dominated the bee garden, not only for its strange habit but also because you could tie knots in the branches, which actually continued to grow despite the knots. It bloomed relentlessly throughout late winter, filling the air with its scent—which, although interesting, was not quite in the same league as a Himalayan daphne in full swing.

In later years, as I became more familiar with this plant, I quickly learned that *Edgeworthia* nomenclature is confused: some authorities quote three species, while others quote two. The culprit for this confusion is *E. chrysantha*, which seems to be synonymous with *E. papyrifera*; both names still appear in nursery catalogues, and some still argue that the two "twins" are different. That said, several cultivars of *E. chrysantha* exist. I am still not convinced they are distinct, and there is certainly cause to bring this group together to trial.

Edgeworthia chrysantha 'Grandiflora' is a form with larger flowers; the specimens I have seen looked exactly like a well-grown *E. chrysantha*, and the more I see, the less convinced I become. *Edgeworthia chrysantha* 'Red Dragon' is among the best forms I have seen, although to call the flowers red is pushing it by any stretch of the imagination: they may give the effect of being red from a distance, but the closer you get, the less red they look. The flowers are, in fact, orange-red. Still, it is a mighty handsome plant, variously offered as *E. chrysantha* f. *rubra*, *E. chrysantha* 'Rubra', *E. chrysantha* 'Ruby Flash', *E. chrysantha* 'Jitsu Red', and *E. chrysantha* 'Akebono' (some of these may be selected reddish-flowering seedlings). *Edgeworthia chrysantha* 'Gold Rush' is a popular cultivar in the USA; I saw it just about everywhere during my last trip there. Quite compact, it may reach only 2m (6ft) tall and has lush blue-green foliage during summer, yellow autumn colour, and in winter is loaded with flowers. I first came across this plant in the garden of Tony Avent (owner of Plant Delights) in North Carolina, where I was impressed by its wonderful silhouette and the sheer quantity of flowers. I introduced a plant into the UK and can only hope that it will soon be more widely available.

The remaining species is *Edgeworthia gardneri*, which also appears in the Himalayas, although I do not know if the paths of the species cross. Philipp von Siebold introduced *E. chrysantha* from China in 1845, while *E. gardneri* from Sikkim was named by Nathaniel Wallich (as *Daphne gardneri*) in 1820, so both plants have been known for some considerable time. *Edgeworthia gardneri* is distinguished by its much larger foliage, 15 to 20cm (6 to 8in) long, with a slightly glaucous or blue sheen to the surface to the leaf. The flowers are also less spectacular than *E. chrysantha* and tend to be more white and silky with little or no yellow.

Both species are used in herbal medicines and as a source of wood, and both are a source of raw material for the unique, traditional handmade paper of central and eastern Himalaya. *Edgeworthia chrysantha* was introduced into Japan, where it is used for making high-quality paper for bank notes.

Cultivation Tips

How I long to have a mature *Edgeworthia chrysantha* flowering in my Hampshire garden. Plants seem to thrive for a short while and then wither in autumn, which must be an indication of the dryness of my soil and the site's exposure to wind during the winter months. Throughout my travels I have met this wonderful species in many different locations, all characterized by two constants: moist, humus-rich soil during summer and protection from cold winds in the winter. It seems to me that in the UK these plants would enjoy the protection and heat of a south-facing wall but would resent the dryness of the soil and reflected heat. With that in mind, a protected, lightly shaded location might be best, especially one where protection is provided all around and from above. The soil must be moisture-retentive; plants do not seem to be very tolerant of drought. In the right conditions they are quick-growing. I have seen single-stem tree-like forms that develop a round head, but I prefer them grown as more natural-looking multi-stemmed shrubs. In the UK both species could be cultivated against a protected wall or in a woodland garden, providing adequate moisture is available. In the USA they seem to enjoy the heat and seem suitable for zones 7 to 9.

Elaeagnus   Elaeagnaceae

Common Names: Silverberry, Russian olive, oleaster.

Flowering Period: Late autumn into early winter.

Flowers: Silvery white, scaly, often hidden by the foliage but very highly scented.

Height and Spread: Fast-growing evergreen shrubs exceeding 4 × 4m (12 × 12ft).

These very useful plants are not for the fainthearted, what with their rate of growth and how difficult they are to prune, but they make wonderful hedges and windbreaks and are especially good for coastal gardens. Flowers are highly scented and are produced in abundance in late October and November.

Elaeagnus ×*ebbingei* is a widely grown hybrid between *E. macrophylla* and *E. pungens*. I am less fond of its several variegated foliage forms; I am more intrigued by what effects its attractive silver foliage forms can bring to a winter garden. But be warned: this quick-growing evergreen shrub will outgrow your garden while your back is turned. In autumn and early winter, this is a fun shrub to have around: the small, silver-white flowers, covered in small brown scales, are hidden beneath the large silver leaves—the last place anyone would look in an attempt to track down the source of the strong scent wafting through the air. It occasionally climbs or scrambles; I have seen it do this up quite tall trees. *Elaeagnus* ×*ebbingei* 'Albert Doorenbos' is named after its raiser, who selected this form from the original hybrid raised in The Hague, The Netherlands, for its much wider (5cm, 2in) leaves, which can reach 10cm (4in) long. The emerging leaves of *E.* ×*ebbingei* 'Coastal Gold', a newer introduction, give the appearance of plain silver foliage but then develop broad, yellow and green margins. Excellent for seaside planting. *Elaeagnus* ×*ebbingei* 'Gilt Edge', undoubtedly the best of the bunch, has brilliant gold margins to the leaves and seldom shows any sign of reversion. *Elaeagnus* ×*ebbingei* 'Limelight', commonly known for its reversion problems, has broad leaves with very prominent silver scales and a large central, deep yellow blotch. *Elaeagnus* ×*ebbingei* 'The Hague' is another original seedling selected for its narrower foliage.

Elaeagnus glabra is a wonderful and very vigorous evergreen shrub with narrow leaves and masses of small, silver and scaly flowers in late October, followed in spring by bright orange berries. *Elaeagnus macrophylla*, a large marauding shrub that reaches quite large proportions when fully grown, provided some of the vigour for the *E.* ×*ebbingei* hybrids. Its foliage has the typical silvery sheen on both the top and bottom surfaces; it flowers in late autumn.

Elaeagnus macrophylla is an unruly shrub best grown into a tree, or pruned annually into a more controllable shape.

Elaeagnus ×*ebbingei* is an underrated winter-flowering shrub as its highly scented paper-like flowers are hidden by the foliage.

Elaeagnus pungens is a large, versatile shrub whose occasionally thorny branches allow it to scramble up and over trees. Leaves are green and shiny above, pale white underneath, with distinctive brown scales. This Japanese treasure has given rise to numerous forms. *Elaeagnus pungens* 'Dicksonii' ('Aurea') is a delightful slow-growing form with an upright habit and a golden yellow margin to the leaf. Somewhat shy to flower. *Elaeagnus pungens* 'Frederici', a very long-cultivated and slow-growing form, has narrow leaves that have an almost entirely creamy yellow surface, with occasional green borders. *Elaeagnus pungens* 'Hosoba-fukurin' is easy to identify with its spiny shoots, and wavy, narrowly yellow-margined leaves; it is somewhat lax in form and is less likely to scorch. *Elaeagnus pungens* 'Maculata' is a Jekyll-and-Hyde shrub that grows quite slowly until established and then with alarming speed. Among the most distinct forms, with a central splash of gold in the middle of the leaf, it is prone to reversion and can turn almost back to green; reverted shoots should be removed quickly before the variegation is lost. *Elaeagnus pungens* 'Forest Gold', a probable variation or sport of *E. pungens* 'Maculata', differs in its more upright habit and large central yellow leaf blotch; it is less likely to revert. *Elaeagnus pungens* 'Goldrim' is, in my opinion, the best of all the silverberries and yet again a sport of *E. pungens* 'Maculata'; it offers quite narrow, shiny green leaves with a very bright yellow margin.

Cultivation Tips

The silverberries are a trouble-free group of attractive evergreen shrubs suitable for a very wide range of soils, from light, free-draining chalk to heavy clay and friable sandy soils; they are exceptionally good for seaside plantings. Their only real drawback is their quick growth, and although some make attractive but large, dome-shaped shrubs, many can prove to be quite unruly if planted in the wrong location. They are best planted as backdrops for other shrubs: their foliage is easily their best attribute, although their scented flowers make an added bonus in autumn.

In the UK they are ultra-hardy and suffer only occasional frost damage; in the USA they are hardy in zones 7 and 8. Site variegated selections in light shade to avoid scorching the foliage.

Erica   **Ericaceae**

Common Names: Winter heath, heath, winter heather, snow heather, spring heather (*Erica carnea*); Darley Dale heath (*E.* ×*darleyensis*).

Flowering Period: Earliest forms flower in November, latest in March and April, but the main season is January to March.

Flowers: Small, bell-shaped, borne in clusters up the stem in shades of white, pink, purple, and red.

Height and Spread: Maximum if unpruned, 20 × 40cm (8 × 16in) for *Erica carnea* but somewhat taller in *E.* ×*darleyensis*.

Over the years the heaths (*Erica carnea*) have fallen in and out of favour with gardeners and garden designers alike, although these days, with the focus on low-maintenance gardening, they are making a comeback. The 2004 edition of the *RHS Plant Finder* lists 130 cultivars of *E. carnea* and a further thirty-one entries for *E.* ×*darleyensis*. This makes it fairly easy to select forms that are either in flower in winter or have striking foliage if not, so that interest can be provided regardless of the month. Traditional associated plantings for heather include dwarf rhododendrons and conifers, both now very much out of favour; but the various foliage effects of heathers and heaths can complement and contrast with many other winter-flowering shrubs, such as *Sarcococca* spp., and they make a wonderful foil against which to show off winter stems. They also provide shade and protection for both winter- and spring-flowering bulbs. In short, heathers are simply too important a group of plants to restrict to the specialist heather garden and should be used wherever hard-wearing groundcover is required.

Many heather hybrids are natural occurring; others originated in nurseries and gardens. One such group are the hybrids between *Erica carnea* and *E. erigena*, *E. ×darleyensis*, aptly named the Darley Dale heath, as it originated at Darley Dale Nursery, Derbyshire, England, in 1890. The hybrids are intermediate between both parents and retain the best attributes of each. They are more vigorous than *E. carnea*, with larger flowers that are occasionally scented; and one can assume that the attractive flecked colouration on some of the spring foliage is a trait from *E. carnea*.

I have selected some of my favourite heathers, and these I have separated into flower colour.

Red- and purple-flowering heathers

Erica carnea 'Adrienne Duncan' is a fabulous heather with deep purple flowers and dark green foliage, tinged purple in winter; it grows to 15cm (6in) high and 35cm (14in) wide. *Erica ×darleyensis* 'Arthur Johnson' is among the best hybrids for cutting in winter. The flowers are slightly scented, bright pink initially and then changing to heliotrope, but on tall stems: this is a tall-growing form, often reaching 60cm (24in) tall and spreading 75cm (30in), and its distinct green foliage is tipped cream in spring. *Erica carnea* 'December Red', 15 × 35cm (6 × 14in), flowers reliably and somewhat longer than just in December: its rose-red flowers can continue into spring. *Erica carnea* 'Challenger', with its very dark magenta flowers and dark green foliage, is similar in all respects to *E. carnea* 'Myretoun Ruby'. *Erica ×darleyensis* 'Kramer's Rote' has very deep magenta flowers and wonderful rich bronzy foliage in spring. A very distinct and compact form, seldom exceeding 35cm (14in) tall. *Erica carnea* 'Myretoun Ruby' offers gorgeous magenta flowers set against deep green foliage, reaching 15cm (6in) high by 45cm (18in) wide. A must for any garden, and long cultivated since it was raised at Myretoun House, Scotland, UK, in 1965. *Erica carnea* 'Nathalie' has fantastic purple flowers in winter against a background of dark green foliage. Arguably one of the deepest and darkest of the *E. carnea* forms, ultimately growing to 15cm (6in) high by 40cm (16in) wide. *Erica carnea* 'Praecox Rubra' is a compact and spreading form, 15cm (6in) high by 40cm (16in) wide, with rich magenta flowers and green foliage occasionally tinged bronze in winter.

Erica carnea 'R. B. Cooke' is among the best pink-flowering winter heathers.

Pink-flowering heathers

Erica carnea 'Ann Sparkes' and 'R. B. Cooke' are two of the best rose-pink flowering heathers around; 'Ann Sparkes', a compact grower to 15cm (6in) high by 25cm (10in) wide, also has bright orange foliage that will turn crimson and bronze during winter. *Erica carnea* 'Aurea' has very bright yellow foliage that is complemented by lilac-pink flowers in late winter; it is the same height as 'Ann Sparkes' but spreads to 35cm (14in), and its foliage tends to scorch in full sun.

Erica ×*darleyensis* 'Darley Dale', a very old cultivar and probably the most widely grown of the heathers, is a compact form, ultimately 30cm (12in) wide and tall, with pale pink flowers borne over a very long period. *Erica* ×*darleyensis* 'Furzey' originated at Furzey Gardens in Hampshire, England, with deep lilac-pink flowers that deepen to heliotrope. Its foliage is tipped in spring with cream and white, and it may spread to 60cm (24in) but will seldom exceed 35cm (14in) in height. *Erica carnea* 'Foxhollow' is a particular favourite of mine as the yellow and bronze foliage deepens to orange and red during winter, just when the shell-pink flowers are produced. A compact but wide-spreading form, ultimately 5cm (6in) tall by 40cm (16in) wide. *Erica* ×*darleyensis* 'Ghost Hills' is a sport selected off *E.* ×*darleyensis* 'Darley Dale' but stronger growing and somewhat taller. Pale pink flowers are produced in winter and spring. *Erica carnea* 'Lake Garda', a favourite with deep green foliage and delightful pale pink flowers during winter, is slightly spreading, often reaching 40cm (16in) wide. *Erica carnea* 'Pink Spangles', a quick-growing and spreading heather, carries its very large, bright pink flowers in late winter. *Erica carnea* 'Rosalie', the most suitable of the winter-flowering heathers for container growing, offers compact, bright pink flower spikes and bronze-green foliage. A hybrid of *E. carnea* 'Myretoun Ruby'.

White-flowering heathers

Erica ×darleyensis 'Ada S. Collins', a compact form resembling *E. carnea* more than *E. erigena* in its growth habit, produces its pure white flowers in abundance; the flowers contrast well with the deep green foliage. *Erica carnea* 'Golden Starlet', 15 × 45cm (6 × 18in), has striking golden yellow foliage that turns lime-green in winter and contrasts against the white flowers; it is less prone to sun scorch. *Erica carnea* 'Ice Princess', a hybrid between *E. carnea* 'Springwood White' and *E. carnea* 'Snow Queen', is very distinct: its tall white flower spikes are held high above the bright green foliage, which will reach 15cm (6in). *Erica carnea* 'Whitehall' is of the same parentage and is very similar in habit, except the flowers are borne higher above the foliage. *Erica carnea* 'Springwood White' is an old but still very popular white-flowering form, and very distinct with its deep green foliage and lax branch habit. *Erica ×darleyensis* 'Silberschmelze' ('Molten Silver') produces masses of scented, silver-white flowers over a very long period in winter—if I had to choose a favourite white-flowering heather, then this would be it. *Erica ×darleyensis* 'White Perfection' grows 5cm (2in) taller than *E. ×darleyensis* 'Silberschmelze' and is somewhat less spreading (70cm, 28in); this extremely good white-flowering form has less-scented flowers but bright green foliage tipped yellow in spring.

Cultivation Tips

Both *Erica carnea* and *E. ×darleyensis* will thrive in alkaline conditions. They will not tolerate shallow chalk soils, unless of course the soil is improved to include additional organic matter, and additional summer irrigation is applied. The best effects are achieved on peaty and acidic soils, although many heathers will grow in less favourable conditions as long as they are not waterlogged in the winter months. The yellow foliage forms do scorch if the pH is too high, or if fully exposed, and are better off in light shade. All other foliage forms are best in full sun and exposure, where the fluctuations between winter and spring temperatures induce foliage colour change.

Prune heathers back immediately after flowering by removing the spent flowers using a pair of garden shears, a Strimmer (Weed Whacker), or rotary lawn mower set on a high setting. For best effect create a landscape that follows the natural undulations of the heather's natural growth. Both these heathers are fully hardy throughout the UK and will thrive in zones 5 to 7 in the USA.

Forsythia   **Oleaceae**

Common Names: Early forsythia, winter-flowering forsythia, yellowbell, yellow
  bells, Korean forsythia (*Forsythia ovata*).
Flowering Period: February and March.
Flowers: Light yellow, bell-shaped, scented, produced before the leaves.
Height and Spread: Varying in height but often reach 3m (9ft) tall and 2.5m (8ft)
  wide.

Although we often associate forsythias with spring, the following two species
flower at the end of winter. Although the beginning of March is the norm, I have
seen them flowering as early as the end of February. Their blooms are less
showy than the more commonly grown hybrid forsythias, but their solitary,
scented flowers are a welcome sight nevertheless.

The first forsythia was introduced in 1833 as *Syringa suspensa*, but it did not
seem to fit comfortably with the lilacs so it was renamed *Forsythia*, in honour of
William Forsyth (1737–1804), a Scot born in Aberdeenshire. Forsyth was
curator of Chelsea Physic Garden, head gardener at Kensington and St James'
Palace (all in London), and a founding member of the Horticultural Society of
London (established in the year of his death), which later became the Royal
Horticultural Society. It is hard to imagine how spring would look in our gardens
without these wonderful shrubs.

Of the two early-flowering species, *Forsythia ovata* and *F. giraldiana*, the latter
is less frequently seen in our gardens, which is a shame: it is a slender-growing
and graceful shrub, with purple new shoots and long, narrow foliage that turns a
rich yellow in autumn. Its hanging flowers are borne singly, not in clusters like
many other types of *Forsythia*, which to me gives it an aristocratic feel, free from
the intervention of plant breeders. Its pale yellow flowers are scented and quite
large, reaching 2.5 to 3cm (1 to 1.5in) long, and are produced in March through
into April, although I have seen it flower in February. *Forsythia giraldiana* is also
the larger of the two: I have seen specimens 4m (12ft) high and wide. It is also
the most drought tolerant of the forsythias, which makes it very adaptable to
warmer climates. *Forsythia giraldiana* 'Golden Times' is a recent introduction
with bright yellow leaves with green speckled centres; the margin may turn
white, a handsome variegation, while some leaves remain yellow. It is a very
attractive shrub both in flower and in leaf but does require some shade
protection, as the foliage may scorch in full sun.

The Korean forsythia, *Forsythia ovata*, is a much smaller affair, a bushy shrub
reaching 1.5m (5ft) tall and spreading by suckering stems to 3m (9ft). E. H.

Wilson first introduced this species from Korea in 1918. It produces masses of amber-yellow, slightly tinged green, solitary flowers early in March (occasionally February), blooming alongside some of the early-flowering rhododendrons; again, the autumn foliage is a pure yellow. One of the hardiest forsythias when in bud, it survived −29°C (−20°F) in controlled tests in Vermont, USA, and so will perform admirably in cold climates. *Forsythia ovata* 'Tetragold', a colchicine-induced selection raised in Holland in 1963, is noted for its large (2 to 3cm, 0.75 to 1.5in long), deep yellow flowers, which are produced in February. *Forsythia* 'Robusta' is a fast-growing hybrid (one parent is unknown, the other is *F. ovata*) with deep yellow flowers; it is worth growing for its red-purple autumn colour. A new form with golden foliage introduced from Korea has been named *F. ovata* 'Seoul Gold'; a seemingly stable form, it will require some protection from sunlight and is best suited to a woodland setting. Cold hardy forms have also been introduced in the USA and Canada. The hardiest form is *F. ovata* 'Ottawa', which originated in Canada, possibly from the Dominion Arboretum in Ottawa; it produces more flowers some ten days earlier than any other form. *Forsythia ovata* 'French's Florence' offers small, light yellow flowers; compact and slow-growing, it is possibly a seed-raised form. *Forsythia* 'Sunrise', a seed-raised hybrid from two different forms of *F. ovata*, originated at Iowa State University; it has small clusters of bright yellow flowers. *Forsythia* 'Meadowlark', *F.* 'Northern Gold', *F.* 'Northern Sun', *F.* 'Happy Centennial', and *F.* 'New Hampshire Gold' (*F. ovata* × *F.* 'Lynwood') are all hybrids of *F. ovata* and *F. europaea* and never fail to flower following temperatures ranging as low as −37°C (−35°F). Arguably the best of the bunch is *F.* 'Northern Sun' with its bright yellow flowers and compact habit.

The Korean forsythia is a wonderful plant, but it has a sinister side: it is on the invasive plant list in a number of states in the USA.

Cultivation Tips

Although forsythias can flower in late winter, branches can be cut, brought inside, and forced, extending the flowering season, and are excellent choices for indoor decorations. It is important that you select a stem with plenty of fat flowering buds; remove any buds that will be submerged in water, or these will rot. Cut the stem and place it in a vase in a cool location for about a week. Then trim the base of the stem again, replace the water with a fresh supply, and move the vase into a warm environment. Stems will flower within a few weeks.

With regard to their garden culture, forsythias are versatile shrubs that will thrive in any soil condition, but they prefer dappled shade or a sunny location. When grown in deep shade they become straggly and seldom flower. If kept in a healthy state, forsythias are relatively trouble-free in the garden and are seldom affected by pest or disease. The best way to achieve a healthy state is by regular pruning, and this should be done immediately after flowering has finished, as they flower on the previous year's growth. Prune back close to the ground about one-quarter of the oldest stems and remove any crossing or weak branches. Alternatively, if your shrub has stopped flowering, it can be cut to within a few inches of the ground in late spring and allowed to regrow. This method allows the plant to reset the balance of flowering wood, but it will result in the loss of flowers for between one and two years.

The forsythias covered here are best planted as foils, where their yellow flowers can erupt through the foliage of other shrubs. They are ideal companions for hellebores and late winter–flowering bulbs, like *Narcissus* 'February Gold' and *Galanthus nivalis*. They are all very hardy throughout the UK and vary in hardiness from zones 5 to 8 in the USA.

Fortunearia   Hamamelidaceae

Fortunearia sinensis

Flowering Period: February and March.

Flowers: Small, insignificant, unscented, similar in appearance and size to those of *Distylium racemosum* (isu tree) but pale green.

Height and Spread: 5 × 5m (15 × 15ft).

This must be one of the most obscure and uninteresting winter-flowering shrubs I have ever come across. It was introduced by E. H. Wilson in 1907 from western China, and I cannot for the life of me think why, unless of course you need one of these to complete your collection of the witch hazel family. *Fortunearia* differs from the witch hazels (*Hamamelis*) by its five-parted flowers, and from the winter hazels (*Corylopsis*) by its narrower, tiny petals—and this is probably the only association *Fortunearia* should have with its fine cousins. In leaf it looks somewhat similar to a witch hazel and produces reasonable yellow autumn colour; it establishes quickly but slows down with age. Its flowers, greenish with red stamens, are again somewhat like those of a witch hazel if you squint hard enough, but nowhere near as showy.

Cultivation Tips

Fortunearia has cultivation requirements similar to those demanded by witch hazels, except that, like the Persian ironwood (*Parrotia persica*), it will tolerate alkaline soils. Excessive drought or waterlogging around the root system will cause rapid death of the root system, as it will for most members of the witch hazel family. Mulching during summer can reduce drought stress within the root system; if your soil drains poorly, plant the shrub slightly proud to reduce waterlogging in the winter.

Pruning *Fortunearia sinensis* is relatively simple and should be done after flowering. Remove crossing and weak branches and, occasionally, some of the oldest shoots close to the ground. I have seen *F. sinensis* grown as a tree-like specimen; in this case, removing crossing branches is all that is required. I would opt for pruning any single-stemmed purchase in spring to create a multi-stemmed specimen. *Fortunearia sinensis* is hardy throughout the UK and in zones 5 to 8 in the USA.

Garrya   **Garryaceae**

Common Names: Silk tassel bush, quinine bush, cuauchichic, tassel bush, coast
    silktassel, silky-tassel.
Flowering Period: January and February.
Flowers: Showy, hanging catkins, green or purple in colour, often reaching 22cm
    (8.5in) in length. Male flowers produce the longest catkins.
Height and Spread: 4 × 4m (12 × 12ft).

All told, fourteen species of evergreen tassel bushes are found in the southern USA, Mexico, and the West Indies. They are all dioecious shrubs (male and female flowers on separate plants) with leathery leaves. The genus was named after Nicolas Garry of the Hudson's Bay Company, who assisted David Douglas on his plant-collecting expeditions in the Pacific Northwest of the USA. The two species most widely grown in the UK and USA are the coast silktassel, *Garrya elliptica*, and the garden hybrid between *G. elliptica* and *G. fremontii*, *G. ×issaquahensis*.

The long (15cm, 6in) spectacular greyish green male catkins of *Garrya elliptica* are borne in January and February and are backed by crinkled green-grey leaves. Often trained against a north-facing wall, this large shrub is far too attractive to sacrifice just to this use. Seldom seen is the female form; although its flowers are slightly smaller at 10cm (4in), it is equally spectacular. *Garrya elliptica* is native to California, where it thrives in coastal locations. Its barks and leaves have been used medicinally to relax muscles and relieve muscle cramps; the drug contained therein is powerful and should be used with caution. I have come across only two cultivars of *G. elliptica*, 'James Roof' and

'Evie'. *Garrya elliptica* 'Evie' was selected by Wayne Roderick of Suncrest Nurseries, California, for its strong-growing but compact habit and its 25cm (10in) tassels, which are pale green and tinged purple. Its leaves are held more closely together than those of *G. elliptica* 'James Roof', making it respond better to pruning—hence, its increased use as a hedge or screen in California. *Garrya elliptica* 'James Roof', a male form, was selected in 1950 by the eponymous director of the Tilden Botanic Garden, California, USA. It has been tried and tested in many locations, and is the only cultivar of *G. elliptica* available in the UK (both it and 'Evie' are available in the USA). 'James Roof' has 20cm (8in) catkins, slightly shorter than those of 'Evie', but the whole appearance of the shrub is different. In 'James Roof', the leaves are spread wider apart, thus exposing the branches and creating a more imposing shrub, especially if grown freestanding.

Garrya ×*issaquahensis* is a large spreading shrub that was first raised in Seattle in 1957, and then some three years later it occurred as an accidental hybrid at the garden of Pat Ballard, Issaquah, Washington, USA. There are three forms available, two USA introductions and one from Ireland. *Garrya* ×*issaquahensis* 'Pat Ballard' is a male selection that originated in 1960 from seed collected from a female plant of *G. fremontii* that had been pollinated by a male plant of *G. elliptica*. It is a vigorous plant, reaching 3.5m (11ft) and spreading about the same; the leaves and habit are intermediate between both parents, but it often flowers earlier than *G. elliptica* and can flower as long as December through to February. The flowers are two-tone, yellowish green and purple, and unfurl to lengths of 20 to 25cm (8 to 10in)—the best of the hybrids, in my view, although it doesn't perform as well in the UK as *G. elliptica*. Similar to 'Pat Ballard', although perhaps slightly hardier, is *G.* ×*issaquahensis* 'Carl English'. *Garrya* ×*issaquahensis* 'Glasnevin Wine', originated at Mallahide Garden, Ireland, was selected for its rich purple catkins, 20 to 25cm (8 to 10in) in length. The shrub seems similar in all respects to 'Pat Ballard', although in my experience it is not as hardy in the UK.

Cultivation Tips
Garryas are not difficult to cultivate as long as you remember some basic rules. Firstly, they will not tolerate waterlogged soils for prolonged periods of time during winter and spring. Secondly, their foliage will be desiccated in winter by cold (especially easterly and northerly) winds. Finally, they dislike being transplanted, so it is worth spending the time to make sure you select the right location in the first place. Garryas have been associated with planting against north-facing walls, where they appreciate the even temperatures and enjoy the protection, and although they look attractive in this location, especially if

The showy, hanging catkins of *Garrya* ×*issaquahensis* 'Glasnevin Wine'.

Garrya elliptica 'James Roof' is among the most widely planted silk tassel bushes.

espaliered or fan-trained, to me this seems a waste of such a fine group of shrubs. Away from the wall, they will thrive in acidic or alkaline soils and in sun or shade (as long as the soil drains adequately and protection from wind is included), and they will develop into mighty, fine evergreen shrubs, providing an excellent foil to other, earlier flowering shrubs, like witch hazels and daphnes, and later proving their worth a second time when in flower.

Protection is key to growing any garrya in the UK, where the lack of summer heat stops their wood from fully ripening before the onset of winter, and makes them prone to spring frost damage. That is why location is critical: if you can find a sunny location, with adequate wind protection, garryas can be grown in many locations in the UK, but without protection they are better planted against a wall. They are also a useful shrub for growing close to the coast, as the foliage is seldom damaged during the summer and autumn. In the USA garryas are best grown in zone 8, but again require wind protection in winter.

Grevillea   **Proteaceae**

Common Names: Cat's claw, mountain grevillea (*Grevillea alpina*); lavender grevillea (*G. lavandulacea*); rosemary grevillea (*G. rosmarinifolia*); royal grevillea (*G. victoriae*).

Flowering Period: November and continuing through winter until summer. Main flower flushes in November and June.

Flowers: Scarlet-red, yellow, and orange, occasionally two-tones of white, yellow, orange, and red.

Height and Spread: Low-growing, seldom reaching 1.5 × 1.5m (5 × 5ft).

Grevilleas are probably the most widely grown of all Australia's plants. They occur in numerous guises and in a multitude of different, vivid flower colours; their unusual, tropical-looking flowers make a welcome surprise in our gardens in winter. They do not flower in response to cold weather but in response to the seasons of the southern hemisphere, flowering in spring and autumn. The genus was named for Charles Francis Greville (1749–1809), who was president and one of the founders of the Royal Horticultural Society, UK; it includes an estimated 280 species found naturally in Australia, New Guinea, Celebes, and New Caledonia, but only a very few are hardy. The following are worth trying.

Grevillea alpina, native to New South Wales and Victoria, is a very variable species in the wild, where its bicolour flowers of white, orange, yellow, or red can be seen in two main flushes, in June or December. Plants are quick-growing, reaching 1m (3ft). Some are erect in habit, while other forms are more lax; the lax forms can reach 2m (6ft) wide. *Grevillea alpina* 'Olympic Flame', whose name commemorates the 1956 Summer Games in Melbourne, is possibly a hybrid between *G. alpina* and *G. rosmarinifolia*; it has rose-pink and cream bicolour flowers and is widely planted in the UK.

Grevillea lavandulacea is a very ornamental and free-flowering dwarf shrub: only the occasional lax branch will reach 1.5m (5ft) in height. Flower colour is typically red or pink with a white centre or limb (the long tube that supports the style), but pure red, white, pink, and even purple forms have been introduced. It is seldom grown in the UK, more widely planted in the USA, where the most commonly grown forms are *G. lavandulacea* 'Victoria Harbour' and *G. lavandulacea* 'Tanunda', both of which bloom almost continuously, forming lax spreading shrubs to 1m (3ft), with grey foliage and reddish pink or red flowers. *Grevillea lavandulacea* 'Adelaide Hills', a dwarf form with light red flowers, grows to just over 1m (3ft) tall.

Grevillea juniperina is native to New South Wales, where it inhabits heavy or light soils. It is a dense shrub with needle-like foliage and red or yellow flowers, growing to around 2m (6ft) tall. Several forms are on the market. *Grevillea juniperina* f. *sulphurea* offers vivid yellow flowers. *Grevillea juniperina* 'Molonglo', introduced into the UK by Raymond Clemo, of Pine Lodge Gardens, St Austell, Cornwall, is a cultivar involving a red-flowering *G. juniperina* and a prostrate yellow form; the result is a very prostrate selection with apricot flowers.

Grevillea rosmarinifolia will flower in December in the UK and again in the spring and summer.

Grevillea rosmarinifolia is among the most widely grown of the grevilleas and probably the hardiest. Native to New South Wales and Victoria, it will reach 2m (6ft) tall with a spread of over 3m (9ft). It is probable that the plants in cultivation are not the true form of *G. rosmarinifolia* but a hybrid with *G. lanigera* or *G. alpina*. The form grown in gardens is compact, seldom reaching 1m (3ft) tall, and if pruned regularly will make a very attractive evergreen groundcover with rosemary-like foliage (hence the epithet) and red, occasionally pink flowers. *Grevillea rosmarinifolia* 'Desert Flame' is a compact form with scarlet-red flowers, while *G. rosmarinifolia* 'Jenkinsii' has slightly greyer foliage than the type and red flowers. It is also a bit more compact, perhaps reaching 1m (3ft) in height. *Grevillea rosmarinifolia* 'Wyalong Wonder', with brilliant red flowers, is even more compact (75cm, 30in) and responds well to pruning. *Grevillea rosmarinifolia* 'Pink Pixie' is very compact, seldom reaching 30cm (12in), and has bicolour pink and white flowers; it seems to be very hardy and very tolerant of hard pruning.

Grevillea 'Canberra Gem' is a vigorous hybrid of *G. juniperina* and *G. rosmarinifolia* with slender, needle-like, aromatic foliage and waxy pinkish red flowers. It will quickly reach 1m (3ft) by 2m (6ft) but can be regularly pruned. *Grevillea* 'Apricot Cream' is similar in stature to *G. alpina* 'Olympic Flame' but has salmon and yellow flowers and more willow-like foliage.

Grevillea 'Robyn Gordon' and *G.* 'Ned Kelly' ('Mason's Hybrid', 'Kentlyn') are vigorous hybrids between *G. banksii* from Queensland and possibly *G. bipinnatifida* from Western Australia. 'Robyn Gordon' is more widely grown, but 'Ned Kelly', raised at a nursery in New South Wales in the 1970s, is increasing in popularity. Both produce very attractive large clusters of red flowers. Both can reach about 2m (6ft) tall and 3m (9ft) wide but are easily kept more compact by regular pruning.

Grevillea victoriae (royal grevillea) is found at high altitudes in the Snowy Mountain area of southeastern Australia, where during parts of winter it is covered by snow. It is among the most versatile of the grevilleas with its showy red flowers; and although it seems to be reasonably hardy in the UK, it truly thrives only in the south of England and the west coast of Scotland and Ireland, in semi-shaded locations, where it quickly reaches 3m (9ft) tall by 2m (6ft) wide.

Cultivation Tips

Grevilleas are pretty easy to cultivate as long as you remember a few golden rules. Firstly, they do best in free-draining acidic soils; the exception to the rule is *Grevillea rosmarinifolia*, which will thrive on shallow alkaline soil and only show a very limited level of chlorosis. Like many other members of the protea family (Proteaceae), grevilleas have a specialised root system that allows them to survive in very acidic nutrient-poor soils; these proteoid roots function similarly to root nodules on leguminous plants, absorbing available nutrients from poor soils. And like many Proteaceae members, grevilleas are phosphorus-intolerant and should be treated only with low-phosphorus fertilisers in slow-release form or not fertilised at all. Secondly, they thrive in hot, sunny locations; most dislike shade and will require little irrigation throughout the growing season. Finally, many respond well to pruning as it produces tight foliage and lots of flowers. Many grevilleas become very straggly if left unpruned, but hard pruning often results in the plant dying, so it is best to prune back hard but taking care to ensure there is sufficient foliage to allow for regrowth. This is best done immediately after flowering.

Grevilleas are limited to gardens in the southern half of the UK and areas affected by the Gulf Stream. They are best planted in spring, after the last frosts, so that they have the entire year to establish and grow. But as our climate continues to change, so does the number of grevilleas that overwinter here: *G. victoriae*, *G. rosmarinifolia*, *G. alpina* 'Olympic Flame', and *G.* 'Canberra Gem' have been recorded as hardy in the Midlands, UK. Some have survived short bursts of temperatures as low as −6°C (20°F), but they continue to dislike chilling winds during the winter and spring. In the USA grevilleas are only really suitable for zone 9, but they will take frost. Grevilleas make excellent accent plants where their evergreen foliage can be used as a foil for other flowering plants. Lower-growing forms make quite exceptional evergreen groundcovers but require full sun to flower best. *Grevillea rosmarinifolia* is a plant I would recommend to anyone wishing to grow grevilleas; if occasionally clipped, it will make a very dense and compact groundcover plant. Many grevilleas are also welcome additions to decorative containers for the cold conservatory or winter patio.

Hamamelis   Hamamelidaceae

The name *Hamamelis* is of Greek descent: *hama* ("together," "with") and *melon* ("apple," "fruit"), a reference to the fact that the flowers appear alongside the previous season's fruit capsules.

The witch hazels belong to the Hamamelidaceae, which flowering plant family includes some other wonderful trees and shrubs, like *Corylopsis*, *Fothergilla*, the Persian ironwood (*Parrotia persica*), and the sweet gums (*Liquidambar*). Most members of this family (with the exception of *P. persica*) prefer humus-rich, moist, acidic soils and will not thrive in shallow chalk soils.

The witch hazels are without any doubt the most valuable group of winter-flowering shrubs, as their spider-like yellow, red, or orange flowers, which are often scented, are seldom damaged by frost. They flower over a long period, too; plant a mixture of witch hazels and you will have flowers from late autumn through to mid March. Many witch hazels also have exceptional autumn colour, which makes them one of the most important landscape shrubs in the winter garden, flowering or not. But I have yet to find the perfect witch hazel package: very large flowers, and scent, together with exceptional autumn colour. The nearest approach to a complete package is *Hamamelis ×intermedia* 'Pallida', which has very large clusters of spider-like flowers that are scented, but its autumn colour is butter-yellow, and not so good as *H. ×intermedia* 'Diane', which has deep red flowers and rich autumn tints but, alas, very little scent. Perhaps perfection resides somewhere in the increasing range of new witch hazel cultivars making their way onto the market, some of which are very good indeed.

Witch hazels are relatively easy to grow, being generally resistant to pests and diseases and tolerating very low temperatures. In fact, they often perform better in a severe winter: if the weather is unseasonably warm, the flowering period can be very short. They are useful in city gardens, as they tolerate polluted air better than most shrubs. Witch hazels thrive on moist, slightly acid, well-drained organic soils in sun or partial shade. Deep soils overlying chalk are acceptable, but if lime-induced chlorosis becomes apparent, plants should be treated with sequestered iron. Organic matter such as leaf mould or well-rotted compost may be incorporated during planting. Their greatest enemy is summer drought. If the soil dries out, the leaves assume early autumn colouration, so it is important to ensure that they are kept moist throughout the growing season. Witch hazels respond well to fertiliser application. A fertiliser high in nitrogen, especially useful in a slow-release form like Growmore, applied before mulching the plants in spring at a rate of 40g per m^2 (2oz sq yd), will aid healthy growth throughout the year, as will an organic option like chicken pellets.

Witch hazels require only occasional maintenance. Pruning is restricted to the removal of dead wood after flowering. If space is at a premium, then they can be kept somewhat smaller by a pruning regime undertaken on a yearly cycle (unless the plant has made little growth during a given year).

Witch hazels flower on the previous year's wood. Close inspection reveals there are no clusters of dense flower buds at the tips of the shoots; instead, there will be a distinct vegetative shoot with a number of leaf buds (or leaves, depending on the season). The annual pruning of witch hazels involves the pruning of each vegetative shoot back to within two or three buds of the flowering wood. A word of caution here: if you were to prune a witch hazel like this from the time it was a young plant, then it would grow very slowly and become very dense. It is better to allow the shrub to reach something like the height of the plant you require, and then begin this method of pruning, which can be done at any time of the year, as its function is to reduce height, not to restrict flowering. I have tried this when the plant is in full leaf, and even when it is in full flower. The only time I would not recommend it is when the leaves are just appearing, as at this time, when sap is rising, any newly cut surface will quickly "bleed" sap. Better to wait until the shrub is in full leaf. It is well worth the effort when undertaking this pruning exercise to remove some of the inner growth from the shrub's centre, as failure to do this will result in a very dense shrub. The major upside of this method: it vastly increases the number of flowers, as pruning back vegetative growth causes denser growth, and hence increases flower bud production.

On grafted specimens, problems may arise from suckering of the rootstock. Any suckers, identifiable by their small, smooth, bright green leaves, should be removed at the base as soon as possible. If you are in doubt, just remember that the most commonly used witch hazel rootstocks are *Hamamelis virginiana* or *H. vernalis*, and as both of these have flowers that are very different from hybrid, Chinese, or Japanese witch hazels, they should be fairly easy to spot. Visit your witch hazels regularly during October to see if you have any branches that have small yellow flowers blooming. If they do, then it is likely they are from the rootstock and not from the desired plants. These can be removed by pruning them as close to the stem as possible. If the suckers originate from below the ground, then carefully excavate the surrounding soil until you discover the union with the root system and simply prune off at this point. Alternatively, if you come back in January or February and see the main plant in flower, and there is evidence that a branch has already flowered, then these too are probably suckers from the rootstock and likewise should be removed. If the rootstock is *H. vernalis* then you may encounter a branch with leaves while the remainder of the shrub is bare; or, if you were to visit your plants in February, you might see two different types of flowers on the same shrub. The vernal witch hazel will have much smaller flowers, and they will have a musky scent. These should also be removed. It is commonplace with the vernal witch hazel that suckers originate from below the soil line, as this shrub tends to have a natural suckering habit. These should be dealt with in the same way as shoots originating from the base in the Virginian witch hazel, *H. virginiana*, rootstock.

Witch hazels make excellent specimen plants when given sufficient room to grow. A dark, evergreen background will show up the flowers and autumn colour, whilst an area with little wind movement will allow the rich scent to linger.

Witch hazels are not difficult to grow if you remember some golden rules. Firstly, they are a woodland species, thriving in the shade of other plants and rooting into the humus-rich layer provided by the trees above. They require a cool root run, and though shade is not essential, they do not like soils that dry out too much during the summer months or that flood during the winter. The most ideal soils are those with a reasonable amount of sand and unimpeded drainage. In more open situations and if summer drought may be a problem, then heavy mulching and occasional watering will allow them to survive.

All witch hazels will sulk for at least one season if they are moved from one part of the garden to another; however, pot or containerised witch hazels establish and grow quite quickly if given adequate aftercare. Planting or transplanting is best done in late winter or early spring, before leaf growth has begun; this also allows witch hazels a full season to establish before the onset of winter. Transplanting or planting in early winter seems to check growth, and it is often a number of seasons before proper growth and establishment begins.

If witch hazels are stressed by drought, or abnormally wet winters, they can become victims of phythophthora root rot or honey fungus (*Armillariella*), both of which cause rapid decline in vigour and health and may result in death. This seems especially to affect old specimens of witch hazels that might be coming to the end of their natural life—in my experience, those around forty-five to fifty years old. Stress might also show itself in other ways. I have witnessed witch hazels in full autumn colour in the middle of summer; this is often followed by flowering in late autumn but, unusually, with flowers of a colour completely different from those normally seen in late winter. This is more common on the hybrids, when a red-flowering form will produce yellow flowers in the autumn. This phenomenon seems to follow abnormally long summers where rainfall has been low.

In the UK all witch hazels are perfectly hardy, and I have yet to see their flowers damaged by frost. There are reports of witch hazel flowers receiving temperatures as low as −23°C (−10°F) with no damage whatsoever.

Hamamelis mollis

Common Name: Chinese witch hazel.

Flowering Period: Will occasionally flower before Christmas and continue through the end of February.

Flowers: Highly scented, yellow, strap-like petals, in multi-clusters.

Height and Spread: Sprawling shrubs to 3m (9ft) tall, often maturing to 5m (15ft) wide.

There is nothing quite like discovering a Chinese witch hazel in full bloom on a frosty January day, its flowers covered in ice crystals and their heady scent filling the air. It is amazing how, even in the face of such adversity, nature finds a way to create such beauty. Of all the witch hazels sold, undoubtedly the most popular are the hybrids between the Chinese and Japanese witch hazel, but it is worth investigating the species, as their hybrid offspring have not always retained the best traits. The Chinese witch hazel is a class act, and several selected forms are currently available. It is easily distinguished from other witch hazels by its highly scented flowers and the short hairs that are borne on its leaves and small branches. This wonderful species was first brought to our attention when, in 1888, Irish botanist Augustine Henry sent specimens back to England from China.

Hamamelis mollis 'Coombe Wood' had been collected in 1879, when Charles Maries was sent plant collecting in China by James Veitch and Sons of London. Maries had previously completed a very successful expedition to Japan, and although his Chinese trip was less fruitful, this first introduction of *H. mollis* did find its way to Britain; however, the seedlings Maries introduced remained unnoticed at Veitch's Coombe Wood nursery until George Nicholson, curator of the Royal Botanic Gardens, Kew, identified them in 1898, not as a superior form of the Japanese witch hazel (*H. japonica*), but as the Chinese witch hazel. At this point Veitch Nurseries began to propagate from this plant, which was somewhat distinct to other forms of the Chinese witch hazel, and which they named *H. mollis* 'Coombe Wood'. E. H. Wilson also collected *H. mollis* during his Veitch-funded expedition in 1900, and did send back seed, although it is unsure whether it was ripe, and there is little evidence that it germinated. Even the herbarium specimen held at RBG Kew does not have viable seed. Wilson did, however, collect and successfully reintroduce both seed and live plants during his 1907 collecting trip for the Arnold Arboretum. A number of plants and seedlings were distributed both in the USA and UK to various institutions and large private estates, and many of the new forms being introduced may originate from this source. Although there are now several forms of the Chinese witch hazel, for the longest time only the 'Coombe Wood' form existed. But in 1961, Lord Aberconway, Bodnant Garden, North Wales, UK, introduced a form from seed probably collected by Wilson from his Arnold Arboretum collection; this *H. mollis* 'Goldcrest' is very heavily scented and is the latest flowering of this group, almost four weeks after 'Coombe Wood', flowering late in February and into late March. It is also somewhat more compact in habit and wider spreading.

Hamamelis mollis 'Boskoop' (a synonym of *H. mollis* Hort.) represents a number of forms that have been distributed in large gardens and collections, probably from the Wilson seed. It is similar in many respects to *H. mollis* 'Jermyns Gold' but less upright in habit; flower colour is a rich, clear yellow, and the scent is good. Even with the increasing number of Chinese witch hazel forms being named, this remains one of the best.

Hamamelis mollis 'Early Bright' is very early to flower, often a month before many other forms; in the USA it blooms in mid January. It originated at Swarthmore College in Pennsylvania and seems similar in habit to *H. mollis* 'Coombe Wood'. *Hamamelis mollis* 'Emily', named in 1990 by Chris Sanders after his mother, has yellow flowers (Chris was heavily involved in plant selections for Bridgemere Garden World, UK). *Hamamelis mollis* 'Bonny Brook', introduced by the University of Washington Arboretum, USA, produces large quantities of scented, golden yellow flowers. *Hamamelis mollis* 'Gold Edge' has the slightest of golden edge to its leaves; when I first saw it, I thought it had a nutrient deficiency. Its variegation makes it a weak growing plant that, in my experience, is shy to flower—an oddity rather than a gardenworthy shrub. Introduced by Richard Nutt, UK, around 1985.

Hamamelis mollis 'Goldcrest' is the most highly scented witch hazel of all.

Hamamelis mollis 'Jermyns Gold' is a fine, heavy-flowering Chinese witch hazel.

Hamamelis mollis 'Iwado', an excellent Japanese form introduced in 1994, has quite large, pure yellow, highly scented flowers. *Hamamelis mollis* 'Jermyns Gold', named by the Sir Harold Hillier Gardens, Hampshire, England, in 1992, is a particularly fine and heavy-flowering form that had long been grown there;

Hamamelis mollis 'Wisley Supreme' was rediscovered at the RHS Garden Wisley following the Great Storm of 1987.

its highly scented flowers with quite wide petals bloom between December and March. The original shrub exhibited an upright habit. There is a distinct possibility that the original plant may have been received from the Arnold Arboretum as they distributed E. H. Wilson's seed. *Hamamelis mollis* 'Kort's Yellow' (originally known as *H. mollis* 'Kort's Select', an invalid name) was introduced in 1998 by Brookside Gardens, Maryland, USA; it performs admirably in UK gardens and is a good all-round performer. *Hamamelis* 'Rochester' (*H. mollis* 'Superba') is a hybrid between *H. vernalis* and *H. mollis*.

Hamamelis mollis 'Wisley Supreme' is a recent introduction from the RHS Garden Wisley, selected in 1995 from a specimen that was somewhat shaded out in its location until the Great Storm of 1987 removed some nearby trees. Since that time the specimen has flourished, flowering profusely. It has a broad spreading habit and quite large, pale yellow flowers that open around the time of 'Coombe Wood', making it one of the first to flower.

Cultivation Tips

In the UK all forms of the Chinese witch hazel can be successfully grown and seem to show very little damage either to the stems or the flowers during cold winters. The exception is *Hamamelis mollis* 'Gold Edge', whose foliage may scorch in summer and which establishes more slowly in gardens due to its slightly variegated foliage and its requirement for slight shade; shade results in less vigorous growth that may be damaged by cold.

In the USA the Chinese witch hazels can be grown successfully in zones 6 to 8 with little or no damage. They do flower somewhat later and are often in bloom during January through to March, depending on the zone; the further south, the earlier they will flower. In Georgia, Michael Dirr (1998) has noted that *Hamamelis mollis* 'Early Bright' is first into bloom, around the end of December; while in the south of England, I have observed it beginning to flower as early as

5 December and in full flower one week later (just as *H. mollis* 'Coombe Wood' is beginning to flower). It is normal to see it in full bloom on Christmas Day in the UK.

I have also noticed that following abnormal seasons—say, a summer that is very dry or an autumn that is mild—some Chinese witch hazel selections retain their leaves long into winter, especially (as a recent study showed) 'Jermyns Gold', 'Early Bright', and 'Gold Edge'. These leaves do detract from the flowers and can almost entirely hide them if not removed, which can be accomplished "manually" on small plants. This unsightly characteristic is also a factor that should be taken into consideration when selecting some of the newer forms of *Hamamelis ×intermedia*.

Hamamelis ×intermedia

Common Name: Hybrid witch hazel.

Flowering Period: Mid December through to March.

Flowers: Colour varies from form to form in hues of yellow, red, and orange.

Height and Spread: 4 × 6m (12 × 20ft).

Hamamelis ×intermedia 'Nina' was one of the first hybrid witch hazels to be named.

Hamamelis ×intermedia is the name given to the hybrids resulting from crossing *H. japonica* and *H. mollis*. With the introduction of the Japanese and Chinese witch hazels into gardens, it was inevitable that garden hybrids between the two species would occur, especially as seed was often collected from plants in large gardens. The first record of this interspecific hybrid appears in 1920 by the Charlottenlund Botanic Garden, where seedlings had been raised from a stand of Chinese and Japanese witch hazels and intermediate plants were noticed. In 1953 a selection was named *Hamamelis ×japollis* 'Nina'; but in 1945 the Arnold Arboretum's botanist Alfred Rehder had named the hybrid group *H. ×intermedia*, after observing seedlings that originated from *H. mollis*, and this earlier name, of course, has priority.

The trend for breeding witch hazels then began. The original crosses aimed to combine the qualities of size and scent with those of colour and profusion. One location has generated more hybrids than anywhere else, and that is Kalmthout Arboretum, Belgium, which began in 1856 as a nursery sited by the famous Ghent grower Charles Van Geert to take advantage of the acid soils. It is probable that Van Geert was sufficiently well connected to receive some of Siebold's introductions from Japan, which included the Japanese witch hazel, *Hamamelis japonica*. In 1896 the nursery changed hands, and by 1902 Belgian nurseryman Antoine Kort had begun to raise thousands of seedlings from the impressive collection of witch hazels he had amassed. Kort was something of a connoisseur when it came to witch hazels, and he published numerous articles in Belgian horticultural magazines; but, sadly, by the 1920s the nursery had fallen into disrepair and was in financial ruin. In 1952 Robert and George de Belder bought the 14-hectare (35-acre) Kalmthout nursery, further developing the witch hazel collection and beginning an arboretum. In 1954 Robert married Jelena Kovacic, a Croatian who had worked in Denmark, Germany, and Holland. Jelena de Belder took an active interest in the arboretum from the start. The de Belders collected seeds from botanic garden catalogues throughout the world, and in 1962 Robert, with his brother, purchased Hemelrijk, in Essen, to accommodate the plants he and his wife were raising. Over the years the de Belders worked and introduced many wonderful garden plants; both had an eye for new forms, and the gardening world is indebted to them for their numerous hydrangeas, crab apples, cherries, and rhododendrons, not to mention witch hazels. Even today, new witch hazels are being introduced from Kalmthout and the de Belders' "overflow" arboretum at Hemelrijk, both of which are open to the public.

The many hybrid witch hazels now available differ greatly in habit, foliage, bloom, and autumn colour. The leaves of those with orange to red flowers tend to turn orange, red, copper, and purple in autumn, whilst the yellow-flowered varieties show rich gold before they fall. I am always asked what my five favourite hybrid witch hazels are, and although from year to year I get the opportunity to evaluate the newer forms, the following have become those that I prefer steadily for different reasons.

Hamamelis ×intermedia 'Pallida', an RHS Wisley introduction.

Hamamelis ×intermedia 'Aurora', introduced in 1985, has distinct two-tone flowers.

1. *Hamamelis ×intermedia* 'Pallida'—the best, largest, and most scented of the yellow-flowering forms. If it had exceptional autumn colour, it would be a hard act to follow.

2. *Hamamelis ×intermedia* 'Aurora'—very large, weird two-tone flowers, yellow and orange, that are scented, with the bonus of good autumn colour. Far superior to the more widely grown *H. ×intermedia* 'Jelena'.

3. *Hamamelis ×intermedia* 'Aphrodite'—flowers when few witch hazels do, during late February, and for a long period. Very large orange flowers that are slightly scented and good autumn colour.

4. *Hamamelis ×intermedia* 'Twilight'—I like this witch hazel just because it is different. Slightly scented red flowers with occasional yellow petals and good autumn colour.

5. *Hamamelis ×intermedia* 'Rubin'—possibly the best red around, deep crimson-red flowers and good autumn colour.

Following are descriptions of hybrid witch hazels I have encountered or grown. Flower colour and bloom time will vary with location and soil type, so the flowering period in particular must serve as a guide only, based on my experience of growing these forms in Hampshire, England.

Hamamelis ×intermedia 'Advent' is a free-flowering yellow form selected from a plant growing at the Sir Harold Hillier Gardens, Hampshire, England, in 1979. It has lemon-yellow flowers, smaller and paler than any of the other forms, and its scent is very light; autumn colour is not worthy of comment, and I have never seen dead leaves retained on it. It is increasingly normal that it flowers during mid January, though flowers can appear around 20 December, occasionally earlier.

Hamamelis ×intermedia 'Allgold' has short-petalled mustard-yellow flowers and a strong but slightly musky scent. It was named by Roy Lancaster of Hillier Nurseries, Hampshire, England, in 1961; he noticed an unusual-looking plant in a batch of received *H. japonica* seedlings. Although the source of the plant is unknown, it remains one of the most distinct forms for its flower colour and scent.

Hamamelis ×intermedia 'Amanon', raised by JHM van Heijningen, Breda, The Netherlands, in 2001, is a hybrid between 'Pallida' and 'Sunburst'. It is in full flower during January and February.

When I first encountered *Hamamelis ×intermedia* 'Angelly', I was immediately taken by its charm and its masses of small, lemon-yellow flowers. Like 'Aphrodite', this wonderful-looking witch hazel originated at JHM van Heijningen, Breda, The Netherlands, in 1985, and although it is a short-petalled form, the fact that the petals have a straight habit and the clustering of the flowers along the stem have led me to surmise that this may be a hybrid that has been "touched" by *H. vernalis*. The combined effect makes it quite distinct in appearance, although that is about as far as my love affair goes, as I have found it a difficult form to grow. Plants often fail to establish, and if and while they do, growth is quite weak. But with that said, if you are a witch hazel fanatic, it is worth persevering with this form.

Bred by JHM van Heijningen, Breda, The Netherlands, in 1985, *Hamamelis ×intermedia* 'Aphrodite' was raised from seed collected from 'Vesna' and possibly pollinated by 'Pallida'. It has large but slender-petalled flowers that are orange- and yellow-streaked, giving it the appearance of having ginger-coloured petals. The flowers are normally produced during February in the UK, and the flowers are very scented, which is not a trait you associate with hybrid witch hazels. None of the leaves are retained in winter, and the autumn colour is as good as (if not better than) 'Jelena'. A true all-round performer, and one that I feel will surpass the benchmark set by 'Jelena'.

Hamamelis ×intermedia 'Arnold Promise' was raised and introduced by the Arnold Arboretum, Massachusetts, USA, in 1945 and named in 1963, from seed collected from the 1907 E. H. Wilson introduction of *H. mollis* that had been pollinated by *H. japonica*. Masses of clear yellow flowers, similar in colour to 'Pallida' and with a strong scent, are borne during late January and continue long into February. Add to this its bold autumn colour, and it is easy to see why it is one of the best all-round performing and most widely cultivated of the witch hazels. In the UK the foliage does tend to hang on in winter, but I have never seen this happen in the USA. Flowers are much smaller than those of many of the other hybrids, and with age the plant develops a more compact shape with a wide-spreading habit. Probably the best witch hazel for the American market but easily outperformed by 'Pallida' in the UK.

As far as newer witch hazels go, *Hamamelis ×intermedia* 'Aurora' is right up there with 'Aphrodite'. It is believed to be a hybrid between 'Vesna' and 'Pallida' that originated at JHM van Heijningen, Breda, The Netherlands, in 1985. The flowers are burnt yellow with an orange basal flush to the splendid long petals, which gives the effect of very large flowers. The scent is reasonable, and the autumn colours are very good, varying from orange-yellow to red. This witch hazel may become the number one choice for general planting, alongside 'Aphrodite' and 'Pallida'.

Hamamelis ×intermedia 'Barmstedt Gold', originated at Baumschule Hachmann, Barmstedt, Germany, around 1975, is a vigorous form with an upright habit and very distinct colour. Its very large deep golden petals are flushed deep red at the base of the flowers and are only very slightly sweet-scented. It flowers in mid January.

Above left: *Hamamelis ×intermedia* 'Aphrodite' is a new breed of witch hazel with distinct flowers and heady scents.

Above: With good autumn colour and distinct yellow and orange two-tone flowers, *Hamamelis ×intermedia* 'Aurora' is a rising star in the witch hazel world.

Left: *Hamamelis ×intermedia* 'Barmstedt Gold' has quite big, rich golden flowers.

Hamamelis ×intermedia 'Diane', the most widely grown red-flowering form, was introduced from Kalmthout Arboretum in 1969. Named by Robert de Belder after his daughter, it was introduced as a considerable improvement over *H. ×intermedia* 'Ruby Glow', which was selected by Antoine Kort in 1946. 'Diane' has richer and deeper red flowers that fade to rusty brown more slowly than 'Ruby Glow'. The flowers are relatively scentless, but this is among the best witch hazels for autumn colour, outdone only by *H. vernalis* 'Sandra'.

Hamamelis ×intermedia 'Dishi' was selected by Jelena de Belder in 2003 from a plant growing at Hemelrijk under the number 10688. A highly scented form.

Hamamelis ×intermedia 'Harry' is a rather strange-looking witch hazel with short, stout petals, giving its flowers an appearance similar to those of *H.* 'Brevipetala' and 'Rochester' only larger, and a delightful rich orange flushed yellow. It originated at Kalmthout Arboretum as a sister seedling of *H. ×intermedia* 'Orange Peel' in 1988 and was named after Harry van Trier, a curator of the arboretum.

Hamamelis ×intermedia 'Diane' is not only among the best reds but has excellent autumn colour.

Hamamelis ×intermedia 'Hiltingbury' has fantastic autumn colour, but alas, its flowers are small and unscented.

Hamamelis ×intermedia 'Hiltingbury' is a large spreading form, raised by Hillier Nurseries in 1945 and named after their acidic nursery near Chandlers Ford, England. The leaves produce exceptional autumn tints of orange and scarlet, equal to that of 'Diane' and 'Jelena', but it is seriously let down by its small, pale copper flowers, suffused with red, which are weakly scented. Far better forms of witch hazels with coppery red flowers are on the market. This form occasionally retains its leaves during the winter.

Hamamelis ×intermedia 'Jelena' is a superb early-flowering form raised at Kalmthout Arboretum and named by Robert de Belder after his wife in 1955. The large flowers, produced in dense clusters, are yellow, suffused red at the base, and hence appear orange. The scent is moderate, and the autumn colour is good, in shades of orange, red, and scarlet. A selection from a group of seedlings made by Antoine Kort in 1937, it was originally named 'Copper Beauty'; Kort supplied cuttings and scions to a nursery in Boskoop, The Netherlands, and it was offered for sale under this name until 1958. It received the RHS's Award of Garden Merit (AGM) in 1993.

Hamamelis ×intermedia 'John' originated from Kalmthout Arboretum in 1998. The flowers are quite large and similar in appearance to 'Aurora' although somewhat smaller overall. This is one of my favourites of the newer witch hazels; I would put this ahead of 'Robert'.

Hamamelis ×intermedia 'Livia' is a stunning deep red form that originated at the de Belders' arboretum at Hemelrijk and was introduced in 1993. The flowers are as red as 'Rubin' and last as long, fading to copper-brown later than 'Ruby

Hamamelis ×intermedia 'Jelena', the petals of its ultra-hardy flowers curled down tightly to protect themselves against frost.

Glow'. Autumn colour is good, but this form will ultimately develop into a wide-spreading shrub.

Hamamelis ×intermedia 'Moonlight' is a strong-growing form whose pale sulphur-yellow, crinkled petals are red-purple at the base. It has a strong, sweet fragrance and in habit is not to dissimilar to 'Pallida', although it is easy to spot in a garden: it retains a large number of dead leaves throughout the winter. This large shrub with ascending branches and yellow autumn colour was named by Roy Lancaster of Hillier Nurseries in 1966, when he discovered it growing in a nursery row labelled *H. ×intermedia* 'Pallida'.

Hamamelis ×intermedia 'Orange Beauty' is an orange and yellow flushed flowering form selected by Heinrich Burns in 1955 from seedlings raised between *H. mollis* and *H. japonica*. A large and wide-spreading shrub, it flowers early in the season, shortly after Christmas. Autumn colour is as good as 'Orange Peel', although in my view this form is not as good.

Hamamelis ×intermedia 'Orange Peel' is another brilliant introduction from Kalmthout, and although it has been around since 1988, the more I get to know this plant, the more I like it. Masses of clear but pale orange flowers, quite large and quite wide, are produced in late December and through into the heart of January. The overall upright shape of the shrub is also very pleasing and can be easily encouraged by regular pruning. 'Orange Peel' seems to have a lot of Chinese witch hazel in it, a direct result of which is its reasonably good scent. The autumn colour is also good. An excellent all-round performer.

Hamamelis ×intermedia 'Pallida' is the most commonly grown yellow-flowered hybrid witch hazel, and if you see a mature shrub in full flower it is not difficult to see why. It produces a reliable flood of explosive, showy, pale pure yellow flowers that are flushed red at the base of the petals. These large flower clusters are often produced before Christmas and continue throughout January, filling the air with a very strong scent. 'Pallida' originated at the RHS Garden Wisley; Wisley's records show only that the seed originated from a Dutch nursery. It was originally grown as *H. mollis* 'Pallida', but although the stems and leaves are hairy, like those of the Chinese witch hazel, the leaves are far too large to be a straight selection of that species. It is still occasionally sold as *H. mollis* 'Pallida', or even *H.* 'Pallida'; some people even suggest that it might be a hybrid witch hazel backcrossed to the Chinese witch hazel, and hence the high traits from *H. mollis*. 'Pallida' received the RHS's Award of Garden Merit (AGM) as early as 1932, although it did not become popular until the 1950s. The flowers are sulphur-yellow, very large and produced in abundance, and its perfume is superior to all but the Chinese witch hazel, *H. mollis*, and hence it remains my number one choice for a yellow-flowering witch hazel. I was amazed to see it hanging on to high numbers of its dead leaves in the USA; only occasionally is such a display seen in the UK.

Hamamelis ×intermedia 'Primavera' is a reasonably well-established cultivar introduced by the de Belders from Kalmthout stock in 1969. It is a vigorous form, and its large primrose-yellow flowers, tinged purple-red at the base, carry the most delightful sweet scent. Dense clusters of flowers are produced in abundance right along the stems in late January and February, but often later. A first-class late-flowering form with a broadly spreading but upright habit.

Hamamelis ×intermedia 'Robert', a wonderful introduction from Hemelrijk, was named by Jelena de Belder in honour of her husband in 2000. It blooms during December, but in the UK its large yellow flowers, flushed with red and orange, are often obscured by the dead leaves hanging on the shrub; thankfully, it loses this trait with age.

Hamamelis ×intermedia 'Rubin', introduced in 1977 by Böhlje Baumschulen, Westerstede, Germany, remains one of the best red-flowering hybrid witch hazels I have ever seen. It flowers slightly later than the similar 'Diane', but its flowers are almost entirely red and slightly larger. It flowered profusely when we first planted it at the Sir Harold Hillier Gardens; in its initial spot, it really stood out in a group of hybrid witch hazels, but when we transplanted it to its permanent location, it took more than three years to regain its vigour. It tends to be similar in leaf to the Japanese witch hazel, and although the autumn colour is good, it is not as good as 'Diane'.

Hamamelis ×*intermedia* 'Twilight' is one of my favourites because its red flowers produce the odd yellow petal.

Hamamelis ×*intermedia* 'Westerstede' is a wonderful, late-flowering German introduction.

Hamamelis ×*intermedia* 'Sunburst' is similar in all respects to 'Pallida' except that it lacks scent. An early-flowering form introduced as an improvement on 'Moonlight' by D. Veerman, Boskoop, The Netherlands, in 1967, it has an upright growth habit and yellow autumn colour. Large, pale lemon-yellow flowers are produced in abundance during January and February; the flowers can be obscured by dead leaves, which may persist through winter.

When I first saw *Hamamelis* ×*intermedia* 'Twilight' in flower, I thought that petals from a nearby yellow flowering form had blown onto the flower. On closer inspection, I was amazed to see that the wonderful red flowers occasionally produce yellow petals within the flower cluster, so from a distance the flower appears two-tone, a mixture of red and yellow. Over the last few years I have become increasingly taken by this witch hazel. Although the flowers are only slightly scented, the autumn colour is quite reasonable. Originated at W. J. van der Werf, Boskoop, The Netherlands, in 1997.

Hamamelis ×*intermedia* 'Vesna' originated at Kalmthout Arboretum in 1970. The large flowers are made up of dark yellow petals stained red at the base, wider and more twisted than other hybrid forms, and with the bonus of a strong and very sweet scent. The base of the flower and the calyx is claret-red, which imparts an overall orange effect somewhere between 'Winter Beauty' and 'Jelena'. The autumn colour is orange and red.

Hamamelis ×*intermedia* 'Westerstede' is still occasionally listed as a form of the Chinese witch hazel under the name *H. mollis* 'Select'. Petals are primrose-yellow, and the blooms appear in late February and last into March, making it one of the latest-flowering of the hybrid witch hazels. Scent is moderate, as is the autumn colour. This form was introduced by Böhlje Baumschulen, Westerstede, Germany, in 1977.

Hamamelis ×*intermedia* 'Winter Beauty' was distributed in Japan by Mr Wada of Hokoneya Nursery, Yokohama, and introduced into The Netherlands in 1963. Flowers are deep golden yellow to orange-yellow and red close to the base, and are almost scentless. Believed to be a hybrid between *H. mollis* and *H. japonica* 'Zuccariniana'.

Cultivation Tips

Hybrid witch hazels are hardy throughout the UK, and in the USA they are hardy in zones 5 to 8. The flowers are less hardy than the stems: flower damage can occur around −26°C (−15°F), while wood is damaged and dies back around −29°C (−20°F).

Flowering period varies from form to form. In the UK flowering can start from early December; in the southern USA flowering can start from mid to late December, but in the northern zones flowering is normal in late January, or early February.

I have had problems establishing hybrid witch hazels in gardens, especially plants that have been open or field-grown, root-balled or burlapped, and then transplanted. This seems to check or halt their growth for at least one season. Although in a suburban garden this can be overcome by regular irrigation and mulching during the growing season, in a larger collection, such checked growth may result in early loss of foliage due to water stress and even abnormal flower production during the autumn period. If problems are left unresolved, the stressed plant can be attacked or invaded by a fungal or viral disease.

Hamamelis japonica

Common Name: Japanese witch hazel.

Flowering Period: Late February into March.

Flowers: Short, pale yellow, occasionally stained red at the base, with wrinkled and twisted petals.

Height and Spread: 4 × 6m (12 × 20ft).

The Japanese witch hazel, *Hamamelis japonica*, was named from a specimen by Siebold in 1843, though he didn't have a chance to collect it until 1862 and didn't introduce it until 1863; by 1874 it was being offered for sale by nurseries in Belgium and Britain. Siebold first visited Japan in 1822 as a doctor for the Dutch East Indian Company; the Dutch had acquired sole trading rights with the Japanese, and although the terms of the arrangement restricted the movement of Dutch employees within Japan, Siebold was fortunate to travel to Edo, a six-hundred-mile trip during which he collected over a hundred plants. On this same trip he also acquired a map, which was considered a military secret and therefore highly valued by the Japanese; for this acquisition, Siebold was imprisoned and tortured and finally forced to leave Japan in 1829, leaving his wife and child behind but retaining 485 Japanese plants (obviously had the right idea to take the plants, but I am not so sure my wife and children would be so forgiving if faced with a similar trade!). Upon his return to Belgium, he deposited his plants at the botanic garden. During the civil war, his beloved plants were distributed among local nurseries and horticultural experts. Later Siebold returned and tried to rebuild his collection, but alas, only eighty of the plants remained. Shortly after (and probably in response to this loss) Siebold opened his own nursery, which by 1842 was regarded as the greatest nursery for imported Japanese plants. Siebold named *H. japonica* in 1843.

The Japanese witch hazel is less frequently seen in our gardens than other witch hazels, although it is a useful addition, as it flowers latest. These shrubs lack the flower size and scent of the hybrid and Chinese witch hazels but are highly prized in witch hazel breeding, as they supply the greatly needed red flower colour. The leaves of *Hamamelis japonica* are smaller than those of *H. mollis*, seldom measuring more than 10cm (4in) long, and are slightly shiny on the upper surface. In autumn they turn a rich orange or red, but in cooler climates they may simply remain yellow.

The tree-like stature and characteristic horizontal branch structure separates *Hamamelis japonica* 'Arborea' from other forms; it also flowers earlier than most forms. It was introduced by Siebold in 1863 from Japan, and in 1881, when exhibited by Veitch's Nursery of Chelsea, England, it was awarded a First Class Certificate by the Royal Horticultural Society. The flowers are quite small but very numerous, deep yellow, touched red at the base, and sweetly but very faintly scented. *Hamamelis japonica* 'Brentry', a very early-flowering form, is often in flower in January (occasionally December); it was selected by Chris Lane, National Plant Collection holder of *Hamamelis* and an authority on the genus, who propagated a virus-free plant at the Sir Harold Hillier Gardens, Hampshire, England, and named it after the area in which he collected it, Brentry Woodland. Flowers, which are large for a Japanese witch hazel, are crinkled, pale yellow, and slightly scented. The original plant, which always flowers alongside the Chinese witch hazels, is now a large, arching shrub, 3m (9ft) high and 5m (15ft) wide.

Hamamelis japonica var. *flavopurpurascens* is one of the largest of this group, occasionally reaching small tree–like proportions but again wider than it is tall.

The flowers are produced in mid February, and are quite large, but instead of being pure pale yellow they are suffused red at the base. The autumn colour is pale yellow. This plant has been widely used to open-pollinate hybrids of the Chinese witch hazel, regularly producing as its offspring vigorous seedlings with flowers ranging from lemon-yellow to burgundy, with characteristics intermediate between both parents. Introduced into the UK and USA by E. H. Wilson, in 1919; Alfred Rehder, botanist at the Arnold Arboretum, distinguished this form by its purplish red petals. *Hamamelis japonica* 'Sulphurea' is a large, spreading form with slightly weeping branches and small, pale sulphur-yellow flowers with extremely crinkled and twisted petals. The scent is sweet but faint, and the autumn colour is a clear yellow. *Hamamelis japonica* 'Pendula' is the only truly weeping witch hazel I have ever come across. (Okay, *H. vernalis* 'Lombart's Weeping' weeps if you train it up a stake or support, but you have to work fairly hard to maintain a nice shape and a central leader on it, whereas the weeping Japanese witch hazel does it all for you.) A strong-growing witch hazel, its masses of small, pale yellow, slightly scented flowers, produced during late January, seem to drip from its heavily weeping branches, and it offers good autumn colour to boot. *Hamamelis japonica* 'Zuccariniana' is a more upright form with twisted, clear butter-yellow flowers, with no tinge of red; often the latest witch hazel to flower, it is occasionally in flower in late February but often in March. This is the most sweetly scented of the Japanese witch hazels, although the scent is not that strong.

Hamamelis japonica 'Zuccariniana' is the most sweetly fragrant Japanese witch hazel.

Cultivation Tips

Japanese witch hazels are hardy throughout the UK, although I have seen occasional damage to flowers, especially in the north of the country. In the USA they are the least hardy of the witch hazels and grow well in zones 5 to 8. In the UK shrubs can flower as early as late January and continue on until March, but flowering mid to late February is the norm. In the southern states of the USA, flowering occurs from late February into early March, and in the northern states, in March. They are relatively easy to grow, provided the conditions demanded by the other forms of the genus.

Hamamelis vernalis

Common Names: Vernal witch hazel, Ozark witch hazel, spring witch hazel.

Flowering Period: Occasionally during December, but more often mid to late January through March.

Flowers: Musky scented, mustard-yellow or orange, small, often almost straight-petalled, borne in clusters.

Height and Spread: 2×2m (6×6ft), often forming masses of suckering stems.

Of all the witch hazels grown in our gardens, the vernal witch hazel is my least favourite due to the size of the flowers and the overall compact habit of the shrub. The flowers do not stand out that well; some are so small that you would easily miss their flowering period. I suppose some have their own charm and grace. This is a hardy witch hazel, second only to the Virginian witch hazel, and holds some of the best traits for autumn colour.

Hamamelis vernalis 'Autumn Embers' is a long-cultivated form selected by Roy Klehm, USA, for its red-purple autumn colour, which in the northern zones it produces reliably. In the southern USA fall colour tends to be orange-red, and in the UK it tends to be orange, occasionally flushed purple.

Hamamelis vernalis 'Christmas Cheer', introduced by J. Gerdemann, Illinois, USA, around 1978, is the only vernal witch hazel that reliably flowers around Christmas Day. Often it will begin to flower in late November, early December and continue on until February. Small, dusty yellow flowers are borne in profusion on this arching shrub.

Hamamelis vernalis 'Lombart's Weeping', originated at Pierre Lombarts, Zundert, The Netherlands, in 1954, is a curious-looking witch hazel with slightly pendulous branches that is best grown up a cane to develop an attractive leader. Flowers are small and orange.

Hamamelis vernalis 'Orange Spangles' is a selection by Pat Edwards, Albrighton, England, one of three National Plant Collection holders for the genus *Hamamelis*. The flowers are two-tone, a mixture of light and darker orange, and are produced during January.

Hamamelis vernalis 'Quasimodo' is a compact selection from Pieter Zwijnenberg, Boskoop, The Netherlands, introduced in 1980. It is noted for its pale orange flowers and compact habit and is often in flower during mid January.

Hamamelis vernalis 'Red Imp' was selected by Peter Dummer of Hillier Nurseries, Hampshire, England, in 1966 from a batch of seed received. It has small red flowers and yellow autumn colour; new leaves are occasionally flushed purple.

It is a pity that the flowers of *Hamamelis vernalis* 'Sandra' are not as good as the autumn colour.

Hamamelis vernalis 'Sandra', autumn colour.

Hamamelis vernalis 'Sandra' is another Peter Dummer selection, named for his daughter in 1962. A strong-growing vernal witch hazel, it offers arguably the best autumn colour of any witch hazel, with leaves in myriad colours, from yellow to red, burgundy, and scarlet through orange; the show is less reliable in the USA. Flowers are pale orange-yellow, quite small but borne in abundance during late January.

Hamamelis vernalis 'Squib' was selected by Peter Dummer from the same batch of seedlings as 'Red Imp' in 1966. Small clusters of cadmium-yellow flowers, green at the base, are borne throughout January. Less vigorous than 'Red Imp'.

Cultivation Tips

I have never seen a vernal witch hazel damaged by cold weather in the UK. In the USA it is hardy in zones 4 to 8. An adaptable species, it is widely distributed from Missouri to Louisiana and Oklahoma, where it grows in various situations, often near river banks or streams, but thrives in free-draining gravelly or sandy soils. In our gardens it is an adaptable plant, thriving even in heavy soils and is more tolerant of drought than the Asiatic species; hybrids involving it or *H. virginiana* have improved drought tolerance compared to *H. mollis* and *H. ×intermedia*. It is widespread through the Ozark Mountains, hence one of its common names, the Ozark witch hazel. It is commonly used as a rootstock for grafting, alas, for its suckering nature is not conducive to this purpose.

In the UK a low percentage of the foliage remains green throughout the year; I have seen this on a number of occasions with 'Autumn Embers'. In the USA, dead leaf retention in the winter can also be a problem.

Retaining a clear stem in an attempt to suppress the suckering habit of *Hamamelis vernalis* is an onerous task and involves judicious pruning on a yearly (and occasionally bi-yearly) basis. Remove crossing and weak branches and try to retain an open crown—a tricky business, as overpruning results in too much new growth and upsets the balance of the shrub, hence more suckering. As a guide, no more than one-third of the existing leaf area should be removed.

Hamamelis virginiana

Common Names: Common witch hazel, Virginian witch hazel, spotted alder, winterbloom, snapping hazelnut.

Flowering Period: October through to late November.

Flowers: Small, pale yellow, occasionally flushed red, borne in small clusters while the leaves are still attached.

Height and Spread: 10 × 8.5m (30 × 25ft).

The origin of the common name for *Hamamelis* lies with this species and early North American settlers, who noticed the similarity between this shrub's leaves and one they were familiar with in England, the hazel or cobnut, *Corylus avellana*. *Wych* is an Old English word meaning "pliable" or "flexible"; like the hazel, *H. virginiana* is used for water divining. The word *wych* has been corrupted to *witch*, hence the common name witch hazel.

The Virginian witch hazel, a large, lax shrub seldom seen in gardens, flowers during late autumn and early winter—and by this feat alone is included in this book. It is commonly used as a rootstock for other witch hazels, as it is easy to grow from seed. It is often in flower

Hamamelis virginiana flowers in autumn, so its flowers are often hidden by its leaves.

early in September, and some of the forms may flower well into December. The fragrant flowers are pale to mustard-yellow, with crumpled petals; they are often obscured by the butter-yellow autumn leaves.

First introduced in 1736 by American naturalist and botanist John Bartram, of Philadelphia, this is the species from which the astringent witch hazel is derived; its leaves, bark, and twigs are used either dried or fresh to produce the astringent, which is used both as a sedative and as a tonic. Its healing properties have been known for centuries by the indigenous peoples of North America, who used it in poultices to treat painful swellings, tumours, cuts, and insect bites. Modern pharmaceutical studies have suggested that its main active ingredients, tannins and volatile oils, can strengthen veins and have anti-inflammatory effects.

Hamamelis virginiana is more commonly grown for the purpose of providing the strong astringent, or commercially, as a rootstock, than as a garden plant in its own right. Throughout my travels along the eastern seaboard of North America I have encountered this shrub growing in dense shade, near water, in hedgerows, at the forest's edge, and even, unbelievably, in almost pure rock in the Appalachian Mountains, where it survived as a dwarf shrub, wind-pruned to the rock face. In gardens I have come upon *H. virginiana* var. *rubescens*, and although there certainly is red pigment in its flower petals, there is still a high percentage of yellow pigment as well. The flowers are small, similar to the vernal witch hazel, and are slightly scented; the tips of the petals are yellow and the base is red. This variety flowers for a long period, with main flush in early November and continuing on into mid to late December. *Hamamelis virginiana* 'Mohonk Red' is an American selection similar to *H. virginiana* var. *rubescens* but flowering over a shorter period; its similarly sized flowers are more red. One can assume that this is a selection from a wild population in the Mohonk Mountains, New York State, USA.

Cultivation Tips

Hamamelis virginiana is native to eastern North America and is widespread from Nova Scotia to Tennessee and in the mountains of the Carolinas. It is an adaptable species, growing in a wide variety of locations, and will thrive in both full sun and shade. It is the most tolerant of the witch hazels to higher pH soils—another reason it makes the best source of rootstocks. As its autumn colour is its trump card and its flowers and scent fall a long way behind, it remains the least seen witch hazel in our gardens; yet, it is hardy, surviving undamaged in the UK even following the coldest recorded winters and hardy in the USA in zones 4 to 8.

Other hybrid witch hazels

Over the years it has become increasingly likely that new witch hazel forms are of hybrid origin, especially where plants have been introduced from large botanic gardens or large collections. The overall habit of these hybrids is intermediate between the Chinese and vernal witch hazel, but the most compelling evidence can be seen within the flowers, which also seem intermediate between both parents: they have straight petals, a dusty yellow colour, and a musky scent, and are borne in dense clusters up the stem. In more recent times, DNA fingerprinting has confirmed that these forms are complexes hybrids that contain *Hamamelis mollis* and *H. vernalis*, the latter being somewhat promiscuous in large collections. Several are worth growing, as they are distinct from many other of the hybrids.

Hamamelis 'Brevipetala', classified as a selection of the Chinese witch hazel when it was first distributed by Pepiniéres Chenault, Orléans, France, around 1935, has since become one of the most widely grown witch hazels of all. Its charm is linked to the quantity of unusual-looking clusters of mustard-yellow, musky-scented flowers it produces in December, and these continue well into late January. Although some of the newer forms are more attractive in flower, this remains one of my favourite witch hazels. It has the twiggy appearance of the vernal witch hazel and is rather scruffy-growing and sprawling in habit, much smaller in stature than the hybrid witch hazels of *H. ×intermedia*.

The hybrid origin of *Hamamelis* 'Brevipetala', once believed to be a selection of *H. mollis*, has recently been proved.

Hamamelis 'Doerak' is another hybrid first introduced as a selection of the Chinese witch hazel, in 1991 by W. J. van der Werf, Boskoop, The Netherlands. This has the best lemon-yellow flowers of any within this group, and they are also quite heavily scented. In appearance this witch hazel is similar to *H. ×intermedia* 'Angelly', with masses of yellow petals, flat but twisted at the tips, borne on short stems in clusters along the branches. Its overall growth habit is quite compact and less straggly than 'Brevipetala', although it does tend to retain dead leaves during the winter months.

Hamamelis 'Rochester' was introduced by Richard Fennichia, Rochester Park, New York. It has slightly larger petals than *H.* 'Brevipetala', but the flowers are more orange in tone, and are borne in compact clusters up the stem. Scent is intriguing: a musky mix between the vernal and Chinese witch hazel. This is a very distinct form when in flower; I have occasionally seen it so as early as late November, although it normally flowers in December and will continue through late January.

This hybrid between the Japanese and vernal witch hazel, as yet unnamed, flowers over a long period from December to late January.

Another interesting hybrid, this time between *Hamamelis japonica* and *H. vernalis*, has only just caught my attention. It flowers very early in the season, often around the first week of December, and will continue to flower late into January. The flowers are quite small and similar in all appearances to the vernal witch hazel except that they are yellow at the tip and orange at the base, and the sepals are stained red. The overall shape of the shrub is quite compact albeit upright in habit.

Cultivation Tips

These hybrid witch hazels are as hardy as those of *Hamamelis ×intermedia*, and seem more hardy than the Chinese witch hazel, thanks to the vernal witch hazel's genes—although 'Brevipetala' failed to flower in the USA at temperatures around −28°C (−18°F), and wood dieback and damage due to freezing of the cambium occurred at around −31°C (−24°F). In the USA they are hardy in zones 5 to 8.

In my experience, hybrids between *Hamamelis mollis* and *H. vernalis* are also susceptible to summer drought (albeit less so than hybrids between *H. mollis* and *H. japonica*). Deep mulching in the summer will help to relieve this, as will occasional irrigation, especially in the first three years following planting.

Jasminum   **Oleaceae**

Jasminum nudiflorum

Common Names: Winter-flowering jasmine, winter jasmine.

Flowering Period: November through to March.

Flowers: Bright yellow, almost scentless, borne on slender, green, leafless stems.

Height and Spread: Seldom taller than 1m (3ft) and spreads as far as you will allow it.

Jasminum nudiflorum is a gangly, low-growing, heavily arching deciduous shrub with green angular shoots that can grow up to 4m (12ft) in a single growing season, forming mounds as the branches arch over. In the UK it will flower in spasmodically during December, but its main flowering flush is in January, when masses of solitary flowers are borne along the branches. *Jasminum nudiflorum* 'Aureum', an interesting form with more summer appeal, is smaller and less vigorous than the species. The leaves are blotched yellow; some are entirely yellow, but luckily these fall before the flowers, as they would mask the pure yellow flowers. *Jasminum nudiflorum* 'Nanum', a compact and slow-growing form, is otherwise similar to *J. nudiflorum*.

Jasminum nudiflorum is a great groundcover for smothering dry, sunny banks.

Jasminum nudiflorum 'Variegatum', a good clear variegated form with a distinct white margin to the leaf, is slightly less vigorous than the green type; *J. nudiflorum* 'Mystique' is similar to 'Variegatum' but with a silvery, rather than white, edge to the leaf.

Cultivation Tips

This deciduous rambler is suitable for a great number of landscape uses. As a freestanding shrub it is somewhat ungainly and is almost impossible to retain in any sort of acceptable habit. It is often best to prune it down to within 15cm (6in) of the ground, and at this time remove those stems that have rooted in (although this is not the easiest thing to accomplish).

This incredibly adaptable plant is very useful for bank stabilisation; it will flourish in areas with relatively little moisture and is not affected by soil pH, thriving in both acidic and alkaline conditions, sun or shade. During the growing season, new shoots will arch over and touch the soil, and where they do, they naturally layer; new roots develop, and so the plant increases its spread across the site. Winter-flowering jasmine will also use other plants as a framework over which to scramble and can bring shrubs like groundcover cotoneasters to life in winter, when the jasmine's bright yellow flowers literally burst through their support. I have seen winter jasmine used in conjunction with *Cotoneaster dammeri* and *C. horizontalis* very effectively indeed.

A similar technique creates an evergreen blanket or dense groundcover below other winter-flowering plants or those whose stems offer winter interest. To achieve this, the jasmine is either mown or clipped two or three times a year after flowering (as it flowers on the previous year's growth), creating a very low but densely growing groundcover. It is then pruned to keep it away from nearby shrubs. It will produce this effect adequately in both full sun and semi-shade; however, in deep shade it is difficult to maintain this habit, and the number of flowers is greatly reduced. This technique provides an excellent foil for witch hazels and works well as a backdrop for many of the more vigorous coloured-stemmed dogwoods, like *Cornus alba* 'Sibirica'.

In gardening history, this rambling shrub, like *Magnolia grandiflora* (bull bay, evergreen magnolia), has been sited by north- or west-facing aspects or walls, a position to which it is well suited. Although the winter jasmine has no natural climbing adaptations like tendrils or sucker pads, it can be kept in place by a series of wires or climbing hooks, or by using another climbing plant as its support. Although the dark and cold of a north-facing wall is not the most glamorous of locations, in it this plant seems to thrive and flowers profusely, as it gets additional protection from the wall. Older specimens can become somewhat unsightly; their long, gangly new shoots can be clipped back after flowering. In some cases, I have seen winter-flowering jasmine pruned two or three times a year to create a very flat screen against a wall, which makes a delightful sight in winter.

One of the strangest uses I have seen for winter-flowering jasmine is that of a narrow hedge which serves as a low boundary, just 1m (3ft) tall and 50cm (20in) wide. Again, this is accomplished by pruning, and it does take several years to create the effect. To create a jasmine hedge, newly planted specimens are pruned regularly between late spring and early autumn to produce bushy plants; these are then allowed to grow to the required height but still pruned three or four times a year to maintain the bushy habit. Once a dense framework is achieved, then the hedge can be pruned three times a year using a hedge trimmer or similar device. Pruning is halted each autumn, to allow the hedge to flower, and begun again in late spring.

The winter-flowering jasmine is hardy in the UK, although, as the bulk of its flowers are produced in February, the flowers can be damaged by winter and early spring frosts. In the USA it is hardy in zones 5 to 10, although flower buds are damaged where temperatures fall below −19°C (−3°F).

Lonicera   **Caprifoliaceae**

Common Names: Winter honeysuckle, winter-flowering shrubby honeysuckle.

Flowering Period: Varies, but most forms begin in late December and continue until February, often March.

Flowers: White or flushed pink, borne in pairs, occasionally in clusters at the node of stems, typical in shape (although much smaller than the climbing honeysuckles) and very sweetly scented.

Height and Spread: Large, straggly shrubs often reaching 3m (9ft) tall and wide but can be kept shorter with regular pruning.

Lonicera fragrantissima, the largest-growing of the winter honeysuckles, may reach a height of 5 × 5m (15 × 15ft) if left unpruned, and at that size it is an awkward-looking shrub in the landscape, with a typical green-blob effect during the summer months. The long, almost hairless stems grow rapidly during the year, and along them are produced masses of pure white, very sweetly scented flowers with very distinct, bright yellow stamens. The foliage tends to hang for a long time during the autumn and winter, and during mild winters, many of the leaves remain green and attached. In the UK flowers are produced from December right through into March and continue into spring, when the flowers begin to be obscured by the emerging foliage. In the southern USA, it flowers in January and lasts around four weeks; in the North it flowers as late as March. Frost quickly kills the delicate flowers, but luckily these are replaced by the many protected by their bud cases and waiting to open. This wonderful species was introduced into the UK by Robert Fortune (1812–1880), who was sent to China to collect "garden worthy" plants by the Royal Horticultural Society, in 1845. Fortune obtained many wonderful plants by buying them from the most prestigious Chinese nurserymen, as well as commissioning people to collect plants from the wild.

Lonicera infundibulum var. *rockii* is a wonderful Chinese variety first introduced to the West in 1983 by Roy Lancaster from Wudang Shan, China, under his collection number Lancaster 1171. It remained unidentified for years, until a specimen was sent from the Sir Harold Hillier Gardens, Hampshire,

England, to Susyn Andrews, a taxonomist at the Royal Botanic Gardens, Kew, Surrey, who identified it. It is similar in habit to *L. fragrantissima* but more compact, and blooms in late winter, when its slender primrose-yellow flowers, flushed pink on the inside, develop. The flowers are funnel-shaped, initially similar to *L. setifera*, but then open. The new shoots are purplish in colour and slightly hairy, and the large leathery leaves are hairy on both surfaces. Although seldom seen, this shrub is beginning to grow in popularity. I first encountered the Lushan honeysuckle, *L. modesta* var. *lushanensis*, at the JC Raulston Arboretum, Raleigh, North Carolina, during January, in full flower. It was an impressive sight: the almost deciduous shrub, 2m (6ft) tall, was covered in masses of pure white, scented flowers, similar to *L. fragrantissima* but smaller. It looked like its long, straggly shoots had recently been trimmed back, which allowed it to retain a more attractive habit. This plant is available but somewhat scarce in the UK.

Lonicera ×*purpusii* was raised before 1920 at the Darmstadt Botanic Garden, Hessen, Germany, as a hybrid between two winter-flowering shrubby honeysuckles, *L. fragrantissima* and *L. standishii*. Both species are fairly widespread in the wild, and where they overlap, the hybrid appears as well. *Lonicera* ×*purpusii* has characteristics from both its parents, although it will outgrow both and may exceed 5m (15ft) in height. The flowers are very highly scented, a creamy white with golden yellow stamens, and the plant is more floriferous than either parent, flowering reliably from December until March. The foliage is retained less in the hybrid than on either parent; on occasion it will appear almost entirely deciduous, although with warmer winters in the UK, it seems to retain more foliage. A considerable improvement on its parents, it was granted the RHS's AM in 1971 and the AGM in 1984.

Lonicera ×*purpusii* 'Winter Beauty' was introduced in 1962, when Alf Alford, then the foreman of Hillier Nurseries, set about improving the characteristics of *L.* ×*purpusii* further still by backcrossing it with *L. standishii*. His hope was to create a more floriferous and compact shrub. The best seedling was *L.* ×*purpusii* 'Winter Beauty', and as its name suggests, it is a real winter charmer. 'Winter Beauty' indeed produces masses of flowers, is more compact in habit, and is very free-flowering, blooming from early December until April. Even if the flowers are damaged by frost, there are still plenty to follow. This selection remains the most popular of the winter-flowering honeysuckles in the UK for its reliability. To gain the maximum benefit from its fragrance, site in a sheltered location, where the scent can linger and slowly drift through the winter garden. In 1993, *L.* ×*purpusii* 'Winter Beauty' was granted an AGM by the RHS, as an improvement on *L.* ×*purpusii*.

Lonicera ×*purpusii* is a very adaptable plant and among the best winter-flowering shrubs for alkaline soils.

Lonicera ×*purpusii* 'Winter Beauty' remains the most widely planted winter-flowering honeysuckle in the UK.

Lonicera ×*purpusii* 'Spring Romance' is a 1980s Alford introduction, a backcross between *L.* ×*purpusii* and *L. standishii* var. *lancifolia*, the narrower and longer-leaved form that produces slightly more flowers. 'Spring Romance' seems even more compact than 'Winter Beauty'. It is difficult to tell the two apart unless you grow them side by side, in which case, in late December, you will notice 'Spring Romance' will only just have begun flowering, while 'Winter Beauty' will have been blooming for weeks. 'Spring Romance' flowers later, yes, but longer into the spring, and it seems to retain less foliage than either of the other hybrids. Stems and shoots are more hairy than 'Winter Beauty', and leaves are slightly longer.

Lonicera setifera—if there were to be a Rolls Royce of honeysuckles, this would be it: the previously mentioned forms are thugs compared to this angelic star. As you can gather, this is my favourite winter-flowering honeysuckle, a beautifully proportioned shrub, not too large, and exquisite when in flower. Scottish plant collector Frank Kingdon Ward originally collected *L. setifera* in 1924, from the Himalayas, during the "golden age" of plant hunting; the form that is grown in our gardens is from the Joseph Rock collection, under number Rock 13250, from the Himalayas. A Viennese by birth, Rock collected in "Tebbuland," which he described as "the Garden of Eden"; his expeditions were funded by the Arnold Arboretum. *Lonicera setifera* is one of the easiest of the winter-flowering honeysuckles to identify as it is shorter, seldom reaching more than 3m (9ft). Its very bristly stems further distinguish this delightful species, whose daphne-like flowers, which pink, flushed white, and deliciously scented, are borne on naked stems during late winter, early spring. It flowers much later than the others, and the flowers are very distinct and un-honeysuckle-like: the flower is made up of an entire tube, whereas two large petals make up the flowers of other species. Roy Lancaster has made a more recent introduction of this shrub from the Himalayas.

Lonicera setifera is my favourite of this group, with its very un-honeysuckle-like flowers and hairy stems.

Fortune also introduced *Lonicera standishii*, the other parent of *L. ×purpusii*, from China in 1845. The introduction of both species, *L. standishii* and *L. fragrantissima*, created much excitement, as prior to 1845 no winter-flowering honeysuckles existed in gardens. Both shrubs are similar in habit, growing to heights of 3 to 5m (9 to 15ft) and tending to be semi-evergreen in mild winters. The flowers of *L. standishii*, as fragrant as those of *L. fragrantissima*, are a creamy white, tinged with pink, but have very distinct, bright yellow stamens. Both species will flower as early as December, although the early blooms may be damaged by frost. *Lonicera standishii* has very bristly stems and leaves and has a tendency to be more deciduous than *L. fragrantissima*. I collected a form of *L. standishii* with light pink flowers from the JC Raulston Arboretum, Raleigh, North Carolina, in the winter of 2001, and brought it back to the UK, where it has survived but hasn't yet flowered. It will be interesting to see how it performs. Its flowers are as fragrant as those of the species.

Lonicera standishii var. *lancifolia* is a long- and narrow-leaved form that produces more flowers than the species, although it tends to hold more of its leaves throughout winter. It was introduced from China by E. H. Wilson in 1908.

Cultivation Tips

All winter-flowering honeysuckles will grow on a wide range of soils: I have encountered these shrubs in everything from heavy clay that waterlogs in winter to light, friable sandy soils that are incredibly dry in summer. On the heavier soils, especially those that waterlog, growth is slower, but even in such harsh conditions, the plant still thrives. With the exception of *Lonicera setifera*, all will grow on shallow, alkaline soils and only show limited levels of chlorosis during the summer months, which again does not affect their growth in any way.

With their large size and lack of interest during the summer and autumn, shrubby honeysuckles are more suitable as back-of-the-border shrubs, where they can be forgotten for the remainder of the year. But don't forget their fragrant scent, which can entice anyone out-of-doors during the winter months. To maximise the scent, they are best planted in areas where scent can linger or where air movement is low. I planted several *Lonicera fragrantissima* to screen the garage wall, and from December through March, the scent lingers close to my front door. If you really enjoy the scent, bring cut branches indoors and force them. Simply cut the stems and place them in a vase full of water, and in a few weeks they will open.

The major drawback with this group of shrubs is their size. Left unchecked, they would quickly outgrow a suburban garden. To retain some sense of scale, I would strongly suggest an annual pruning regime whereby older shoots are removed, allowing new shoots to regenerate from the base of cut stems. To achieve this, select three of the oldest flowering stems and remove them immediately after flowering, making sure you never remove more than one-third of the total growth in one season. The following season, prune all the emerging growth and another third of the oldest wood; removing the growing tips forces the plant to bush. In time the shrub is balanced and continues to flower unhindered. This method can then be used continually to keep the growth compact. Alternatively, if you encounter a very overgrown specimen, it can be cut back hard to within a few inches of the ground in late spring and allowed to regenerate.

All the winter-flowering honeysuckles are hardy in the UK, but flowers will be damaged when temperatures fall below freezing. In the USA they are hardy in zones 4 to 8, with the exception of *Lonicera setifera*, which is hardy zones 5 to 8.

Magnolia   **Magnoliaceae**

Magnolias are my favourite group of winter- and spring-flowering plants; their amazing flowers and history inspire me. Fossil evidence carbon-dated to around eighty million years ago confirms the presence of magnolia-like plants during the reign of the dinosaurs. Today's magnolias have changed little and still provide a link to prehistoric times, when magnolia-like trees grew on several continents. It is no surprise that the primary pollinators of these wonderful plants are beetles, one of the oldest insect groups. In late winter and throughout the main part of the magnolia season (which can, through a succession of species, continue until autumn), small pollen beetles can be found gorging themselves on the flowers. A favourite occupation during this time is opening up flowers in search of beetles, of course in the company of my children!

Magnolias flower as early as February, when *Magnolia campbellii* comes into flower. It is a breathtaking sight to see such a majestic tree in full flower. But the flowers are short-lived and are easily damaged by frost; in many seasons, I have seen magnolias in full flower on one day and their flowers collapsed on the next, destroyed by freezing temperatures, nothing left but limp, black flower petals, dangling from the branches—such beauty destroyed so quickly.

Magnolias are best suited to those areas in the UK that are influenced by the Gulf Stream, like the West Coast of England, Scotland, and Ireland, where mild temperatures and frost-free conditions prevail. The most suitable areas are in the south of England, including Sussex, Surrey, Dorset, Devon, and Hampshire, and no magnolia enthusiast should miss the flower extravaganza in Cornwall during February and March, when 30m (90ft) plus magnolias bloom and light up Cornish valleys with their aristocratic flowers. In the UK magnolias can be

The waterlily-like flowers of *Magnolia campbellii* can range from pure white to magenta.

grown outside of these specialised microclimates, but growth will be reduced and flowers prone to damage. In the USA they are less frequently grown, seen only in large gardens or arboreta where the temperature rarely falls below freezing, restricting them to the west coast of North America in special microclimates from San Francisco to British Columbia. Other great magnolia-growing climates include Korea and New Zealand.

Magnolia campbellii

Common Name: Campbell's magnolia.

Flowering Period: Mid February into March.

Flowers: White, dark rose-purple, and pink, very large and waterlily-like.

Height and Spread: In its native habitat of the Himalayas this is a very large "shrub" indeed, exceeding 45m (150ft), and the dominant tree above rhododendrons in the landscape.

Magnolia campbellii is a large tree introduced in 1865 from the Himalayas, where it is native to Nepal, Sikkim, and Bhutan, and its wood is prized for matchsticks and tea chests. It also occurs in southwest China. Flowers are massive, up to 30cm (12in) across or often larger. The flowers are produced on naked branches during February. The flowers first open into a waterlily shape, and then, after a few days, they flop and spread wide. A large tree will have literally hundreds of these blooms, which are often deep pink inside the flower with the outer tepals being rose-pink—an interesting contrast when you first see the flowers in bud and watch them change colour as they open. In the wild, colour variation can be anything from pure white to rose-pink to pale pink to magenta, with pure white being the dominant colour.

Magnolia campbellii Alba Group represents the most common form in the wild: those plants with pure white flowers. Although the pink-flowered form was first introduced and is the most commonly grown form in our gardens, the white form—first planted in England in 1925 at the garden of J. C. Williams, Caerhays Castle, Cornwall—is a real showstopper.

Magnolia campbellii 'Darjeeling', a wonderful form with very dark rose-coloured flowers, was introduced from the Darjeeling Botanical Garden, India, and is the least hardy of the selections. It survived for many years planted against the wall of Jermyns House, the home of Sir Harold Hillier, in Hampshire, England. *Magnolia campbellii* 'Betty Jessel' is a delightful selection with very large, deep crimson flowers raised by Sir George Jessel around 1967 from seed collected from *M. campbellii* 'Darjeeling'; it is named after the raiser's wife. *Magnolia campbellii* 'Ethel Hillier' was a selection made by Hillier Nurseries

The magenta flowers of *Magnolia campbellii* subsp. *mollicomata* 'Lanarth' are a breathtaking sight, appearing as they do during the last throes of winter.

from seed collected in the wild; the flowers are very large, and there is a trace of pink on the outside of the flower tepals. *Magnolia campbellii* 'Strybing White', an American introduction with very large, pure white flowers, originated at the Strybing Arboretum in San Francisco.

Magnolia campbellii subsp. *mollicomata* was first introduced into the UK by George Forrest under the collection number F.25655 in 1924. A scaled-down version of *M. campbellii*, it seems more compact and hardier, with smaller flowers reaching 20 to 25cm (8 to 10in) across; it also flowers earlier and often after ten to fifteen years from seed. The taxonomic distinction between this subspecies and the type is that Campbell's magnolia has less hairy leaves and does not have hairy flower stalks. The flower colour of *M. campbellii* subsp. *mollicomata* is rose-purple, although paler pink forms do exist. From the Forrest seed 25655, three seedlings have been selected and named after the gardens where they were raised: Borde Hill in Sussex, and Lanarth and Werrington in Cornwall, England. The flower colour, which has been described as port wine, is very deep on all three and once seen against a clear blue February sky will never be forgotten. The Borde Hill form died out, but not before it was propagated and distributed to other gardens; it is the lightest of the three. 'Lanarth', the most widely grown, has the deepest purple flowers but is the weakest grower of this group. 'Werrington' has the most intense deep reddish, cyclamen-purple flowers.

A number of *Magnolia campbellii* × *M. campbellii* subsp. *mollicomata* hybrids have originated in gardens from seed collected from open-pollinated plants. *Magnolia* 'Sidbury' originated at the home of Sir Charles Cave, Sidbury Manor,

Magnolia campbellii subsp.
mollicomata 'Werrington'.

Devon, in 1946. The early-flowering habit of *M. campbellii* subsp. *mollicomata* is retained, but 'Sidbury' is much more vigorous, and the flowers are very large rose-pink, to pale pink in bud, opening pinkish white or pink-purple with a strong white flush. *Magnolia* 'Charles Raffill' was named from a tree growing at Windsor Great Park, England, from an original seedling given Charles Raffill of the Royal Botanic Gardens, Kew, in 1946, who deliberately crossed the two species; the flowers are very similar to 'Sidbury', a pale pinky white on the outer petals and soft pink on the inner petals. *Magnolia* 'Kew Surprise', named from a tree growing at Caerhays Castle, Cornwall, has large, deep purple flowers; the flowers are also distinct as they are a much richer pink in bud than when fully open. *Magnolia* 'Wakehurst', a wonderful hybrid with the deepest rose-purple flowers of this group, is named after a tree growing at Wakehurst Place, West Sussex, England.

Cultivation Tips

Campbell's magnolia is a large tree and probably unsuitable for most suburban gardens. Most plants are propagated by grafting or cuttings, so as to reduce the thirty-year wait until flowering; plants thus propagated take between eight and ten years to flower. They are relatively quick-growing and are really suited only as an upper-canopy tree, or as a specimen in the middle of a lawn.

Campbell's magnolias thrive best where they are afforded protection by nearby trees; they dislike open, windy sites, as their stems and branches are brittle when young. A neutral to acidic soils is best, and although they thrive in heavy clay soils, they prefer those with a more free-draining nature. They require large volumes of water when young; years with below-average rainfall can cause their growth to be seriously checked and may lead to invasion by fungal or decay organisms. Mulching is critical to their survival when they are young; deep mulching is preferred, with well-composted bark chips or leaf mould or another type of organic matter. This is best placed around the plant out to the drip line in spring, as this is when the roots are most actively growing. Magnolias are best planted in spring; their root system puts on very little growth during autumn and winter, hence they will establish more readily in spring, when the soils warm up. This group of magnolias has few problems, the exceptions being bark stripping by squirrels and fungal diseases, such as honey fungus.

In the UK Campbell's magnolias are best grown in the south of the country; in the USA they are a zone 7 to 9 plant, although they have not yet been fully tested. *Magnolia campbellii* subsp. *mollicomata* may prove to be even hardier in the climate of the USA.

Although large if left unpruned, these magnolias can be reduced in size by an annual pruning from a young age to the new growth of vegetative (nonflowering) buds, which will result in a multi-stemmed shrub rather than a tree with a single trunk; magnolia flowering buds are very fat and easy to distinguish from the much slimmer leaf or vegetative buds. To achieve a multi-stemmed shrub, cut down a young, newly purchased magnolia to force buds to grow out near the base but above the graft union (a bulge, close to the base of the plant, where the two plants, rootstock, and scion are joined). Allow several selected shoots to develop and grow out; I would suggest no more than five, with possibly three being the best number. Once a year, prune back the vegetative shoots at the very top of the plant, leaving two or three shoots above the previous year's growth. After four or five seasons of this, allow the shrub to grow out, pruning it only to reduce crossing, weak, or damaged branches. This will yield a shrub magnolia about a third of its normal tree height and one with a lower framework of branches—hence, flowers are carried lower down.

This technique, which allows this wonderful magnolia to be used in the place of a large shrub (or medium-sized tree), was modified from a system used upon plants damaged by the Great Storm of 1987. In its wake, decimated magnolia trees along the south coast were cut down close to the ground; these cut stumps regenerated quickly, producing multi-stemmed plants that, with careful pruning, could be balanced into worthwhile specimens. So quick was the new growth that within five years many of these now medium to large shrubs were, amazingly, flowering again.

But a warning: overpruning of any magnolia's canopy results in an eruption of very vigorous vegetative shoots, as the tree or shrub tries to reset the balance and replace lost leaf area. As a guide, never reduce the canopy by more than 20 to 25 percent.

Magnolia breeders are still trying to produce the ultimate Sino-Himalayan magnolia, one that produces huge flowers after the last frosts have passed, and *Magnolia campbellii* figures strongly and importantly in the gene pool available to them for this end.

Mahonia   Berberidaceae

All mahonias are easy to identify. Belonging as they do to the barberry family, they have bright yellow wood just below the bark, which is obvious when pruning or cutting them. Also, the flowers of many members of this family have spring-loaded stamens: when a pollinator (usually a bumblebee) alights on the flower and pushes its head toward the flower and touches the style (the female part of the flower, which receives the pollen), the stamens curl forward and deposit pollen from the anther onto the bee's head. The bee then flies off in search of another flower and pollinates it, transferring pollen to the next style. You are probably wondering where all this is going. Well, here's a neat (but slightly anorakic) trick that you can show your friends during the late winter or spring: using the tip of a ballpoint pen, tickle the style in the centre of the flower and watch the stamens close quickly toward it. Your friends will be amazed.

Mahonia aquifolium

Common Names: Oregon grape, Oregon grape holly, grape-holly, Oregon holly grape.

Flowering Period: As early as February and continuing on until March and April.

Flowers: Bright yellow, lightly scented, borne in dense clusters above evergreen foliage.

Height and Spread: Seldom exceeds 1m (3ft) in height, but can vary from form to form; width too can vary, as the shrub produces suckering stems, depending on the space it is given.

Oregon grapes are fun to play with in the garden as well, as hugely adaptable subjects that can be used in a multitude of situations. Their attractive evergreen foliage often colours crimson, red, and yellow in the autumn and winter. In late winter and early spring, dense clusters of vibrant yellow flowers bloom just above the foliage, and these are followed by large, drooping clusters of blue-black berries that resemble bunches of grapes, hence the common name. Add this all together, and you get a highly useful but compact evergreen plant for the general landscape. Its main attribute is its large, somewhat holly-like, glossy evergreen foliage; its large, compressed panicles of scented yellow flowers are a massive bonus. In the USA, flowering is often a month or two behind the UK: March and April in the South, and as late as April in the North. In the UK, flowering begins during February and continues on into March. The Oregon grape in its various forms is widely used in broad sweeps in town landscapes, whereas in our gardens, its dwarf forms make delightful groundcover plants in sun or shade, and the taller forms will illuminate and grace those dull and dank forgotten areas of our gardens. Most forms of the Oregon grape will spread, some slowly and some more quickly.

For me there are only two real runners in the race for most attractive Oregon grape, and the clear winner is *Mahonia aquifolium* 'Apollo', among the earliest of the Oregon grapes to flower in the UK (and always the first to flower in the south of England): its dense clusters of scented, pure yellow flowers occasionally appear as early as January. This compact form seldom grows more than 1m (3ft) tall and is adorned with good, clean foliage and red leaf petioles. In my view, this is the best Oregon grape for general planting, although it doesn't produce as many fruits as other forms. It can be cut back hard after flowering to retain an even more compact habit, and although I have seen this accomplished with a flail mower or bush hog, it is not a method I would recommend, as it often weakens the shrub; a more acceptable method is to reduce its height by half

Mahonia aquifolium is known as the Oregon grape for the masses of berries that follow its yellow flowers.

using a hedge cutter. A very close second in the race is *M. aquifolium* 'Green Ripple' with its funky, wrinkled green leaves, which again turn purplish in late autumn and complement its rich yellow flowers perfectly; another compact grower, it seldom reaches 1m (3ft) in height and flowers in late February.

Mahonia aquifolium 'Atropurpurea' is a delightful form taller than 'Apollo' or 'Green Ripple', often reaching over 1.5m (5ft), with foliage that turns a luscious deep reddish purple in autumn as the temperatures fall; by late winter, its colour intensified, it provides a wonderful backdrop for the dense clusters of yellow flowers. It is often one of the last to flower in the UK.

Mahonia aquifolium 'Golden Abundance' is an American introduction selected for its floriferousness; I have been told it is a sight to behold in full flower. It is probably the most ornamental of the forms when in bloom, as its dense panicles of bright yellow, scented flowers are complemented by its bright green foliage; and it is also among the best for fruit set, which in the USA is far better than in the UK. This form produces masses of pendulous clusters of deep blue fruits the size of small grapes. Another American introduction is *M. aquifolium* 'Mayhan Strain', a compact selection seldom reaching 1m (3ft) introduced by Mayhan Nursery, Veradale, Washington, who claim that it comes true from seed. *Mahonia aquifolium* 'Orange Flame', which is patented in the USA, produces wine-red foliage in winter if planted in full sun and protected from desiccating winter wind; it reaches 2m (6ft) in height and has attractive orange new growth that slowly turns a luscious green during summer. *Mahonia aquifolium* 'Moseri' is a popular selection in the USA. Given hot summers and cold winters, new growth emerges apricot and changes to rich orange and red before turning green. But alas, I have never seen it do this in the UK, where its new foliage is bronze-red, not an interesting apricot. Nevertheless, it is a compact form, seldom growing over 1m (3ft) tall (although I wish it would). *Mahonia aquifolium* 'Smaragd' is, in my experience, the very first to flower in the UK, blooming about seven to ten days earlier than 'Apollo'; it is compact, with large clusters of yellow flowers and bright green foliage.

Several cultivars within this group of mahonias are possibly hybrids with *Mahonia pinnata*. I say "possibly" because *M. pinnata* is incredibly (or seems to be) rare in gardens (many plants thought to be *M. pinnata* turn out to be *M. ×wagneri* 'Pinnacle'). *Mahonia pinnata* does somewhat resemble *M. aquifolium* in habit, although it is a much stronger-growing shrub, often exceeding 3m (9ft); *M. pinnata* may be further distinguished from *M. aquifolium* by its small clusters of flowers, which appear along the stem and originate from leaf axils, whereas *M. aquifolium* has only terminal flowers. To add fuel to the fire, the natural ranges of *M. aquifolium* and *M. pinnata* overlap in northern California, and seed collected from plants growing in this area yield plants that exhibit some traits of both parents. And to really muddy the water, hybrids collected from the native hybrid stand in California do match some of the plants collected from the "pure" stand in California. The name *M.* ×*wagneri* is now used to cover several hybrids that are probably of this parentage. I strongly suspect that *M. aquifolium* 'King's Ransom' has at some time been "touched" by *M. pinnata*, as the shrub has a taller, more erect presence and its leaves are more spiky than those of *M. aquifolium*; too, its flowers are produced along the stem and not just at the tips. It is a fine form, reaching 2m (6ft), and its foliage turns red-purple in the winter in response to cold temperatures. *Mahonia* ×*wagneri* 'Hastings' Elegant' is the most compact of this group, seldom reaching 2m (6ft), and produces very dense clusters of bright yellow flowers in March, occasionally very late February. *Mahonia* ×*wagneri* 'Pinnacle' was a selection made from a group of seedlings grown as *M. pinnata*; it stood out with its vigorous growth and larger clusters of bright yellow flowers. *Mahonia* ×*wagneri* 'Undulata' was distributed by Nottcutts Nursery, England, from propagation material collected from the National Trust's Garden at Rowallen in Northern Ireland (the material was labelled *M. aquifolium* 'Undulatum Nanum', but it is unclear where the original plants came from); this selection carries more traits of *M. aquifolium* than any—and flowers later than many—of the other forms in this group; still, in my opinion, it is the best of them.

Cultivation Tips

Oregon grapes are very hardy groundcover shrubs that can take a considerable amount of "landscape" abuse as long as you remember some golden rules. Like many relatively large-leaved evergreens, winter can cause them considerable problems, especially when the ground is frozen and the air temperature rises quickly. Such environmental conditions can lead to the drying out of foliage; drying winds compound the trouble, causing considerable damage in a relatively short period of time. In extremes cases, the desiccation results in the death of the plant. Such winter troubles are more of a threat in the USA, in both the southern and northern states along the East Coast but also inland. To overcome them, some form of winter protection is advisable, not only from wind and sun but also from winter drought, which can be problematic on soils that freeze easily. Now for the paradox. Bold evergreen shrubs are often planted against a north-facing wall, where protection from sun and wind is almost guaranteed; however, in such protected situations where even temperatures are experienced, the soil may remain frozen for long periods of time. To avoid the risk of this happening, mulch the plant's root system (or better yet, the entire border) with composted bark or well-rotted farmyard manure or some other form of organic matter.

In more open situations within our winter landscape, evergreens with bold foliage can be awarded the protection of established plantings; site them below the canopy of a deciduous tree, or where they are protected on all sides by mature shrubs. In such a situation and if adequate water is available throughout the year, these evergreens will flourish. Protection from sunlight during the heart of a Georgia summer is also important, as again drying winds can cause considerable damage to the foliage.

In the UK the Oregon grape is often used as a landscape plant for bank stabilisation, and in our climate seems well suited to this practice; however, in a more continental climate, such a use would place the plant under severe stress. In more continental climates, the Oregon grape is best placed at the very outer edge of a protective canopy, where foliage will fully colour during winter and spring but where protection sufficient to limit foliage damage is available.

For normal landscape use the Oregon grape will grow in semi-shade to full sun as long as there is enough moisture available during periods of drought; otherwise the foliage will dry out. The best foliage colour is achieved on neutral to acidic soils. Shallow chalk soils are problematic for both their pH and lack of moisture retention; in such soils, Oregon grapes seem short-lived and look somewhat chlorotic. Stressed plants seem to be susceptible to powdery mildew and rust.

Growing Oregon grapes is fairly easy. They are very hardy in the UK and are only occasionally damaged during winter by temperatures below freezing and drying winds. In the USA they are hardy in zones 4 to 8; some forms are less hardy than others, so knowledge of your local microclimates is important.

Leggy and overgrown plants can be cut back after flowering and the old growth reduced by one-half to two-thirds. Recovery is slow, and the plants look awful for a season or two, but it is still the best way of regenerating an old plant—unless, of course, you want to replant the whole group.

Other winter-flowering mahonias

Common Names: Leatherleaf mahonia (*Mahonia bealei*); Japanese mahonia (*M. japonica*).

Flowering Period: Late winter for *Mahonia bealei* and *M. japonica*; late autumn, early winter for *M. ×media*.

Flowers: Long panicles of pendulous, often scented flowers in *Mahonia bealei* and *M. japonica*; *M. ×media* has flowering spikes intermediate between *M. lomariifolia* and *M. japonica*, often lax rather than pendulous, with scent varying from form to form.

Height and Spread: Mature specimens of almost tree-like proportions, yet exhibiting multi-stems, can reach 5m (15ft) tall and 3m (9ft) wide.

I have fond memories as a student of horticulture at the Royal Botanic Garden Edinburgh, Scotland, of trying to separate, let alone identify, these imposing evergreens; their different forms were then, to me, almost indistinguishable. But over the years I became more familiar with this wonderful group of plants, and now the sight of a fully grown hybrid mahonia fills me with excitement, as it heralds the arrival of winter, flowering alongside *Camellia sasanqua*—no two plants better complement each other. I often look back and wonder why it took me so long to enjoy their beauty. Could it be a simple case of plant snobbery, that mahonias are far too commonly grown to be a plantsman's plant? I am almost ashamed to admit that this might be pretty close to the truth. Isn't it odd how you can be so blind to something so beautiful when it is staring you in the face!

Picture this. If I was to enthuse about an imposing yet tough, deep green evergreen shrub with bold, architectural foliage, one that in autumn and winter bore masses of lightly scented, pure yellow flowers in pendulous racemes over 30cm (12in) long, you can bet your bottom dollar you would rush out and buy one. And many people are doing just that: one of the most widely purchased non-coniferous, medium-sized evergreen shrubs is the Japanese mahonia, *Mahonia japonica*. When you meet one up close, you'll be forced to agree. It is hard to find anything that can possibly outperform one, particularly in a winter garden setting: they are reasonably quick-growing, they provide a deep green foil for other plants to flower against, they make attractive windbreaks, and they are spiny enough to stop anyone from trying to shortcut through your shrubbery.

The two most commonly misidentified mahonias are the Japanese and leatherleaf, *Mahonia japonica* and *M. bealei*, and even today the latter is often listed as *M. japonica* 'Bealei'. *Mahonia bealei* is a much coarser-looking plant; the leaflets overlap and give a denser look. The margins on the leaf are more pronounced than they are on the Japanese mahonia, and the centre leaflet has a long, pronounced spine, longer than the leaflet itself. But the giveaway is that the flower spikes on *M. bealei* are erect, not lax or pendulous as in the Japanese mahonia. *Mahonia japonica* also produces red and orange tints in autumn and winter, an attribute I have not seen on *M. bealei*. Of the two, you are more likely to encounter the Japanese mahonia in gardens, nurseries, plant centres, and public places.

Mahonia bealei was introduced by Robert Fortune from China in 1848; by 1858 plants were available. Fortune clearly distinguishes the erect flowering habit of *M. bealei* in his description of the species (which he named for Thomas C. Beale, a Shanghai merchant) but also comments on its similarities with *M. japonica* in both leaf and habit. *Mahonia bealei* is widely used in the USA as a landscape plant, taking the place of *M. japonica* in many states. I witnessed

Mahonia japonica not only has very beautiful late-winter flowers, but it also produces good autumn tints.

quite large plants in Athens, Georgia, in full bloom during one visit in January and on another occasion in full flower in February, their sweet scent filling the air—something I had not experienced with plants in the UK. I was also considerably impressed to see them in the fall of the following year, with masses of glaucous blue fruits weighing down the flower stalks and a feeding frenzy of various birds stripping the ripe berries. Though *M. bealei* is reasonably widespread in China, there have been relatively few introductions; however, Japanese plant explorer Mikinori Ogisu recently reintroduced a form of *M. bealei* with a silver-white underside that equals that of another Chinese species, *M. gracilipes*. I have seen a number of propagated plants, and I for one am hoping they will shortly find their way into cultivation and be more widely available.

The Japanese mahonia, *Mahonia japonica*, is a common plant in our gardens in the UK; it is wide-spreading (3m, 9ft) but still shorter than many of the hybrid mahonias covered later in this section, a slightly more compact 2m (6ft) in height. This species is somewhat of a mystery: it has been grown for centuries in Japan but has not been discovered in the wild for many years. Although it will flower from late autumn to early spring, I always associate this mahonia with late winter: it blooms alongside sarcococca, from late January to March. Its flowers are as sweetly scented as those of *M. bealei*, but they are much more lax in habit and a paler yellow; the overall length of the spike seems much longer, too, easily reaching over 30cm (12in). The foliage appears to be somewhat softer but if you grab it, you get the same shock you'd receive from touching any other mahonia. The autumn colour on *M. japonica* is sometimes explained away as a nutrient deficiency; I find this hard to believe as I have witnessed many different plants on many different sites, and they all exhibit the same types of colour—bright red and orange, occasionally yellow, and some purple, usually coinciding with the lower light levels and temperatures of autumn. This mahonia's autumn colour is a wonderful addition to an already superb display of attributes.

An important introduction of recent times must be the hybrids between *Mahonia lomariifolia* and *M. japonica*, *M. ×media*. As we have already sung the praises of the Japanese mahonia, it is worth stopping to discuss the finer points of what many people recognise as the finest mahonia. *Mahonia lomariifolia* was introduced from Yunnan in 1931 by Major Lawrence Johnston, of Hidcote Manor, Gloucestershire, England. It is easily distinguished from other mahonias by its open, leggy habit, with most of its arching foliage, over 1m (3ft) long, at the top of bare stems. Its leaflets occur in pairs, between fourteen and twenty, and its bright lemon-yellow flowers are borne in dense clusters, 20cm (8in) long; flowers are slightly scented and are produced in October and November. But this most spectacular-looking mahonia is also the least hardy of this group. In Edinburgh, Scotland, it is regularly damaged and requires protection both from cold and from wind. In the south of England it will survive almost undamaged; it was reportedly severely damaged during the winter of 1978, but it did regrow from the base.

Mahonia lomariifolia, with its long, arching foliage and bright yellow flowers, is a welcome sight during early winter.

The attraction of crossing this fine-foliaged mahonia with a more hardy form was obvious, and in October 1957, The Crown Estate Commissioners, Windsor, England, exhibited at the RHS's show at Vincent Square, London, one 'Charity', a plant that seemed intermediate between *Mahonia lomariifolia* and *M. japonica*—and here begins the *M. ×media* story. The origins of 'Charity' and several similar hybrids can be traced to Slieve Donard Nursery, County Down, Northern Ireland, where a large batch of seed-raised *M. lomariifolia* had been grown. About a hundred of these seedlings were acquired and grown on by Richmond Nursery, Windlesham, Surrey, England, in 1951; about a year later, they were seen by Sir Eric Savill and Mr Hope Findlay of Savill Gardens, Surrey, who noticed that three of the young plants showed some seedling variation and appeared to be intermediate between *M. lomariifolia* and *M. japonica* or *M. bealei*. These were planted out at Savill Gardens, and it was here, in 1957, that they first flowered. It seems that although other people had tried to deliberately cross *M. japonica* and *M. lomariifolia*, this happened accidentally at Slieve Donard's Nursery, and it is believed that *M. japonica* was the pollen parent.

The hybrids between *Mahonia lomariifolia* and *M. japonica* bring together the best attributes of both parents, as can be seen here.

Mahonia ×media 'Arthur Menzies', a distinct form that originated in the USA.

The best and probably most complete collection of *Mahonia ×media* material remains somewhat intact at Savill Gardens and Windsor Great Park, England; 'Rebecca', 'Roundwood', and 'Sarah'—all seedlings selected from 'Charity'—are still hiding in the collection. All seem to me to be similar to 'Charity' ('Sarah' has an interesting, somewhat more compact habit); flowers are canary-yellow and only slightly scented. None of the three are in commerce, and they really should be fully evaluated, to see if they are improvements on their parents.

Mahonia ×media 'Arthur Menzies', a spectacular form selected by the Washington Park Arboretum, Seattle, USA, in 1961, is sometimes listed as a hybrid of *M. lomariifolia* and *M. bealei*. It was named for Arthur Menzies, the supervisor of plant accessions at the Strybing Arboretum, California, in whose garden the cross arose. In the UK it is a large evergreen, reaching over 3m (9ft) and retaining something of the habit of *M. lomariifolia*, with that tufted-looking foliage at the tips of the stems. Its semi-erect spikes of slightly scented, lemon-yellow flowers appear in late autumn and early winter.

Mahonia ×*media* 'Charity' remains among the best forms. Indeed, it is a hard act to follow, as it retains the best attributes of both parents; I have seen specimens over 4m (12ft) tall, with 3m (9ft) being the norm. The foliage is also very attractive and has the look of *M. lomariifolia*, each branch over 0.5m (1.5ft) in length and a rich green. Long panicles of arching clusters of flowers emerge from the tips of the shoots during autumn and early winter, often alongside

Mahonia ×*media* 'Charity', first exhibited in 1957 and still among the most widely grown forms of this group.

those of *M. lomariifolia*, but differing by being slightly scented and a deep yellow. An impressive sight both in foliage and flower. *Mahonia* ×*media* 'Winter Sun', a seedling left behind at Slieve Donard Nursery, is similar to 'Charity' but more compact, with flower spikes similar to those found on *M. lomariifolia* (erect, scented, and a clear yellow) but flowering a few weeks later. It is a more suitable selection for a smaller garden or anywhere space is at a premium. *Mahonia* ×*media* 'Charity's Sister', a selection of one of the original seedlings grown at Savill Gardens from plants received from Richmond Nursery, is very similar to 'Charity' but slightly taller and somewhat lax in habit. Its flowers, which appear during December, are more scented than those of 'Charity'.

Mahonia ×*media* 'Faith' and 'Hope' are named selections from open-pollinated seed of 'Charity' that were grown on at Savill Gardens in 1961. 'Faith' bears a stunning resemblance to *M. lomariifolia* and has erect spikes of bright yellow flowers. Both plants are mildly scented and compact, possibly reaching 2m (6ft) in height with an upright habit. 'Faith' flowers some three weeks earlier than 'Charity'; I have seen it in flower during mid October. 'Hope' is usually in flower during late November and flowers over a long period, often three months in duration.

Although the Slieve Donard plants were accidental hybrids, the same cross was deliberately made in England by Lionel Fortescue at Buckland Monachorum, Devon, and by Norman Hadden, Porlock Gardens, Somerset. Although some of the resulting selections are very distinct, it is difficult to justify so many similar-looking shrubs. *Mahonia* ×*media* 'Lionel Fortescue', originated from a Fortescue seedling that was grown on at Savill Gardens, is the earliest of this group to flower; I have seen it in flower at the beginning of October, although with the weather often so mild at this time in the south of England, flowering is relatively short, seldom lasting a month. The flowers are quite scented, upright, and in clusters, but the overall size of the shrub is quite large, somewhat reminiscent of *M. lomariifolia*, but not as tall as some of the other clones. *Mahonia ×media* 'Buckland' is an outstanding form with a strong slant toward *M. japonica*, with long, arching racemes of yellow scented flowers that are produced over a long period from December onward. *Mahonia ×media* 'Underway', originated at Porlock Gardens, is quite compact and leans toward *M. japonica* in habit and in flower, with lax clusters of bright yellow, scented flowers.

Cultivation Tips

All these mahonias are quite large, bold-foliage evergreens and are highly desirable landscape plants. They are useful for creating shade and as windbreaks, if not too exposed to the elements themselves; and they have proven extremely useful planted below the canopy of mature trees. It is in fact this ability that made them so popular, as where else can you find such an imposing evergreen that will take dry shade? They will thrive in most soils; some chlorosis and leaf colouring will occur on shallow chalk soils, and if this is linked to drying winds, some desiccation of the foliage may occur.

Growing conditions similar to those demanded by *Mahonia aquifolium* are required, especially in the USA, where these mahonias will thrive in zones 6 to 8 (although in the southern states, some summer protection may also be required, especially where temperatures are high). In the northern states plants get obliterated by winter thaws and freezes, especially when soils are frozen and the air temperature rises quickly, which causes the plant to transpire. In such conditions, the foliage can be severely damaged. Dirr (1998) reports leaf and stem damage on *M. ×media* 'Arthur Menzies' at Callaway Gardens in Georgia with temperatures between −5 and 0°F (−20 and −18°C). I would surmise that with damage at that latitude and at those temperatures, *M. lomariifolia* would undoubtedly fry (and probably explode). I have, however, often been amazed by where I have encountered large-leaved mahonias, and the lengths some people will go to to grow them. I came across a rather shabby-looking *M. lomariifolia* at Adelaide Botanical Gardens, Australia, that was planted in a lathe house, with rhododendrons and orchids—I assume for protection from summer heat; its distinctive foliage was half the size of normal and almost hidden behind masses of blue-black berries. I could only imagine that the flower set must have been something else. On the west coast of Scotland I met a mammoth-sized *M. lomariifolia*, around 5m (15ft) tall, with the most amazing furrowed bark and foliage over 2m (6ft) long. Such specimens never cease to amaze me and give an insight into the adaptability of these mahonias; although, as with their relatives, the Oregon grapes, wind exposure and freezing temperatures are a factor to consider—and possibly avoid—when cultivating these wonderful plants. Placing them in shady positions will not only protect their foliage from hot sunny weather and provide adequate wind protection but also allows the scent—of those that have it—to build and linger in the landscape.

It is worth knowing how to prune these big plants. People who have walked out of a garden centre with a baby mahonia in tow are always horrified when they are later confronted by a fully mature specimen exceeding 2m (6ft) tall. All this group will, if left unchecked, grow into very large shrubs, often as high as wide; some of us may have the room to accommodate such a monster, others will not. So a bit of judicial pruning from the off will save some fairly strenuous hacking later on.

The trick to retaining a more compact shrub is to select the tallest shoot every three to four years and cut this back hard, leaving just a short stub near the base of the plant. This will force any buds near the base into growth and create a branching effect close to the base. Select the strongest growing stems from the new branching and allow them to grow out and up. Foliage and branches can be pruned to let this new material through as it reaches the existing canopy of the shrub.

It is possible to conduct a similar type of pruning on mature specimens, but instead of removing only one of the dominant stems, all can be reduced by two-thirds of their overall length. This will give the appearance of an "upside down" spider, and it may take over three years for the plant to fully recover, but the improved end justifies the means.

Oemleria   Rosaceae

Oemleria cerasiformis
Common Names: Oso berry, Indian plum.
Flowering Period: In the UK February and March, in the USA March and April.
Flowers: Small, whitish green, scented, borne in long, pendulous racemes.
Height and Spread: 2.5 to 3.0 (7.5 to 9ft) tall by 4m (12ft) wide.

The oso berry, *Oemleria cerasiformis* (formerly *Osmaronia cerasiformis*) is one of the last true winter-flowering shrubs to bloom here in Hampshire, England. Like many winter-flowerers (the shrubby honeysuckles, *Lonicera*, for instance), it is a rather straggly-looking shrub, which its suckering habit perpetuates, so it is not particularly attractive when in leaf—looks like a large green blob. When in flower, however, the long chains of heavenly scented, whitish green pendulous flowers are quite something, and although the genus is closely related to the cherries (*Prunus*), the flowers are more reminiscent of the flowering currants (*Ribes*). A fairly rare plant in our gardens in the UK, the oso berry is more widely used in the USA, where it is native to California, as a landscape plant for reclaiming land: it is an excellent pioneer species, growing in nutrient-poor soils and especially tolerant of sites with little tree canopy.

Both males and females are required for the oso berry to produce its fruits, and they are best sited in close proximity to each other. At the Sir Harold Hillier Gardens in Hampshire, we had two plants growing some 500m (1640ft) apart, and the bees never seemed to hook the two plants together, so we never had fruit. The fruits are quite small, 10mm (0.25in) long, damson-like, at first peach-coloured then turning a glaucous blue; they are edible and can be eaten fresh, cooked, or dried. The berries have some astringent properties. Native Americans made tea from the bark and used to store dried fruits for winter consumption, hence the other common name, the Indian plum. Male plants undoubtedly have the largest and most-scented flowers; the racemes measure 10 to 15cm (4 to 6in) and can begin to flower in February and continue into March. In the various locations in the USA flowering is normally March into April and is seen as the harbinger of spring. For me it heralds the end of the winter-flowering period, as the flowers emerge just before the foliage.

Oemleria cerasiformis in bloom.

Cultivation Tips

The oso berry is not a difficult shrub to grow as long as you give it enough room to fully establish and bear in mind that it is a wide-spreading suckering shrub. It will grow on a wide range of soils; I have seen it growing on dry acidic soils, humus-rich soils that waterlog in winter, and very shallow alkaline soils (this last will produce some chlorosis and result in leaf burn). I would select a male form for its showier flowers; it is unlikely that in a normal garden situation both a male and a female could be grown, and to be fair, the fruits are not that decorative.

As garden shrubs go, this is definitely a back-of-the-border shrub, one to impress your friends with during winter and then to be forgotten, hidden somewhere behind a big clump of herbaceous perennials. But don't get me wrong: this is not a shrub to be ashamed of—far from it. It just isn't pretty for the rest of the year, unless of course you wish to adorn it with a deciduous climber, something along the lines of *Dicentra scandens* 'Athens Yellow', a particularly good form selected by Allan Armitage of the University of Georgia, Athens, with the typical flowers of the bleeding heart, of a rich yellow.

The main problem with the oso berry is its willingness to increase by suckers each year. Placing a retaining barrier of some kind around the outer edge of the plant may help, or you can dig up the outer circle of suckers and give them away to friends. But spreading with age is something that affects us all, and the oso berry is no exception. To halt the progress of its "middle-age spread," undertake regular pruning when it is young. On a yearly basis, remove about one-quarter of the oldest stems and allow new stems to develop from their base; this seems to stop the production of suckering stems. Such pruning is best accomplished after flowering and once the foliage has fully expanded. This regular maintenance should keep your shrub in good condition; it will thrive throughout the UK and is hardy in the USA to zone 5.

Osmanthus   Oleaceae

Early winter–flowering osmanthus

Common Names: Fragrant tea olive (*Osmanthus fragrans*); holly tea olive, false holly (*O. heterophyllus*); Fortune's osmanthus (*O. ×fortunei*).

Flowering Period: Late October through to early December, and occasionally spasmodically in the spring.

Flowers: Small, white, highly scented, often obscured by the holly-like foliage.

Height and Spread: Variable, with many making large shrubs.

Your first encounter with osmanthus can certainly lead you up the holly garden path, as many have foliage resembling that of the common or English holly, *Ilex aquifolium*. You'll see upon closer inspection, however, that the leaves are arranged opposite each other, in pairs, whereas in holly they are alternate. Several *Osmanthus* species, such as *O. americanus* (American devilwood) and *O. decorus*, do not have spiny foliage; some species can exhibit both heavily toothed and entire leaves, but we are not here to discuss the finer points of leaf arrangements. All are imposing evergreens grown mainly for their foliage, which varies immensely from species to species.

A particular favourite of mine, *Osmanthus armatus*, is not for the fainthearted: it reaches 5m (15ft) in height and often spreads as wide, with some of the biggest leaves found within this group, often exceeding 18cm (7in) in length and edged with hook-shaped teeth. The highly scented, small, pure white flowers are produced in abundance from October through into late November. I have not encountered this shrub anywhere on my travels in the USA, but in my

Osmanthus armatus is not for those short of space, as it will attain almost tree-like stature.

view it should be much hardier than *O. fragrans*, which is classed as hardy in zones 9 and 10, but will grow in zones 7 to 10 (and I would support the 7 to 10 range). It is certainly worthy of more attention than it presently gets, especially when you consider it was introduced in 1902 by E. H. Wilson, and he knew a thing or two about quality garden plants. One more commonly planted in our gardens is Fortune's osmanthus, *O. ×fortunei*, a hybrid between *O. fragrans* and *O. heterophyllus*, introduced from Japan in 1862 by Robert Fortune, although the original introduction was made by Thomas Lobb in 1852. Yet another large shrub reaching 6m (20ft) tall and forming a dense mound of spiny foliage that, given age, becomes spineless. The flowers, which are produced in abundance during November (occasionally late autumn in milder areas), are very highly scented, small, pure white, and hidden by the foliage. A controlled cross of the two species was undertaken in the USA at San Jose, California; although the resulting offspring resemble the plants grown in our gardens, two distinct selections were made. *Osmanthus ×fortunei* 'San Jose' has longer and narrower leaves than the form commonly grown and flowers a week earlier; *O. ×fortunei* 'Fruitlandii' is supposed to be more compact and hardier than the other two forms and also has curious ivory-yellow flowers rather than the true white of Fortune's osmanthus. I have encountered both selections in Georgia, and they certainly do look different when you see several hundred lined out in nursery rows, their foliage deep, glistening green and undamaged by a Georgia summer, in which climate they certainly grow and flower better than in the UK.

But, if I had the opportunity to grow a plant in the UK that we currently cannot, then close to the top of my list would be the fragrant tea olive,

Osmanthus fragrans, which is widely planted in Mediterranean regions (and which I have seen flowering itself almost to death in North Carolina and Georgia). This delightful evergreen has finely toothed leaves; and in early autumn (September) and continuing until early winter (often longer), the tips of the foliage have clusters of creamy white, very highly and sweetly scented flowers that certainly make it a shrub to die for! It will thrive in all but the heaviest waterlogged soils, and the hotter it is, the better it does: the high temperatures ripen the wood and harden it off before the onset of winter, and it is this fact which has restricted this plant to south-facing walls or glasshouses in the mildest areas of the British Isles. Even in the USA, it is restricted to zones 9 and 10, where it attains a height of 5m (15ft); however, severe damage can occur when temperatures fall below −18°C (0°F). Don't be misled—even though it doesn't get that cold in the UK that often, we don't get the 100°F (38°C) summers either. I trawled the Internet in search of named forms of *O. fragrans* and was astounded to discover nine cultivars; the following are ones I have encountered. *Osmanthus fragrans* f. *aurantiacus* is amazing; it doesn't repeat bloom and seems less hardy than the white-flowering form, but does have vivid, almost barberry-like orange flowers. *Osmanthus fragrans* 'Conger Yellow' has bright yellow flowers and attractive glossy foliage. *Osmanthus fragrans* 'Nanjing's Beauty' ('Fudingzhu'), introduced from China to the USA, is a very floriferous white-flowering form that blooms from fall until spring and has slightly smaller foliage. Reputedly the hardiest form available (a possible zone 6 plant), it is probably the form to introduce in the UK.

Osmanthus heterophyllus, the holly tea olive, is probably the most widely grown species and is undoubtedly the hardiest. It offers amazing depth and variety: some forms have spiky, holly-like foliage, some provide the most beautiful shades of colour within the foliage—and then there are those that look like they have survived some kind of weird science experiment. All are slow-growing (the variegated, golden, and multicoloured forms are very slow) but remarkably hardy and will survive in full sun to deep shade and in all kinds of soils (but not in high pH and waterlogged conditions). Brief description of the various forms on the market follow. All flower from late October through into late November, depending on the season. Flowers are pure white, highly scented, and often hidden by the foliage.

It is always good to start off with some controversy. *Osmanthus heterophyllus* 'Aureus' is sometimes listed as being synonymous with 'Aureomarginatus', which I do find a bit difficult to fathom, having seen for myself a form with bright yellow foliage labelled 'Aureus' at the JC Raulston Arboretum, Raleigh, North Carolina, and a bright golden–edged form in Georgia, clearly labelled

'Aureomarginatus'. There seems to be some mix up here; however, I am clear in my own mind that 'Aureus' has emerging golden yellow foliage that fades to green-yellow and then pale green by late summer. It is very distinct—one of the most beautiful selections of the species. 'Aureomarginatus' (which may itself be synonymous with 'Aureovariegatus') is also distinct, with a clear golden yellow edge to the leaf and new growth that is occasionally tinted purple; the variegation is very stable. *Osmanthus heterophyllus* 'Goshiki' is the most unusual selection, with five different colours—pink, bronze, gold, green, and yellow—splattered across the leaf. A compact plant, to 2m (6ft), with a good constitution and delightful purple-tinted new growth, it is the jewel of the crown in this bunch. The most holly-like of this group is *O. heterophyllus* 'Gulftide'; the foliage of young plants is very spiky, but with maturity the holly-like foliage is lost. It is a large shrub, becoming more open with age and exceeding 4m (12ft) tall and quite wide. 'Purpurea' is the purple-foliaged equivalent of 'Aureus': the emerging foliage is purple-black, and the hotter the weather is, the blacker it becomes. Fantastic grown as a hedge or clipped every so often, when it is almost reminiscent of *Pittosporum tenuifolium* 'Tom Thumb'. With age the foliage fades to a green-purple but is still attractive and provides a more than attractive foil for the white flowers. Originated at the Royal Botanic Gardens, Kew, Surrey, in 1860, 'Purpurea' is arguably one of the hardiest selections of *O. heterophyllus*, apart from the green-foliaged forms, and will eventually make a shrub 3m (9ft)

Osmanthus heterophyllus 'Variegatus' is one of the best variegated plants on the planet.

tall and wide, if unclipped. 'Sasaba', a remarkable form that was selected and raised in Japan and then distributed to the UK and USA, is in my view a typical Japanese collector's plant with deeply cut foliage, heavily spiked at the tips, that looks like a cross between a gnarled holly leaf and a barberry (and I am informed that sasaba means "bamboo leaf" in Japanese). It flowers regularly and, what with the deformed nature of the leaf, the flowers seem to show up more. Similar in size and stature to 'Purpurea'.

Some variegated plants should be put down at birth. *Osmanthus heterophyllus* 'Variegatus', a delightful and widely available form, is not one of them: it has such stable, well-pronounced variegation that it falls firmly into the category of plants to die for—or, dare I say, trade your wife for (see *Hamamelis japonica*)! Its rich, creamy white leaf margin often extends into the leaf area, contrasting beautifully against the deep, glossy green centre.

Cultivation Tips

Osmanthus armatus is in my experience a very easy shrub to grow, as are all the early-flowering tea olives listed here. Of course, there is a lot of experimentation left regarding hardiness. One must find the most appropriate local growing conditions for *O. armatus* and *O. fragrans*; *O.* ×*fortunei* and *O. heterophyllus* should prove equally easy to cultivate in most areas of the UK, and in the USA should be cultivated in zones 6 to 10 without any serious problems. Unlike many other evergreens, these are adaptable plants, taking a variety of soils and not fazed by sun or shade or lack thereof, although those with variegated or golden foliage may need slight protection from extremely high summer temperatures.

All the early-flowerers covered in this section are best as background plants: they should remain on the periphery of any planting scheme, as backdrops for other plants. They also make excellent hedges and can be clipped into a number of different shapes, but please retain some dignity: I can take hedges, meatballs, and toadstool-like shapes, but please do not subject this wonderful group of plants to the ignominy of being turned into poodles or flamingos or the plethora of other shapes that infect our gardens. Any clipping to maintain a nice symmetrical shape should be done in late autumn or mid spring, when the risk of winter damage to the emerging foliage has passed. Certainly, clipping of the new foliage maintains juvenility and keeps the spiny-foliage effect.

Early winter–flowering osmanthus require very little routine maintenance. They fall into the desirable category of low-maintenance, high-impact landscape plants—nothing left but to simply sit back and enjoy them.

Late winter–flowering osmanthus

Common Names: Himalayan osmanthus (*Osmanthus suavis*); Yunnan osmanthus (*O. yunnanensis*).

Flowering Period: January through to March.

Flowers: Pure white to ivory-white, highly scented, borne in clusters around the stems.

Height and Spread: 4m (12ft) for *Osmanthus suavis*; 10m (30ft) for *O. yunnanensis*.

I first encountered *Osmanthus suavis* at the Royal Botanic Garden Edinburgh, Scotland, when I stumbled across a plant in full bloom during late February, and I can tell you it was a heartwarming sight—the branches were literally covered in small clusters of sweetly scented, pure white flowers. Its growth habit was unlike any osmanthus I had encountered before, with very upright branches, not the mounded habit I had come to expect with other species. Several years later I came across this same species again, hidden in the darkest recesses of the Sir Harold Hillier Gardens, Hampshire, this time a much larger and more mature specimen, and flowering a few weeks earlier in this more southerly location. It is not among the more attractive species in the genus, as its habit is slightly more open and leggier than many of the others, but considering its erect growing habit, it is more than suitable for general planting.

Osmanthus yunnanensis is a much bigger affair, and, given age and adequate protection from nearby trees and the benefit of a sunny location, it can attain almost tree-like size. The very scented flowers are borne in late winter (February) but are almost totally obscured by the large leaves, 15cm (6in) long, which are either toothed or not. A single-stemmed specimen close to Jermyns House, Sir Harold Hillier Gardens, has survived for many years; it is around 11m (33ft) tall and is growing in a semi-woodland setting in a free-draining, acidic, sandy soil; I have never seen any damage to the foliage. There are reportedly larger specimens in some of the Cornish gardens, and a fine specimen at Hidcote Manor, Gloucestershire.

Cultivation Tips

Osmanthus suavis is the hardier of these two species; it should be as hardy as *O. serrulatus*, which is reckoned to be hardy in zones 7 to 10. *Osmanthus yunnanensis* is still fairly rare in gardens and is easily too large for an urban garden—but just imagine how far the scent from a round-headed tree-sized (11m, 33ft) osmanthus in full flower would travel. This imposing landscape plant is probably only as hardy as *O. fragrans* and I suspect it will not have the same heat tolerance, but only experimentation will tell.

Once again, both these later-flowering species require minimal attention and very little pruning, apart from removing the occasional dead, damaged, or crossing branch to maintain shape. This operation is usually undertaken after flowering in early summer.

Parrotia   **Hamamelidaceae**

Parrotia persica

Common Name: Persian ironwood.

Flowering Period: January and February.

Flowers: Small clusters of bright red stamens protruding (just) from chocolate-brown flower buds.

Height and Spread: Varies, but this is a stately shrub, often as wide as tall. The largest recorded in the UK, at Westonbirt National Arboretum, Gloucestershire, England, is 15m (45ft) tall; in the USA a massive multi-stemmed specimen at the Arnold Arboretum, Jamaica Plain, Massachusetts, is 20m (60ft) tall by 25m (75ft) wide.

The Persian ironwood, *Parrotia persica*, is a widely planted shrub native to northern Iran (Persia); many of the plants grown in cultivation are more tree-like, often multi-stemmed specimens, often wider than taller. It is mainly grown for its autumn colour, which is breathtaking—a long-lasting display of vibrant oranges, purples, reds, and yellows, similar in intensity to *Fothergilla major*. The Persian ironwood is one of the few members of the witch hazel family that will thrive on alkaline soils and also colour well at the same time. Its unusual-looking flowers, which are produced between January and February, are nowhere as showy as those of the witch hazels; the furry brown flower buds simply split to reveal bright red stamens, giving a reddish haze to the ends of the branches.

The Persian ironwood was first introduced into the UK, to the Royal Botanic Gardens, Kew, in 1841 from St Petersburg Botanic Gardens. It is widely planted in parks and larger gardens and is now a fairly common landscape shrub, distinct in both autumn and winter. The bark is also highly ornamental, flaking to reveal variously coloured underbark and resembling that of *Cornus kousa*, to my mind. A number of selections are on offer, most originating from seedling selections in Holland, the UK, and the USA. The following are descriptions of the plants I have seen firsthand.

Parrotia persica 'Burgundy', a selection made by Karan Junker of PMA Plant Specialists, Somerset, England, offers purple young growth and exceptional autumn colour; its habit is the same as the straight species. *Parrotia persica* 'Biltmore' is a selection from a fine round-headed specimen more than a century old, growing close to the Azalea Dell at the Biltmore Estate in North Carolina and distributed under this name by Earth Shade Nursery, Warne, North Carolina, USA. *Parrotia persica* 'Select' offers lime-green leaves with a very distinct purple edge; this attractive form is also reported to have exceptional autumn colour. *Parrotia persica* 'Lamplighter' (originally distributed as *P. persica* 'Variegata') is a slow-growing Persian ironwood with broadly white-margined leaves that are flushed purple; in autumn the foliage's purple tint intensifies and becomes the dominant feature. It was discovered as a branch sport by Stephen Taffler, a UK fanatic of variegated plants. The variegation can occasionally revert (a close eye is needed to ensure that it is not lost entirely), and as is often the case with such highly variegated plants, shade is required to stop the foliage from burning up in the sunlight. A difficult plant to establish: lack of vigour is this selection's main downfall.

I know of two forms of the pendulous ironwood, *Parrotia persica* 'Pendula'. The first, a slow-growing, strongly pendulous form first introduced by the Royal Botanic Gardens, Kew, Surrey, in 1934, was distributed to several large gardens, although few specimens of this very slow-growing form exist today. It seldom grows any taller than 1.5m (5ft) and seems to have no apical dominance whatsoever: branches are completely pendulous, growing out from the main trunk and creeping along the ground, producing a shrub some 2m (6ft) wide. The autumn colour is a pale yellow, and it flowers sparsely. The other form of the pendulous ironwood is a much taller affair, possibly a top-grafted form, and is considerably more vigorous;

Parrotia persica 'Lamplighter' is a new introduction with white variegated foliage and purple tints.

it will eventually grow to the same height as the normal Persian ironwood. The branches are semi-pendulous, growing down slightly in an arching manner but retaining their ability to grow upright, giving a saggy-branched effect. The shrub otherwise has the typical Persian ironwood autumn colour and winter flowers. *Parrotia persica* 'Vanessa', a seedling selection, has been cultivated in Holland since 1975; sufficient nursery stock was finally built up, and it was introduced into the UK and USA, in 1995, where it is distributed by Twombly Nursery, Monroe, Connecticut. A distinct tree-like form, it develops a clear central leader

Parrotia persica 'Vanessa' offers an interesting habit and gorgeous autumn colour.

but also has slightly weeping side branches; its delightful foliage is edged bronze in early summer, intensifies to a rich bronze in late summer, and then produces exceptional autumn colour. Considering its various seasons of interest, I feel that this could become the best Persian ironwood for general planting, especially where size is a problem. 'Vanessa' will not disappoint, particularly when called upon to help to fill the difficult call for a small tree for chalk or high pH soils.

Cultivation Tips

Parrotia persica is one of the best autumn-colouring shrubs for high pH soils and will grow in full sun and semi-shade. It can be used as a specimen shrub or, if pruned regularly, can be developed into a smallish specimen tree. The tree-trained versions show off their attractive bark to a far greater extent but require annual pruning to retain their shape. As a general guide, it is wise never to remove more than one-quarter of the total leaf area during any seasonal pruning operation; removing more will result in the production of masses of epicormic shoots as the shrub tries to reset the root-to-shoot balance. It is often best to prune simply to retain shape, removing crossing and weak branches and those required to retain a central trunk.

Large, unpruned, mature Persian ironwoods have a special, almost magical feel to them. There is something Alice-in-Wonderland about them, their large branches sweeping down to the ground and a mass of crossing branches making up their canopy. A pruner's nightmare, they are probably best left to their own devices. This is how I enjoy the Persian ironwood, its gnarled branches silhouetting the winter sky. Use them as big landscape plants, as a specimen in a lawn (that is, if you have a lawn that big), as a woodland-edge shrub, or even massed in a landscape, where the beauty of their autumn colour, shape, and winter blooms can be fully appreciated. They are remarkably hardy throughout the UK and best grown in suitable soils in zones 4 to 8 in the USA.

Rhododendron   **Ericaceae**

Of all the plants we grow in our gardens, none are better known than the rhododendrons, introduced into the West from India over 350 years ago. Probably the most remarkable introductions were those made by Joseph Hooker, who travelled in Sikkim and the Himalayas between 1848 and 1850; the forty-three species sent back and propagated by his father, William Hooker, at the Royal Botanic Gardens, Kew, swelled the rhodic ranks and fired a generation with their beauty and importance. Rhododendrons were subsequently collected by most of the great plant explorers—Forrest, Wilson, Kingdon Ward, Purdom, Farrer, Ludlow and Sherriff, Rock— and even now, nurseries and private collectors are always on the search for new species to introduce.

The range of rhododendrons available in the market has increased a hundred-fold, and breeding programmes to increase hardiness, improve flower colour, and instill compactness are underway throughout the world. And although a number of raised forms will allegedly thrive in neutral conditions, the major drawback to rhododendrons' being a widespread garden plant is their dependence on acidic soils. Many newer hybrids are more compact and contain the best traits of many of the species, with bigger flowers, cleaner foliage, and increased adaptability as garden plants; yet, you simply do not see rhododendrons used within the winter landscape.

One of their main weaknesses as landscape plants is that their flower petals are incredibly susceptible to winter or spring frost. Anyone who has tried to exhibit rhododendrons at horticultural shows will know how delicate those petals are: the simplest pressure, and a brown bruise appears. The same damage occurs when temperatures fall below 0°C (32°F); one or two nights of such temperatures and an entire flush of flowers will be lost, even to closed buds. This can be soul-destroying—one waits in anticipation for the blooms to unfurl, only to have them destroyed in one fell swoop …

That said, a great number of exceptional rhododendrons are, in my view, essential if somewhat ephemeral players in the winter garden. These range from small compact plants, growing little more than 1m (3ft) tall, to those of tree-like stature with large, bold foliage that requires the protection of dappled shade from nearby trees throughout the summer. What they bring to the winter show are flower colours and shapes that no other plant provides. Most require protection from frost; during the summer months, protection from direct sunlight is essential.

Our garden rhododendrons come from all corners of the globe; the genus *Rhododendron* is large, containing well over eight hundred species specialised to various habitats, including alpine tundra, forest edge, mountainous forest, dense forest, rocky outcrops in mountain ranges, and subtropical rain forest. With such a variety of plants to whet our appetite, it is hard to believe that rhododendrons have gone the route of conifers and heathers in the UK: they are a group of plants out-of-vogue with the British public. The bubble has burst for rhododendrons; where in the 1960s and 1970s rhododendrons were the talk of flower shows (especially during their season, March through June), now we see only a few specimens, relegated to dark corners of the hall. What a poor end for such a remarkable group of plants, and one so entrenched in the history of our garden plants.

The rhododendrons I have selected for special mention are divided into two groups, stately (larger-leaved, larger-growing species and hybrids that, if given sufficient room and conditions, will develop into quite large shrubs, occasionally small trees) and compact forms. These flower in January and February and only very occasionally earlier than this; I have encountered them in bloom within the rhododendron collections at the Sir Harold Hillier Gardens and Exbury Gardens (both in Hampshire, England) and at the RHS Garden Wisley. Flowering periods do vary from year to year, and in a mild winter, which often happens in the south of England, considerably more than those included here will flower. For ease of classification, all winter-flowering rhododendrons mentioned will (in the south of England) flower before the end of February (even if their flowers are destroyed by early frost), hence their inclusion here. For the classification of hardiness, I have used either the USDA hardiness zones (where I can track down the necessary information) or the equivalent UK zones as given in *The Rhododendron Handbook* (RHS, 1998), which is widely used in the cultivation of *Rhododendron* species in the UK. These winter hardiness ratings do not, however, take into account the extremes faced within a continental climate, especially those with very high summer temperatures.

Stately winter-flowering rhododendrons

Rhododendron arboreum (H2-3, zone 7) is among the most important species ever introduced and one of Joseph Hooker's primary introductions, in 1810; it was initially distributed to a wide range of private collectors and landowners. It is very early to flower, often blooming in mid January, its blood-red flowers unmistakable in the winter landscape. Its leaves are quite small, but the underside can be covered in smooth silver- or copper-coloured indumentum.

In the wild, *Rhododendron arboreum* has a massive distribution range, across the temperate Himalayas through Kashmir to Bhutan. It is separated into several different forms identified by distinctive foliage or flower colour. *Arborea* means "tree-like," and given the right conditions this species can indeed make an imposing shrub, growing from 5 to 30m (15 to 90ft) tall. Such massive specimens occur in the wild as well as in areas with Sino-Himalayan conditions, where the average rainfall is high and air temperatures are even throughout the year. In such places you will find the best rhododendron collections—areas like Cornwall, the west coast of Scotland, Ireland, parts of southern England, the western seaboard of the USA, especially Oregon, and New Zealand. Here the true size of the species can be encountered. *Rhododendron arboreum* subsp. *arboreum*, the most common form, is found in the Himalayas and is widespread across northern India, Nepal, and Sikkim, yet is surprisingly one of the least hardy forms; it has a distinct white to silvery underside to the foliage and crimson flowers. *Rhododendron arboreum* subsp. *cinnamomeum* (H3-4a, zone 8) has very distinct cinnamon indumentum on the underside of the leaves. *Rhododendron arboreum* subsp. *cinnamomeum* 'Roseum' (var. *roseum*) (H3-4a, zone 8) represents those forms with pale flowers, often of a rich rose-pink, with darker spots. 'Tony Schilling' (H3-4a, zone 8) has deep pink flowers with distinct darker spots; collected by Tony Schilling, then curator of RBG Kew at Wakehurst Place, West Sussex. 'Album' (var. *album*) (H3-4a, zone 8) encompasses those forms with white flowers; these are among the hardiest of this group, often coming from the highest elevations. 'Blood Red' (H3-4a, zone 8) has very striking blood-red flowers and is quite early to flower.

Rhododendron fulgens (H4a, zone 7) is a delightful species from eastern Nepal, Bhutan, and Sikkim, where its height varies from 1 to 4.5m (3 to 12ft). It flowers in late February in the south of England, early March further north, where it is quite hardy. Flowers are similar in colour to *R. arboreum*, although the overall effect is carried on a much smaller shrub. This is one of my favourite winter-flowering species for the reddish brown indumentum on the underside of the leaves. *Rhododendron* ×*geraldii* (H4b, zones 7 and 8) is a real corker, a beautiful early-flowering hybrid between *R. praevernum* and *R. sutchuenense* that occurs in the wild where the two species meet. It is a large, somewhat straggly-looking shrub, with quite large trusses of pure white flowers with a distinct purple basal blotch; it is a rare treat when in flower (as early as the end of January, although February is the norm), as many late winter–flowering rhododendrons tend to be in the red and pink ranges.

Rhododendron grande (H2-3, zones 6 and 7) is a rhododendron with attitude written all over it! Given sufficient rainfall, the leaves will reach 30cm (12in) long, with a shiny upper surface and silvery indumentum on the underside, on a shrub reaching up to 12m (36ft). You can imagine Joseph Hooker's excitement when he first saw this species (which he introduced from Sikkim in 1850), its pink-budded flowers opening ivory-white and each with a distinct purple basal blotch. The flowers themselves are an impressive 5cm (2in) across, with fifteen to twenty-five making up a truss. But alas, this one requires protection from both wind and sun and is only for woodland settings in the mildest areas, where it will flower in February and March.

The vivid flower colour of *Rhododendron ririei* will surely turn a few heads in late winter.

The delicate white and pink flowers of *Rhododendron watsonii* are a sight to behold in late February.

Rhododendron praevernum (H4b), one of the parents of *R. ×geraldii*, is more compact than its offspring, between 2 and 5m (3 and 15ft) tall. A delightful early-flowering species from China, its large white or pink-suffused flowers, occasionally speckled and with a distinct purple eye, are produced in February and March. *Rhododendron ririei* (H4, zone 7) is a real eye-catcher, with purple-blue flowers in quite large trusses. The foliage is also attractive and quite long, around 15cm (6in), with a silvery underside. Introduced to our gardens by E. H. Wilson in 1904, this Chinese species can get quite large, 10m (30ft) tall. Once seen, never forgotten. *Rhododendron strigillosum* (H4a, zones 6 and 7) is a small tree, never taller than 6m (20ft) and native to China, where it is found between elevations of 2200 and 3350m (7200 and 11,000ft). Flowers are produced early in February in clusters of eight to twelve; they are quite small and a deep brilliant red, if provided a sheltered woodland in which to grow. Two final Chinese natives, each introduced by E. H. Wilson, are *R. sutchuenense* and *R. watsonii*. *Rhododendron sutchuenense* (H4b, zone 6) is arguably the best of the winter-flowering rhododendrons, reaching 5m (15ft) with age; foliage is distinctly drooping and in February is joined by the ten-clustered trusses of rose-pink to rose-lilac and often spotted flowers, but without a blotch, which distinguishes it from *R. ×geraldii* and *R. praevernum*. *Rhododendron watsonii* (H4, zone 8) can be distinguished by its flattened petioles; it is a small tree to 6m (20ft) but often smaller in cultivation, when, during February and March, it will bear white flowers, tinged pink and with distinct crimson basal blotch, in clusters of twelve to fifteen.

Compact winter-flowering rhododendrons

Rhododendron eclecteum (H3-4a, zone 6) is one of the first rhododendrons I ever exhibited at the RHS's Early Rhododendron and Camellia Show at Vincent Square, London. It is a beautiful, variable species, growing 1 to 3m (3 to 9ft) tall, with fleshy flowers that are easily damaged. It offers a complete range of flower colours, from white or pink to pale purple, red, or yellow, and flowers that can be spotted, mottled, or clean. Several hybrids masquerade under this name.

Rhododendron lapponicum (H4b-c, zones 6 and 7) is a very distinct species native to Alaska, Canada, Greenland, Scandinavia, and Arctic Russia, and as such is very hardy. It is low-growing, seldom exceeding 1m (3ft) tall, and flowers in February and March in mild seasons, with purple flowers in clusters of two or three. Although it is ultra-hardy, it is a difficult species to keep alive, as many of the Arctic tundra species are.

Without forcing, *Rhododendron* 'Christmas Cheer' flowers in February.

Rhododendron 'Christmas Cheer' (H4, zone 6), a hardy hybrid bred in 1908, was widely used in the pot plant industry, where under artificial conditions it could be forced into flower for Christmas. In the south of England, its white to pale pink flowers, white in bud, open in February. It grows to over 2m (6ft) with age, although it can be retained as a more compact plant: regular pruning produces a dense shrub with pale green foliage.

Rhododendron moupinense hybrids are even more compact. *Rhododendron moupinense* (H3-4, zone 7) itself is a real sweetie, a delightful low-growing species from Sichuan seldom reaching over 1.3m (3.5ft) tall and bearing quite large, bell-shaped, scented, white, pink, or deep rose flowers, occasionally spotted red or crimson, and leaves with hairy edges. It will require protection from frost and early morning sun when the delicate flowers are blooming in February and March. *Rhododendron* 'Cilipinense' (H3-4, zones 7 and 8), a deliberate hybrid between *R. ciliatum* and *R. moupinense*, was raised at Bodnant Garden, North Wales, UK, in 1927. Like many of this parentage, it is a compact rhododendron, 1m (3ft) tall, with glossy evergreen, purple-tinted, bristle-margined leaves and slightly floppy flowers, 6cm (2.5in) across, of a crystal white, tipped or flushed pink, appearing deeper pink in bud. Flowers are a joy to see in late winter but are easily damaged by frost. *Rhododendron* 'Bo-peep' (H3-4, zone 7), raised at Exbury Gardens, Hampshire, England, in 1934, is a hybrid between *R. moupinense* and *R. lutescens*. Again, it is a compact grower, with masses of primrose-yellow flowers produced late in February to early March; the flowers are large, 3cm (1.5in) across, and are delicately speckled orange. *Rhododendron* 'Seta' (H3, zone 7), raised at Bodnant Gardens, North Wales, in 1933, is another charming hybrid of *R. moupinense*, this time crossed with *R. spinuliferum*. Its flowers are the most unusual of this group: they are trumpet-shaped, 3cm (1.5in) long, borne in clusters at the tip of the foliage, pure white at the base, and shaded a rich pink at the tips. This shrub flowers at the end of February into March and often reaches 1.5m (5ft) in height.

Rhododendron leucaspis (H3, zone 7) is a delightful low-growing species from the borders of Tibet and Burma, whence it was introduced by Frank Kingdon Ward in 1925. It seldom reaches over 1m (3ft) tall and requires some shelter,

Rhododendron moupinense, an exquisite species, is a parent of several stunning hybrids.

especially when in bloom: the paper-like, pure white flowers, 5cm (2in) across and produced in clusters of two or three during February and March, are highly susceptible to frost damage. *Rhododendron* 'Bric-à-brac' (H3, zone 7) is another widely used Exbury hybrid, this time between *R. moupinense* and *R. leucaspis*, raised in 1934. In flower it resembles *R. leucaspis*, but its pure white, open-mouthed flowers measure 6cm (2.5in) across and have very distinct chocolate-brown stamens. In my view, it is one of the best of this group, albeit one of the least hardy; it requires a sheltered location and its flowers especially are easily damaged if the temperature falls below freezing.

Rhododendron 'Praecox' (H4, zone 6), a cross between *R. ciliatum* and *R. dauricum*, was bred in 1855 by Isaac Davies of Ormskirk, Lancaster, England. Its rosy-red flowers have an open trumpet shape and are borne in clusters at the tips of the foliage. This is one of the earliest rhododendrons to flower (it can be in full bloom during early February) and often retains its foliage, which is scented when crushed or rubbed, throughout winter. *Rhododendron dauricum* (H4c, zone 4) is a straggly but nevertheless charming, semi-evergreen compact rhododendron native to Russia, Mongolia, northern China, and Japan, where it thrives at elevations above 1600m (5250ft); pruning after flowering can encourage bushiness and create a less straggly habit. This species usually flowers alongside *R. mucronulatum* in January and February; in fact, *R. dauricum* is closely related to *R. mucronulatum*, but it retains its leaves and has smaller flowers, 2.5cm (1in) in diameter. Its solitary pale to rich pink-purple flowers appear at the end of branches. Flowers are quite frost-resistant but can be damaged; happily, there are usually plenty of flowering buds to take their place, making this one of the best and hardiest rhododendrons for winter planting. There seem to be two white-flowering forms (often labelled simply as *R. dauricum* 'Album'): *R. dauricum* 'Arctic Pearl' and *R. dauricum* 'Hokkaido'. Both are quite compact plants, reaching 1.5m (5ft) tall, with pure white flowers in January through to March; 'Hokkaido', a selection from Japan, has very large flowers. *Rhododendron dauricum* 'Hiltingbury' exhibits flowers in clusters of three to four at the tips and seems to retain almost all its leaves, which bronze in the winter; flowers are a rich rose-purple, and darker purple on the reverse. It was selected by the late John Bond, Keeper of the Crown Estates, Windsor and Savill Gardens, from a plant growing at Hillier Nurseries' acidic nursery at Chandlers Ford, Southampton, England. *Rhododendron dauricum* 'Midwinter' is a hardy form with deep purple flowers that are borne in January and early February; it is less evergreen than 'Hiltingbury'. *Rhododendron dauricum* Sempervirens Group is the name given to seed-raised plants that retain their foliage throughout winter and have multiple flowers of rose-purple. All the

The delicate flowers of *Rhododendron dauricum* need protection from winter frosts.

various forms of *R. dauricum* are likewise hardy in H4c, zone 4. *Rhododendron sichotense* (H5, zone 5) is very closely allied to *R. dauricum* (and indeed is often listed as *R. dauricum*) but is somewhat taller and has pale purple flowers in January and February.

Rhododendron mucronulatum (H4b-c, zone 5) is similar in many respects to *R. dauricum*; however, its foliage can be completely deciduous, and its flowers, 2.5cm (1in) in diameter, emerge before the leaves in late January. This is another hardy species, native to Russia, China, Mongolia, Korea, and Japan, where it is found at elevations above 300m (985ft). Numerous forms are available, in flower colours ranging from bright rose through to purple and occasionally white. *Rhododendron mucronulatum* var. *taquetii* (var. *chejuense*), a high-altitude form found in southern Korea, seldom grows any taller than 50cm (20in); it has rose-purple flowers, totally deciduous foliage, and good autumn colour. *Rhododendron mucronulatum* 'Album' flowers in early January and has pure white flowers with the faintest tint of pink. *Rhododendron mucronulatum* 'Hollaido', a Danish selection, is another pure white form, this time without any pink tints; it flowers one month later than the species, blooming in late February. *Rhododendron mucronulatum* 'Cama' has quite large, soft pink flowers that slowly fade to white and semi-evergreen foliage—most unusual. *Rhododendron mucronulatum* 'Cornell Pink', named by Henry T. Skinner, of Cornell University, Ithaca, New York, in 1952, produces its tissue-like, phlox-pink flowers early in the season; it is among the most widely grown of this group and, in my view, the

Many a winter planting includes the compact *Rhododendron mucronulatum* 'Cornell Pink', a quality act.

best. *Rhododendron mucronulatum* 'Gros Jacques' is similar to *R. dauricum* 'Midwinter' in overall habit, but its flowers are slightly larger, a deeper purple-pink, and are produced in abundance and very early, often at the beginning of January. *Rhododendron mucronulatum* 'Mahogany Red', with rich red-mahogany flowers, was selected by plant geneticist August Kehr, who introduced many wonderful magnolias, camellias, and rhododendrons from his garden in Hendersonville, North Carolina, USA. *Rhododendron mucronulatum* 'Winter Brightness' is a long-cultivated form with rich rose-pink to purple flowers. Double-flowering forms have reportedly been selected in Japan; from the early descriptions, these would make very welcome introductions into our gardens.

Cultivation Tips

If you can provide the conditions demanded by rhododendrons, their inclusion in the winter landscape is a welcome surprise. A soil with a pH of between 4.5 and 5.5 is recognised as optimum for their successful cultivation. Attempting to grow rhododendrons outside this soil range is an expensive mistake and will result in the rapid death of your prize possessions. At this pH range, most or all the nutrients required by rhododendrons are available in a soluble form for the plants to use. As the pH rises, iron and manganese—which are required for the development of chlorophyll, the green pigment in plant leaves—begin to break down, and as plants use chlorophyll to absorb sunlight and thus manufacture energy, this can have devastating effects. Lack of chlorophyll results in the yellowing of leaves, or chlorosis. Not only is unavailability of nutrients a problem; their over-availability can be a problem too, and as the pH rises higher, calcium and magnesium become so available in the soil, they become toxic to plants used to a lower pH.

Other areas of concern include drainage, moisture, and shade. As many (but not all) rhododendrons are woodland dwellers, they require the shelter of dappled shade from trees above and cool, moist soils for their roots below. Shade is an important factor: it provides a lower temperature for your plants to grow in but also lessens the risk of damage to the flowers, by protecting delicate blooms from an early morning sun that might cause them to thaw too quickly. As a general rule, the larger the leaf, the more overhead protection is required; many of the larger-leaved species come from forested areas, where high rainfall and moist soils are the norm, and it is these conditions that we are trying to emulate.

Many *Rhododendron* species hail from areas where the air is saturated with moisture. It is difficult to provide this in an open, exposed garden location, and it is often said that rhododendrons enjoy each other's company, thus creating to some extent their own microclimate. One element they do not enjoy is very hot weather, especially where temperatures rise above 32°C (90°F); in such conditions, additional shade is a must, and the hotter it gets, the more shade is required. Summer temperatures can vary dramatically; in a maritime climate, it is not the norm to have such high temperatures, whereas in a continental climate it is. So, a sunny, summer day in Athens, Georgia, USA, is very different from one in Romsey, Hampshire, England: considerably more protection would be required in Georgia than in Hampshire.

Both humid air and a moist soil are important requirements in the cultivation of *Rhododendron* species; but, as you quickly discover when growing rhododendrons, the more you think you know, the more the rules will change on you. The hardy hybrids (HH), for example, are suited for much wider landscape use and were especially bred for a wider tolerance of wind, sun, and, to a lesser extent, dryer soils. *Rhododendron* 'Christmas Cheer' is one such complex hybrid; it can be grown as a hedge in a fully exposed location, in quite dry soils, without suffering any detriment whatsoever. Conversely, this hybrid can also be grown where many of the large-leaved species would thrive, in deeper shade and moist soils. One thing is clear, however: few rhododendrons will thrive in very wet soils, especially those that become waterlogged during winter and spring. Rhododendrons require well-oxygenated soils that retain moisture throughout most of the season but that do not become flooded for long periods in the winter. A small period of waterlogging is acceptable, but long periods are not.

Such a large group of plants will obviously be afflicted by a number of pests and diseases. Deer, rabbits, mice, and voles can eat bark and leaves and ring-bark newly planted shrubs; if such pests are problems and eradication is not an option, every plant should be protected by anti-deer/rabbit fencing and guards. Weevils can be problematic and difficult to control in both the root-eating grub and leaf-eating adult stages; a predatory eelworm is widely used to control this pest, as are additives to composts and soils. Aphids, caspid bugs, and rhododendron aphis can also be problems. Phytophthora root rot, honey fungus, and rhododendron mildew can be controlled and kept in check by using good hygiene; better yet, avoid species that are very prone to these diseases in the first place, or replace them with those that are more resistant. Phytophthora root rots (those caused by *Phytophthora cinnamomi* in particular) have long been associated with rhododendrons; these infections cause wilting in young and newly planted rhododendrons, especially where soils are wet and cold in the winter. In recent years, containerised plants of certain *Rhododendron* species have become infected by *P. ramorum*, which causes sudden oak death, a notifiable disease in many countries. This pathogen has now been found on a very wide range of plants. Readers wishing to get the most up-to-date information should check with their local or state government agency, as sudden oak death manifests itself in a myriad of different symptoms on a variety of hosts.

Pruning of the more compact species and hybrids is best done after flowering; remove any developing seed heads as well, as these take energy from the plant, reducing its vigour. Simply tip the top growth to force the plant to bush, creating a more dense habit. With larger plants, more traditional pruning techniques can be adopted; this involves the regular removal of spent flowers and pruning out weak, old, and crossing stems and shoots. If a more bushy plant is required, the central growth bud can be pinched out using one's finger and thumb; a much better method, however, is to cut an entire stem back to the next whirl of foliage, as this will produce a more balanced array of new shoots. This last should be accomplished after flowering has finished.

Large rhododendrons can also be cut back hard after flowering and after the last risk of frost. Regeneration is slow; it often takes five to ten years for the shrub to become a suitable specimen once again. This technique involves cutting all the major stems back to within 50cm (20in) of ground level, allowing them to reshoot over the coming years and then selecting and pruning out a suitable shape from the developing shrub. Best results are gained where plants are in a reasonably open location and the developing shoots get plenty of indirect sunshine.

Rhododendrons can be used in many ways in the winter garden. The larger-leaved species make excellent background plantings in shady spots or below trees, where their presence can itself create some shade and provide a foil for other plants to flower against. Then, when it is their turn to bloom, their flowers are protected from sunlight and the risk of frost damage, and they can light up dreary corners of the garden. Smaller, more delicate species are, in my view, best planted in small colonies, where the flowers can be seen en masse and the risk of the whole lot being damaged is greatly reduced. A wonderful setting for them is beneath the shelter of mature trees; if they are further protected by other, larger plants, that is a bonus. I have found that many of the larger species of mahonias and their hybrids work well to provide this cover (*Mahonia ×media* and *M. lomariifolia* are good candidates). Camellias, too, are good complements for smaller rhododendrons.

As garden plants go, rhododendrons require little pruning and aftercare. With careful selection, it is possible to have these beautiful and varied plants flowering throughout the year.

Sarcococca   **Buxaceae**

Common Names: Winter box, Christmas box, fragrant box.
Flowering Period: January through to March.
Flowers: Very small, off-white, almost insignificant, borne in the leaf axils and
   hidden by the foliage. Female flowers sit atop the larger male flowers, which
   have pink stamens and are highly scented.
Height and Spread: Low-growing, slowly suckering evergreen shrubs, seldom
   reaching 1m (3ft) tall.

Can you imagine the utility of a dwarf, scented, evergreen shrub adaptable to the most inhospitable places, like that fated spot at the base of your Leyland or Lawson cypress hedge? Well, here it is, and once established in such a location, winter box will thrive and spread, forming a dense mass of evergreen stems. Hardy throughout the UK and in the USA in zones 6 to 8 unless otherwise stated.

Sarcococca confusa, an extremely useful, luxuriant-looking evergreen shrub with deep glossy foliage, highly scented flowers, and deep black fruits, is the true owner of the common name Christmas box. This species is possibly native to China, where it has been widely cultivated and whence it was introduced in 1916. It is similar to *S. ruscifolia*, which has bright red fruits.

Sarcococca hookeriana, native to Himalayas and a Tony Schilling introduction under his collection number 1260, is fairly rare in our gardens. It is quite an erect species and among the quickest-growing of this group, producing numerous highly scented, ivory-white flowers during February and March, followed by black fruits. Not as hardy as *S. hookeriana* var. *digyna*, a much more slender form originated from western China, whence it was introduced in 1908 by E. H. Wilson. I have seen quite tall clumps of this, with widely arching stems up to almost 1.5 (4ft) tall. It flowers in February and March, its highly scented flowers almost totally hidden by the foliage; these are followed by glossy black berries. *Sarcococca hookeriana* var. *digyna* 'Purple Stem', a wonderful and erect form with new stems and leaves flushed purple and larger flowers, was named by Hillier Nurseries, Hampshire, England, in 1968; its heavily scented flowers appear in late February. *Sarcococca hookeriana* var. *humilis* is a particular favourite of mine: not only is it a lot more compact, seldom reaching any taller than 1m (3ft), but it has a suckering habit, which produces dense colonies. Its highly scented flowers are almost visible among the very glossy green foliage; the male flowers have pink stamens, and the fruits are black. This is the hardiest winter box, a form of it collected by Christopher Grey-Wilson and Barry Phillips from the Himalayas, under collector initials GWP, is just exquisite. Hardy throughout the UK, and possibly hardy to zone 5 in the USA.

Sarcococca hookeriana var. *digyna* 'Purple Stem', a Hillier Nurseries introduction, has purple-tinted new stems and larger flowers.

Sarcococca hookeriana var. *humilis* (GWP), a wonderfully compact form with dark glossy leaves, should be named and made more widely available.

Sarcococca orientalis is the cream of these winter flowerers. It is shrubbier and less suckering, almost dome-forming in habit, reaching little more than 0.5m (1.5ft) tall and seldom spreading wider. It has the biggest leaves of the group, often measuring 9cm (3.5in) long; they are light green (in light sun) to deep green (in more sun). Male flowers are tinged a pale shade of pink and are borne in the leaf axils from mid February well into March. Fruits are black. A native to China introduced by Roy Lancaster in 1980, its popularity increases every year. Although the flowers are tiny, their tantalizing scent is strong. It will tolerate semi- to very dense shade; if planted in full sun, it will quickly turn yellow and slowly die over a number of years.

Sarcococca ruscifolia, seldom seen in our gardens, is a slow-growing, compact, slowly spreading form with red fruits and thick-looking, shiny, deep green leaves. Native to central China, it was introduced in 1908 by E. H. Wilson. *Sarcococca ruscifolia* var. *chinensis* is much more commonly planted and a much more vigorous garden plant. It can grow quite tall; I have encountered 1.5m (5ft) tall specimens, but these were very old, and the centres were starting to die out. The flowers are produced in abundance in early February and are followed by bright red-purple berries. *Sarcococca ruscifolia* var. *chinensis* 'Dragon Gate', a selection made by Roy Lancaster in 1980 from the Dragon Gate in the mountains above Kumming, Yunnan, is a lax-growing plant with quite fine, linear foliage of a deep green. Scented flowers are off-white and produced in late February.

Sarcococca saligna and *S. wallichii*, Himalayan species both, are not widely grown. *Sarcococca saligna* is the least scented of all the winter boxes, which is a real shame, as it has the most delightful leaves, lance-shaped and 13cm (5in) long, and a reasonable overall habit. Flowers are greenish white and followed by purple berries. *Sarcococca wallichii*, a native of Nepal, is the tallest of all the species; it can reach 2m (6ft) if grown in moist conditions, where it will develop rich green glossy foliage. Flowers are borne in late February and are followed by black fruits.

Cultivation Tips

All sarcococcas are best grown in semi- to deep shade: their foliage is bleached by sunlight, and they dwindle somewhat in full sun. This does not necessarily mean direct overhead tree shade; surrounding light shade from nearby shrubs is sufficient to grow this plant in a more open location. One of the main bonuses of this group of evergreens is that they will not only grow in quite dense shade, but they are ideal for that dread difficulty, dry shade, in both acidic and alkaline soils.

So long as they are not grown in too much sunshine, winter boxes are pretty well behaved. Often they will go unnoticed until they are in flower, at which time, people will wander around sniffing every plant in search of the source of the intoxicating scent. They are best sited close to a path or in an area of slow air movement, where their strong scent can build and drift. I like to use them in bold blocks, to maximise the benefit from their fragrance, and as they are adaptable to deep shade, they are useful groundcover plants under trees, where little else will grow.

No routine maintenance is required. If plants become too gangly, they can be reduced in size by pruning them any time between April through to September; the very bushy plants that result may need some of their stems thinned to the ground. This brings us to another method of pruning, whereby all the stems are cut down to the ground after the last frost in spring, to prevent the new growth's being killed or damaged; this allows new stems to develop from ground level. This can be done every other year, to contain the height of the plant.

The only other problem that occasionally appears is that old plants begin to lose vigour, and as they do, the centre of the plant begins to die out, and the whole plant looks unsightly. This is easily remedied. Divide the plant, just as you would an herbaceous perennial, and discard the old centre. This operation can be undertaken either in March or April or in November. Newly divided plants will require care and maintenance, and those planted in December will require protection from winter wind to stop foliage from drying out.

Stachyurus   Stachyuraceae

Common Names: Chinese spiketail, Japanese spiketail, early spiketail.
Flowering Period: February and March.
Flowers: Pendulous racemes, 13cm (5in) long, made up of fifteen to thirty-five
  individual flowers.
Height and Spread: 2 to 3.5m (6 to 11ft) tall and often wider.

Some five or six *Stachyurus* species are native to China, Japan, and the Himalayas, but of those only two are moderately hardy and neither is that well known in our gardens. This to me seems a real shame as the flowers of these deciduous shrubs are distinct and unusual (albeit unscented), and the sight of their foxtail-like flower spikes, hanging proud from naked stems, is most welcome in late February. Both species are hardy in the UK and thrive in sheltered woodland situations, where flowers may be damaged by early spring frosts. In the USA they are hardy in zones 6 to 8 but, again, require some shelter.

The first of those cultivated is *Stachyurus chinensis*, a large spreading shrub native to China and introduced by E. H. Wilson in 1908. It has long, tapering foliage and good yellow autumn colour, which contrasts well with the purplish tints to the branches and veins in the leaf. Long racemes of thirty to thirty-five

Stachyurus chinensis has long, pendulous flowers in late winter.

soft yellow flowers appear in early March, earlier in milder years. *Stachyurus chinensis* 'Celina', selected for its exceptionally long flower spikes, has the added advantage of rich butter-yellow autumn colour. *Stachyurus chinensis* 'Goldbeater' originated at Mark Bulk's nursery, Rein & Mark Bulk, Boskoop, The Netherlands. It has delightful golden yellow new foliage that fades to a pale off-green during the summer. I have not yet seen it in flower, but I am told that the flowers are similar to those of the species in appearance, although the length of the spike is shorter (this probably has something to do with this selection's lack of chlorophyll—hence, lack of vigour). It requires semi-shade to retain its golden colour; deep shade turns foliage a light green. *Stachyurus chinensis* 'Joy Forever' too has a shorter flower spike, like 'Goldbeater', but is somewhat stronger growing; it is similar to *S. praecox* 'Magpie', except that it has a golden yellow leaf margin, making it the best of the variegated spiketails: its variegation is very pronounced and stable, whereas 'Magpie' reverts. A nomenclatural aside: I have seen 'Magpie' listed as a form of *S. chinensis* in several publications, but I have no doubt in my mind that it is *S. praecox*, not *S. chinensis*. I also have my suspicions about 'Joy Forever' and 'Goldbeater' being *S. praecox* but have not yet been unable to verify this.

The second, *Stachyurus praecox* (Japanese spiketail), is more widely grown than *S. chinensis*—probably as it is easier to cultivate, although it is somewhat more difficult to acquire. Compared to the Chinese spiketail, the Japanese is shorter, with smaller and shorter flower spikes and no purple-tinted shoots; its mature height and spread is 3 × 3m (9 × 9ft) and its overall presence is less

Stachyurus praecox 'Magpie' has great autumn colour.

vigorous. Pale yellow flowers are produced earlier, in late February, occasionally in mid February, in long racemes of fifteen to twenty-four flowers. *Stachyurus praecox* 'Magpie', one of the most widely grown Japanese spiketails, was introduced by Hillier Nurseries, Hampshire, England, in 1945; its white to creamy white variegated foliage is flushed pink and splashed pale green. It does, however, tend to revert, producing not only pale green shoots but also shoots that are completely white, with no green colouration whatsoever. *Stachyurus praecox* 'Rubriflorus' is an interesting form with pale yellow flowers that do look pinkish from a distance; its growth habit and stature is the same as *S. praecox*.

Cultivation Tips

The spiketails are relatively easy to cultivate if you follow their simple growing requirements. They all require a sheltered site, preferably in a semi-shaded location. They generally prefer acid soils to shallow chalk soils; in my experience *Stachyurus chinensis* is more tolerant of alkaline soils. Poor drainage, especially in the winter, can cause even established specimens to fail, and considerable problems occur in exposed locations, as this often results in frost destroying the delicate flowers and, occasionally, the stems. If a woodland setting with free-draining soil can be found below the dappled shade of deciduous trees or shrubs, then this group of plants will bring considerable years of pleasure.

A little regular pruning will encourage flowering and create a more attractive shrub with a more bushy habit. Both species produce widely arching, nonflowering branches that can quickly develop during the summer months, growing over 2m (6ft) in a year and giving the plant a rather unsightly look. Prune one or two of the longest, most flimsy-looking of these stems to within a few inches of the ground; these will then regrow, replacing some of the older flowering shoots the following year. Any pruning should be undertaken after flowering has finished in late spring. Any weak or poorly growing nonflowering shoots can also be removed at this time, as can any crossing branches.

Sycopsis and ×*Sycoparrotia*   Hamamelidaceae

Sycopsis sinensis and ×*Sycoparrotia semidecidua*

Common Name: Chinese fig hazel (*Sycopsis sinensis*).

Flowering Period: February and March.

Flowers: Petal-less, borne in small clusters; yellow stamens, flushed red, protrude from chocolate-coloured buds.

Height and Spread: 6 × 4m (20 × 12ft).

Sycopsis sinensis is the only one of the seven species of *Sycopsis* native to China and the Himalayas that we grow in the West. Its leathery, rich deep green foliage provides a foil for its yellow, red-tinted stamens, which from a distance appear almost ginger-yellow, poking out of chocolate-coloured flower bud cases. Although related to the witch hazels, the flowers do not have any petals and are made up of stamens, just like those of *Parrotia persica*—indeed, the flowers of these two species are very similar in appearance. This tall and widely spreading evergreen shrub is hardy in the south of England but can suffer frost damage; I have seen plants growing at the Royal Botanic Garden Edinburgh, Scotland, but these were planted in a protected location and even so had some visible frost damage. In the USA plants are hardy in zones 7 to 9, with some experimentation required in zone 7.

If you take two fantastic parents like *Parrotia persica* (Persian ironwood) and *Sycopsis sinensis*, you would expect to get the most amazing offspring, but this is not the case with ×*Sycoparrotia semidecidua*. In fact, this bigeneric hybrid is more of a novelty than an out-and-out landscape plant; it is largely confined to botanical collections and is only really recognised when in flower. Although intermediate, it did not retain the best traits of each parent. Great bark and fantastic autumn colour on a compact version of *P. persica* would have been an attractive proposition indeed, but alas, Mother Nature isn't that predicable, and what we have here is a semi-evergreen shrub that occasionally has yellow foliage that falls in autumn, with a high tendency in growth toward *S. sinensis*. It is an interesting plant, nevertheless, with coarse, leathery foliage that it retains to a greater or lesser extent, depending on the weather: the colder it is, the more leaves it will shed. The influence of *P. persica* seems to have made it hardier, and ×*S. semidecidua* can therefore be more widely planted, solidly into zone 7.

Its best feature is its winter flowers, which are produced in February and March: small yellow flowers protrude from dark brown flower buds, producing an effect similar to that of *Parrotia persica* but differing in colour (the Persian ironwood has red stamens). This is a broadly growing shrub, up to 4m (12ft) tall and 6m (20ft) wide.

Cultivation Tips

I have heard some people rave about these two shrubs, but I fail to get excited about them. Both are easy to grow if given a moisture-retentive but free-draining acidic soil, in full sun or semi-shade; in such a location, both will make imposing shrubs with dense foliage. They are most noticeable when in flower and will have little impact during the remainder of the year, so are best planted as a backdrop to a border. A group planted en masse is somewhat more interesting, especially when in flower; the evergreen *Sycopsis sinensis* is better for this use.

Neither requires any specialised pruning apart from some formative shaping of the shrub. Both can be lightly clipped into informal hedge shapes after flowering has finished.

Viburnum   **Caprifoliaceae**

Flowering Period: Deciduous species flower from November through to spring; evergreens, late winter through to spring.
Flowers: White or pink, borne in clusters, often scented.

Most gardens, I'll bet, have a viburnum planted somewhere in their midst. The genus encompasses more than 150 named species and forms from many temperate regions of the world; with so much beauty and diversity, it is hardly surprising that these plants are favourites. In the maritime climate of the UK, the deciduous viburnums are important winter-flowering shrubs; for me and many others, they, along with *Mahonia* ×*media* cultivars, herald the arrival of winter. I drift-planted a group of *Viburnum* ×*bodnantense* 'Dawn' through

Mahonia ×*media* 'Hope' in the Winter Garden at the Sir Harold Hillier Gardens, Hampshire, England, to unexpectedly good effect. The mahonias provide an exquisite foil for the pink flowers of 'Dawn', and for some reason, the scents seem to complement each other rather than compete. Some might find pink and yellow flowers an odd mix, but it worked and certainly brightened up a dull area of the garden. Deciduous winter-flowering viburnums are very much at the mercy of the winter elements in UK gardens. If conditions are relatively frost-free and mild during late autumn and early winter, masses of pink or white flowers—no display is more breathtaking—will be borne on naked stems, exuding a heavy, sweet scent that lingers in the damp winter air. These are first-rate plants for the winter landscape, but as the flowers are so susceptible to winter frost, any blooms not damaged after Christmas are a pure bonus. In the continental climate, however, with greater fluctuations in temperatures, these plants do not fare well. I have seem them shrivel and wilt in the heat of a southern summer and their flowers massacred in the heart of winter by freezing temperatures—not a pretty sight. To subject such a wonderful group of plants to such purgatory is sacrilege.

The evergreen forms of *Viburnum tinus* (laurustinus), however, are much different. These will flower from late winter into early spring, and even later than this. In the UK they are relatively hardy, but in the USA, where frosts come early, there is insufficient time for the wood to ripen before the onset of winter. Where frost develops later in the year, this is not a problem.

Viburnum ×*bodnantense* flowers spasmodically from late summer, with the main flowering in winter. Although the epithet suggests the plants were first raised at Bodnant Gardens in North Wales, this is not the case. This hybrid cross, between *V. farreri* (*V. fragrans*) and *V. grandiflorum*, was first attempted at the Royal Botanic Garden Edinburgh, in 1933. The Edinburgh form, still grown in gardens, is *V.* ×*bodnantense* 'Charles Lamont'; however, Edinburgh considered the hybrid no improvement on either of the parents so decided not to take the matter further. In 1935, the same cross was undertaken at Bodnant Gardens, North Wales, the garden of Lord Aberconway, by his head gardener, F. C. Puddle. Access to seed coming in via plant hunters of the Golden Age provided Puddle with a wealth of new material. He set out for and achieved an improvement on both species, and it was Puddle who first published the name *V.* ×*bodnantense*. The two commonly grown Bodnant hybrids are 'Dawn' and 'Deben'. *Viburnum* ×*bodnantense* 'Dawn' is similar to 'Charles Lamont' but is paler in bud and somewhat more straggly in habit, although neither shrub is that pretty or tidy in growth. I have encountered a number of very large, unpruned specimens of 'Dawn'; they are over 3m (9ft) wide and about the same in height, producing widely arching stems. Of the three forms, 'Dawn', 'Deben', and 'Charles Lamont', 'Dawn' is the closest to *V. grandiflorum* in habit and stem and in flower, with its distinct pink stamens.

Viburnum ×*bodnantense* 'Deben' is the shortest and most compact form, reaching 2m (6ft) in height and the same in width. It is easily distinguished by its pink-budded flowers that open pure white, with white stamens. I have seen many plants labelled 'Deben' but on closer inspection they are usually *'Dawn'*. *Viburnum* ×*bodnantense* 'Charles Lamont' remains the only selection introduced by the Royal Botanic Garden Edinburgh; it is named after the garden's curator. The flowers are pinker than 'Dawn' and somewhat shorter, but unless you are comparing

Viburnum ×*bodnantense* 'Dawn' remains the most widely grown of the Bodnant hybrid viburnums.

both flowers side by side, knowing this is of little help. In habit, again, there are strong similarities to 'Dawn', although 'Charles Lamont' arches less and is not as tall, seldom reaching 2.5m (8ft) tall and wide, and its bark is more mahogany in colour than either of the other forms. 'Charles Lamont' also seems to have a

strong tendency toward *V. farreri*, making it in my view the best of this group of hybrids for the UK climate. Several years ago in England, a golden-foliaged sport from 'Charles Lamont' arose, with a proposed name of 'Landsdown Lucy'. I saw an entire shade tunnel full of this in spring, as plants were being bulked up; its golden yellow, purple-tinged foliage contrasted luridly with the hot-pink flowers, and I am ashamed to say I could see the marketing appeal for such a weird plant. Luckily, its foliage fried in any level of sun, and it never made it past the trial stage. I have a single plant in my garden, in quite medium shade, and by the end of summer the foliage is wrinkled and brown. It seldom flowers and when it does, fortunately, there are no leaves around.

Viburnum farreri, one of the parents of *V.* ×*bodnantense*, is a beautiful shrub in its own right.

Although the Bodnant viburnums are welcome additions to our gardens, they are quite big and flower somewhat later than some of the species. The real star,

Viburnum farreri 'Nanum', a compact form of Farrer's viburnum.

in my view, is Farrer's viburnum, *Viburnum farreri*. Originally named *V. fragrans* for its highly scented flowers, its name was later changed to *V. farreri*, in honour of Reginald Farrer (1880–1920), who collected this viburnum in China; the original introduction was made in 1910 by William Purdom (1880–1921), who had been sent to China to collect plants for Harvard University's Arnold Arboretum, USA, and Veitch's Nursery, in London. Both men met and collected in China between 1914 and 1916. It is a delightful species, considerably smaller and more "twiggy" than the hybrids mentioned earlier, occasionally reaching 2m (6ft) tall and 1.5m (5ft) wide. The flowers, which are produced from late November along the naked stems, are pink in bud, opening white, and very highly scented. In mild winters, shrubs are adorned with an eye-catching display of flowers. As with many winter-flowering viburnums, the foliage is strongly toothed, and is tinged pink-purple in spring and autumn. *Viburnum farreri* 'Candidissimum' ('Album') has pure white flowers; it seems less vigorous than the other forms and is a lot more compact. *Viburnum farreri* 'Farrer's Pink' is a real gem; its flowers are very deep pink in bud and open to reveal pink-tinted white flowers that are even larger and more showy than those of the species, if that is at all possible. *Viburnum farreri* 'Nanum' ('Compactum') is a very dwarf and suckering form that flowers well if given sufficient sunlight and moisture to do so. Seldom reaching 1m (3ft) tall and wide, this is an odd-looking form: it always reminds me of a viburnum chewed to the ground by deer and struggling to regrow—that is, until you see it in flower. The viburnum for those of us with space limitations.

Viburnum grandiflorum 'Snow White' is a real treasure.

Viburnum grandiflorum is the Himalayan version of *V. farreri* but much bigger and more erect. It flowers mainly after Christmas, often in late February and March, as air temperatures begin to rise. The flowers are larger than those of *V. farreri* and look more pendulous; they are a deep reddish pink in bud and open to a rich deep pink, fading with age. Its leaves have more than the three pronounced veins of *V. farreri* and are not flushed pink-purple in spring. *Viburnum grandiflorum* f. *foetens* bears its pure white flowers at the tips of the branches, which gives it a somewhat curious look when in flower. *Viburnum grandiflorum* 'Snow White' is my all-time favourite of this batch, with very large pink-tipped and -backed flowers that are pure white in the centre. Collected in Nepal by Donald Lowndes in 1950, under his collection number Lowndes 1409, it is a strong-growing form, far superior to and easier to cultivate than *V. grandiflorum* f. *foetens*, which can be somewhat temperamental.

Viburnum tinus (laurustinus), native to the Mediterranean region, has been grown in the UK for over three hundred years, although it is most associated with the southern half of the country, where the first frosts are far enough into winter and therefore do little damage to its foliage. It is widely planted and is used in various ways, including as a coastal hedge or as a specimen plant in open or shady positions. It looks quite good when trained up a single stem; I have come across such tree-like specimens over 4m (12ft) tall. Many forms have been selected for their shape, form, and flowers, which are produced in late winter. *Viburnum tinus* 'Spring Bouquet' ('Compactum') is a floriferous selection used predominantly in the cut flower market and widely marketed in the USA. Its abundantly produced flowers are reddish purple in bud, opening pure white; the plants I have seen are compact, dome-shaped evergreen buns, 2m (6ft) tall and wide. *Viburnum tinus* 'Eve Price' is one of the most widely grown forms in the UK, selected for its dense habit and numerous flattish clusters of flowers. These are a rich purple in bud and open white, tinted pink. Leaves are smaller than many other forms and a rich green, occasionally tinted purple. It can make a large 3 × 3m (9 × 9ft) shrub—a real showstopper, in leaf and in flower. *Viburnum tinus* 'French White' is a very large form with exceptional large clusters of pure white flowers. Occasionally a small tree, it can be easily clipped or sheared so that it retains a more compact habit. *Viburnum tinus* 'Gwenllian' is another compact form with small leaves, selected by the Royal Botanic Gardens, Kew, Surrey, England. Its delightful habit, more dense than that of 'Eve Price', complements its flowers perfectly: these too are in compact clusters, deep pink–budded and –backed and opening pure white. *Viburnum tinus* 'Pink Prelude' is quite a tall-growing form with pure white flowers that fade to pink with age. *Viburnum tinus* 'Purpureum' has pink-budded opening off-white flowers and attractive purple-tinted new growth. *Viburnum tinus* 'Pyramidale' is a long-cultivated form with an upright habit, dense foliage, and pinkish purple–budded flowers that open off-white. *Viburnum tinus* subsp. *rigidum* is a semi-tender form with very hairy foliage and pure white flowers opening in early February; it is the best-flowering form in my opinion but survives only in a sheltered, almost frost-free location. *Viburnum tinus* Spirit, a recent Dutch introduction that flowers from autumn to spring, produces masses of pure white flowers all over its compact form. Flowers are followed by blue, then black fruits, which suggests that this form is self-compatible, as generally groups are needed to produce fruits. *Viburnum tinus* 'Variegatum' offers exquisite foliage with a creamy yellow variegation and creamy white flowers. It is somewhat shy to flower, and the foliage is very susceptible to both sun scorch and frost damage: this plant requires a sheltered, semi-shaded location.

Cultivation Tips

Viburnums are relatively easy to cultivate if a couple of essential requirements are met. All the plants covered here will grow in alkaline and acidic soils, although their tolerance to shallow alkaline soils varies. Laurustinus, *Viburnum tinus*, will grow on such soils but does show some minor leaf colouring in the height of summer. In the UK, this species and its various forms are best grown in southern counties, where—with lower rainfall in autumn, winter, and spring, and higher summer temperatures—they will thrive. I have encountered specimens growing well as far north as Scotland, but these were in sunny

Viburnum tinus Spirit, a recent introduction from Holland

microclimates, away from drying winds and frost, where they could flourish. In the USA, they are hardy in zones 8 to 10, and may be hardy in zone 7 if in a location where the first frost in winter is sufficiently far into the winter that the plant's wood has had enough time to harden. If this is not the case, a freeze can be devastating. Again, the variegated form, *V. tinus* 'Variegatum', is suited only to protected locations.

For a first-rate fruit set, mixed plantings are recommended. Some forms are not self-compatible: to plant a group of 'Eve Price' together would not necessarily produce fruit, but to mix in another form would. The inwardly and outwardly compatible Spirit may prove to be a good pollinator for all the other forms, but this has yet to be tested. With the exception of the compact forms, most forms of *Viburnum tinus* will grow quite large. Although few require regular pruning, many can be trained into informal hedges or round, compact domes with yearly pruning. This is usually done when the last risk of frost is over, after the plant finishes blooming in late spring or early summer. Plants can be trimmed with hedge cutters or pruning shears to create the desired effect, which is to force the foliage to thicken and create a dense shrub. Overgrown plants can be ruthlessly cut back to bare stems and allowed to regenerate. Generally for this type of pruning and shaping, a single yearly application is all that is needed.

Viburnum farreri and its selections will also grow on alkaline soils, but without some level of irrigation or deep mulching during the summer months, their foliage will shrivel and die. It seems that many species of viburnums that flourish in temperate woodland settings in the wild will fail if moisture around the root system falls to such a level that water is unavailable to the plant. If you can provide these viburnums with conditions similar to their native habitat in the garden, then they are relatively easy to accommodate. In the UK, all the deciduous winter-flowering viburnums can be grown quite successfully in deep, humus-rich, moisture-retentive soils. They will also grow in shallow chalk soils, but in these soils it will take a bit more work to alleviate problems associated with summer drought. These problems are not insurmountable, however, as the benefits easily outweigh them. In the USA, however, it is a different story, especially in areas associated with high summer temperatures: summer drought problems are a real issue here. Zones 5 to 8 are recommended, but with some experimentation, as winter frosts too will wreak havoc and destroy any open or partially open buds.

With such a long flowering period, viburnums can be used in many different ways, from specimen plants in a woodland setting to group-planted to maximise their scent. They also make a fine addition to a mixed (herbaceous and shrub) border; for this purpose, I would recommend *Viburnum farreri*, for its flowering ability, more graceful habit, and smaller stature. For larger plantings I would use *V.* ×*bodnantense* in its various forms, as these are quicker-growing and seem to be more sun tolerant in the UK. *Viburnum grandiflorum* is much happier in a woodland or semi-shaded setting, in which cooler situation it will thrive; in such settings, you might even be able to successfully grow the temperamental *V. grandiflorum* f. *foetens*, but good luck.

All this group, if left unpruned, can develop into unwieldy shrubs with long, arching branches; once they have finished flowering, they are an eyesore in the landscape. They can look more "tidy" and are easy to contain if pruned on a regular basis. Pruning of deciduous winter-flowering viburnums should be undertaken after they have finished flowering in late spring, with the aim of reducing by a third the very old flowering wood, which may be identified as the thickest branches. Such pruning also retains a tighter shape, as inevitably the tall and widely spreading branches are among the oldest. Once these thick branches have been selected, they can be cut close to ground level using a pruning saw or pair of lopping shears. Cutting branches close to ground level allows new shoots to develop close to the base of the shrub; these will replace the older wood in future years. Flowering is not interfered with so long as two-thirds of the older wood is retained—this percentage assures there will be plenty of flower buds for future seasons.

Where To See Winter-flowering Shrubs

Anglesey Abbey Gardens, Cambridgeshire, England, UK

Arnold Arboretum of Harvard University, Jamaica Plain, Massachusetts, USA

Atlanta Botanical Gardens, Atlanta, Georgia, USA

Cambridge Botanic Garden, Cambridgeshire, England, UK

Morris Arboretum of the University of Pennsylvania, Philadelphia,
  Pennsylvania, USA

Mullestein Winter Garden, Cornell Plantations, Ithaca, New York, USA

Royal Botanic Garden Edinburgh, Scotland, UK

Royal Botanic Gardens, Kew, Surrey, England, UK

Royal Botanic Gardens, Kew, Wakehurst Place, West Sussex, England, UK

Royal Horticultural Society Garden, Rosemoor, Devon, England, UK

Royal Horticultural Society Garden, Wisley, Surrey, England, UK

Sheffield Park, East Sussex, England, UK

Sir Harold Hillier Gardens, Hampshire, England, UK

Bibliography

Bloom, Adrian. 1993. *Winter Garden Glory*. Harper Collins.

Brickell, C. D., and B. Mathew. 1976. *Daphne: The Genus in the Wild and in Cultivation*. Woking: The Alpine Garden Society.

Brickell, Christopher, ed. 1996. *A–Z Encyclopedia of Garden Plants*. London: Dorling Kindersley, in association with The Royal Horticultural Society.

———. 1995. *Garden Plants*. London: Pavilion, in association with The Royal Horticultural Society.

Callaway, Dorothy J. 1994. *The World of Magnolias*. Portland, Oregon: Timber Press.

Campbell-Culver, Maggie. 2001. *The Origin of Plants*. London: Headline.

Clarke, Graham. 1986. *Autumn and Winter Colour in the Garden*. London: Ward Lock Ltd.

Coombes, Allen, and Kim Tripp. 1998. *The Gardener's Guide to Shrubs*. London: Reed Books Ltd.

Cox, Peter A. 1993. *The Cultivation of Rhododendrons*. London: B. T. Batsford Ltd.

Dirr, Michael A. 1998. *Manual of Woody Landscape Plants: Their Identification, Ornamental Characteristics, Culture, Propagation and Uses*. 5th ed. Champaign, Illinois: Stipes Publishing.

———. 2002. *Dirr's Trees and Shrubs for Warm Climates: An Illustrated Encyclopedia*. Portland, Oregon: Timber Press.

Griffiths, Mark. 1997. *The New Royal Horticultural Society Dictionary Index of Garden Plants*. Portland, Oregon: Timber Press (reprint of book originally published by Macmillan Press 1994).

Grounds, Roger. 1998. *The Plantfinder's Guide to Ornamental Grasses*. Newton Abbot, Devon: David and Charles.

Hillier, John, and Allen Coombes, eds. 1972. *The Hillier Manual of Trees and Shrubs*. Newton Abbot, Devon: David and Charles.

Houtman, R. T., and W. J. van der Werf. 2002. "Hamamelis". *Dendroflora* 39:30–59.

Hunt, David, ed. 1998. "The Magnolias and Their Allies." Proceeding of an International Symposium, Royal Holloway, University of London, Egham, Surrey, UK, 12–13 April 1996.

Jacobson, Arthur Lee. 1996. *North American Landscape Trees*. Berkeley, California: Ten Speed Press.

Johnson, Owen, ed. 2003. *Champion Trees of Britain and Ireland.* Stowmarket, Suffolk: Whittet Books.

McClure, F. A. 1993. *The Bamboos*. Washington: Smithsonian Institution Press (reprint of book originally published by Harvard University Press 1966).

Morley, B. D., and H. R. Toelken, eds. 1983. *Flowering Plants in Australia*. Willoughby, Australia: Rigby Publishers.

Oudolf, Piet, with Noël Kingsbury. 1999. *Designing with Plants*. Portland, Oregon: Timber Press.

Poor, Janet Meakin, and Nancy Peterson Brewster, eds. 1996. *Plants That Merit Attention.* Vol. 2, Shrubs. Portland, Oregon: Timber Press.

Reiley, H. Edward. 2004. *Success with Rhododendrons and Azaleas*. Revised ed. Portland, Oregon: Timber Press.

Royal Horticultural Society. 1997. *The Rhododendron Handbook 1998: Rhododendron Species in Cultivation.* London: The Royal Horticultural Society.

———. 2004. *RHS Plant Finder: 2004–2005.* London: Dorling Kindersley.

Trehane, Jennifer. 1998. *Camellias: The Complete Guide to Their Cultivation and Use*. London: B. T. Batsford Ltd.

US Department of Agriculture
Hardiness Zone Map

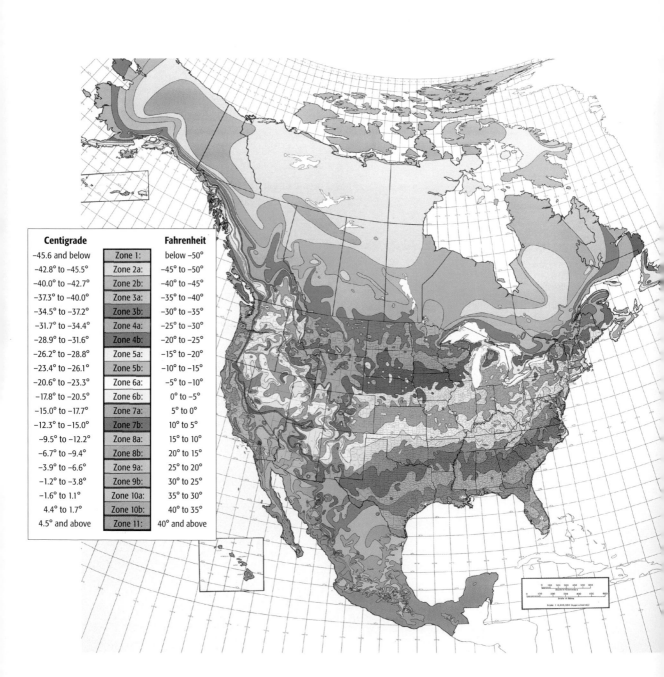

Centigrade		Fahrenheit
−45.6 and below	Zone 1:	below −50°
−42.8° to −45.5°	Zone 2a:	−45° to −50°
−40.0° to −42.7°	Zone 2b:	−40° to −45°
−37.3° to −40.0°	Zone 3a:	−35° to −40°
−34.5° to −37.2°	Zone 3b:	−30° to −35°
−31.7° to −34.4°	Zone 4a:	−25° to −30°
−28.9° to −31.6°	Zone 4b:	−20° to −25°
−26.2° to −28.8°	Zone 5a:	−15° to −20°
−23.4° to −26.1°	Zone 5b:	−10° to −15°
−20.6° to −23.3°	Zone 6a:	−5° to −10°
−17.8° to −20.5°	Zone 6b:	0° to −5°
−15.0° to −17.7°	Zone 7a:	5° to 0°
−12.3° to −15.0°	Zone 7b:	10° to 5°
−9.5° to −12.2°	Zone 8a:	15° to 10°
−6.7° to −9.4°	Zone 8b:	20° to 15°
−3.9° to −6.6°	Zone 9a:	25° to 20°
−1.2° to −3.8°	Zone 9b:	30° to 25°
−1.6° to 1.1°	Zone 10a:	35° to 30°
4.4° to 1.7°	Zone 10b:	40° to 35°
4.5° and above	Zone 11:	40° and above

Index

A

Abeliophyllum 83–85

Abeliophyllum distichum 83–85

Abies concolor 54

Abies nordmanniana 55

Abies pinsapo 54

Acacia 85–86

Acacia baileyana 85

Acacia dealbata 85

Acacia pravissima 86

Acer ×conspicuum 38, 49

Acer davidii 49

Acer griseum 38, 39, 40, 48, 87

Acer maximowiczianum 48

Acer negundo 49

Acer nikoense 48

Acer palmatum 49

Acer pensylvanicum 48, 49

Acer rufinerve 49

Acer tegmentosum 38

American angelica tree 67

American devilwood 188

American holly 77, 79

Amur cherry 49

Aralia elata 67, 68

Aralia spinosa 67

Arbutus 87–88

Arbutus andrachne 87

Arbutus ×andrachnoides 87, 88

Arbutus unedo 45, 87–88

Arbutus unedo f. *rubra* 88

Aucuba japonica 56

Australian fuchsia 110, 111

B

bamboo 64

barberry 73, 88

beautybush 69

Berberis 88–89

Berberis aggregata 73

Berberis ×carminea 73

Berberis darwinii 89

Berberis dictyophylla 74

Berberis koreana 75

Berberis linearifolia 88

Berberis ×lologensis 89

Berberis trigona 88, 89

Berberis wilsoniae 73, 75

Bergenia 10, 42

Betula albosinensis 37

Betula ermanii 37, 46

Betula nigra 46, 47

Betula papyrifera 47

Betula pendula 47

Betula utilis 46, 47

Betula utilis var. *jacquemontii* 37, 46

Betula utilis var. *occidentalis* 46

black bamboo 64

black mondo grass 34, 38

bleeding heart 188

Bodnant viburnum 216, 217

box elder 49

bronze sedge 36

bull bay 164

butcher's broom 37

buttercup winter hazel 111

C

Callicarpa americana 69

Callicarpa bodinieri var. *giraldii* 70

Callicarpa japonica var. *luxurians* 70

Calluna 89–91

Calluna vulgaris 54, 63, 64, 89–91

Camellia 15, 18, 43, 91–104, 208

Camellia brevistyla 103

Camellia cuspidata 93, 103

Camellia granthamiana 104

Camellia ×hiemalis 97, 98

Camellia japonica 91–94, 97, 99, 101, 103

Camellia oleifera 44, 94–95, 98

Camellia reticulata 93, 98

Camellia saluenensis 91, 93, 94, 99, 101, 103

Camellia sasanqua 44, 94, 95–99, 100, 101, 104, 180

Camellia sinensis 99–100, 104

Camellia sinensis var. *sinensis* 99

Camellia taliensis 104

Camellia tsaii 104

Camellia ×*vernalis* 100, 101, 102

Camellia ×*williamsii* 93, 98, 101–102

Campbell's magnolia 171

canoe birch 47

Carex comans 36

cat's claw 136

Caucasian fir 55

cherry laurel 54

Chimonanthus 104–106

Chimonanthus praecox 7, 43, 104–106

Chimonanthus praecox var. *luteus* 105, 106

Chinese fig hazel 214

Chinese paperbark maple 38, 39, 40, 48

Chinese red birch 37

Chinese silver grass 42, 59

Chinese spiketail 211

Chinese witch hazel 11, 140, 142–145, 151, 156, 162

Choisya 106–108

Choisya dumosa var. *arizonica* 107

Choisya ternata 106–108

Christmas box 38, 40, 115, 118, 208

coast silktassel 133

cobnut 159

Colorado white fir 54

Cootamundra wattle 85

coral-bark maple 49

cornelian cherry 16, 43, 45, 108

Cornus 108–110

Cornus alba 15, 32, 38, 49, 50, 65, 70, 71, 164

Cornus alternifolia 58

Cornus amomum 70

Cornus kousa 194

Cornus mas 43, 45, 108–109

Cornus officinalis 108, 109

Cornus sanguinea 28, 50, 51, 52, 70

Cornus sericea 50, 70

Cornus stolonifera 50

Correa 110–111

Correa alba 110–111

Correa backhouseana 111

Correa ×*harrisii* 110

Correa mannii 110

Correa pulchella 110

Correa reflexa 110, 111

Cortaderia 62

Cortaderia fulvida 62

Cortaderia selloana 62, 63

Corylopsis 111–113, 132, 139

Corylopsis coreana 111–113

Corylopsis gotoana var. *coreana* 112

Corylopsis pauciflora 111

Corylopsis sinensis var. *calvescens* 111

Corylopsis spicata 111, 112

Corylus avellana 159

Cotoneaster 71, 72

Cotoneaster dammeri 71, 164

Cotoneaster frigidus 71

Cotoneaster frigidus f. *fructuluteo* 71

Cotoneaster horizontalis 164

Cotoneaster microphyllus 71

Cotoneaster salicifolius 71

Cotoneaster ×*watereri* 71

coxcomb willow 53

crack willow 53

crape myrtle 20

Crocus 36

cuauchichic 133

×*Cupressocyparis leylandii* 54

D

Daboecia 113

Daboecia cantabrica 113

Daboecia cantabrica subsp. *scotica* 113

daffodil 36

Daphne 114–120

Daphne bholua 15, 40, 114–117

Daphne bholua f. *alba* 114, 116, 117

Daphne bholua var. *glacialis* 114, 116

Daphne gardneri 123

Daphne jezoensis 117, 118, 120

Daphne laureola 117, 118, 120, 121

Daphne laureola subsp. *philippi* 117, 118, 120

Daphne longilobata 117

Daphne mezereum 117, 119, 120

Daphne mezereum f. *alba* 119

Daphne mezereum var. *autumnalis* 119

Daphne mezereum var. *rubra* 119

Daphne odora 116, 117, 119, 120

Daphne odora f. *alba* 120

Daphne odora var. *rubra* 120

Daphniphyllum himalaense subsp. *macropodum* 55

Daphniphyllum macropodum 55

Darley Dale heath 126

David's maple 49

Decaisnea fargesii 76

devil's walking stick 67

Dicentra scandens 188

Dirca 121

Dirca occidentalis 121

Dirca palustris 121

Distylium racemosum 132

E

early forsythia 130

early spiketail 211

Edgeworthia 122–123

Edgeworthia chrysantha 122

Edgeworthia chrysantha f.
   rubra 122

Edgeworthia gardneri 123

Edgeworthia papyrifera
   122–123

Elaeagnus 124–126

Elaeagnus ×*ebbingei* 124, 125

Elaeagnus glabra 124

Elaeagnus macrophylla 124,
   125

Elaeagnus pungens 124,
   125–126

English holly 7, 77, 188

English yew 54

Erica 126–129

Erica carnea 126–129

Erica ×*darleyensis* 126–129

Erica erigena 127

Euonymus europaeus 71

Euonymus grandiflorus 71

Euonymus japonicus 55

Euphorbia characias 38

evergreen magnolia 164

F

Fagus sylvatica 31

false holly 188

Farrer's viburnum 218

Fatsia japonica 68

February daphne 117

flowering currant 187

Forsythia 130–132

Forsythia europaea 131

Forsythia giraldiana 130

Forsythia ovata 130–132

Fortunearia 132–133

Fortunearia sinensis 132–133

Fortune's osmanthus 188

Foster's holly 78, 79

Fothergilla major 194

fragrant box 208

fragrant daphne 117, 119

fragrant paper bush 122

fragrant tea olive 188

fragrant wintersweet 104

G

Galanthus nivalis 132

Garrya 133–135

Garrya elliptica 133–135

Garrya fremontii 133

Garrya ×*issaquahensis*
   133–135

Gaultheria mucronata 75, 76

Gaultheria procumbens 75

golden mimosa 85

golden weeping willow 7

grape-holly 175

Grevillea 136–138

Grevillea alpina 136, 137

Grevillea banksii 136, 138

Grevillea bipinnatifida 137

Grevillea juniperina 136, 137

Grevillea juniperina f.
   sulphurea 137

Grevillea lanigera 137

Grevillea lavandulacea 136

Grevillea rosmarinifolia 136,
   137, 138

Grevillea victoriae 136, 138

H

Hamamelis 104, 132, 139–162

Hamamelis ×*intermedia* 40,
   44, 139, 145–154, 158, 161

Hamamelis ×*japollis* 145

Hamamelis japonica 112,
   142, 145, 146, 147, 151,
   154–156, 162, 192

Hamamelis japonica var.
   flavopurpurascens 155

Hamamelis mollis 11,
   142–145, 151, 152, 153,
   154, 155, 158, 161

Hamamelis vernalis 112, 140,
   144, 148, 149, 156,
   157–159, 161, 162

Hamamelis virginiana 140,
   141, 158, 159–160

Hamamelis virginiana var.
   rubescens 160

hazel 159

heath 126

heather 15, 54, 89, 113

Hebe albicans 36

Hedera helix 42

Helleborus ×*hybridus* 38

Hercules' club 67

Himalayan cherry 38

Himalayan daphne 15, 19, 40,
   114–117, 122

Himalayan osmanthus 193

Himalayan white-stemmed
   birch 37, 46

holly tea olive 188

I

Ilex aquifolium 7, 54, 77, 188

Ilex ×*attenuata* 78, 79

Ilex cassine 78

Ilex cornuta 77

Ilex decidua 79, 80

Ilex opaca 78, 79

Ilex serrata 81

Ilex verticillata 80, 81

Indian plum 186

isu tree 132

ivy 42

J

Japanese angelica tree 67
Japanese camellia 91, 93, 101
Japanese mahonia 53, 179, 180
Japanese spiketail 211
Japanese spindleberry 55
Japanese winterberry 81
Japanese witch hazel 140,
    142, 154–156
Jasminum 163–165
Jasminum nudiflorum
    163–165

K

Killarney strawberry tree 87
knot plant 122
Korean abelialeaf 83
Korean forsythia 130, 131
Korean winter hazel 111, 112

L

Lagerstroemia indica 20
laurustinus 57, 216, 219, 220
lavender grevillea 134
leatherleaf mahonia 179
leatherleaf viburnum 58
leatherwood 121
Leyland cypress 54
Ligustrum ovalifolium 54
Liquidambar 139
Liriope 36
London plane 45
Lonicera 11, 165–169, 186
Lonicera fragrantissima 38,
    43, 165, 166, 168, 169
Lonicera infundibulum var.
    rockii 165
Lonicera modesta var.
    lushanensis 165
Lonicera ×*purpusii* 19, 38,
    166, 167
Lonicera setifera 166, 167, 169
Lonicera standishii 166, 168

Lonicera standishii var.
    lancifolia 167, 169
Lushan honeysuckle 166

M

Magnolia 170–175
Magnolia campbellii 170,
    171–175
Magnolia campbellii subsp.
    mollicomata 172–173
Magnolia grandiflora 164
Mahonia 175–186
Mahonia aquifolium 28,
    175–179
Mahonia bealei 179, 180,
    181, 182, 183
Mahonia gracilipes 181
Mahonia japonica 53, 73, 95,
    179, 180, 181, 182, 183, 185
Mahonia lomariifolia 179,
    182, 183, 184, 208
Mahonia ×*media* 59, 95, 179,
    182–185, 208, 215
Mahonia pinnata 177, 178
Mahonia ×*wagneri* 177, 178
Manchurian cherry 49
Mexican orange 106
Mexican orange blossom 106
mezereon 117
mimosa 85
Miscanthus 62
Miscanthus sacchariflorus 62
Miscanthus sinensis 11, 36,
    37, 42, 43, 59, 60, 61
Miscanthus sinensis var.
    condensatus 60
Molinia caerulea 36
Molinia caerulea subsp.
    caerulea 63, 64
mondo grass 36
mountain grevillea 136
mountain pine 54
Mrs Wilson's barberry 75
Muscari armeniacum 34

N

Nandina domestica 66, 67
Nandina domestica f.
    leucocarpa 67
Narcissus 36, 132
Nepalese cherry 38, 49
New Zealand flax 42
New Zealand pampas grass 62

O

Oemleria 186–188
Oemleria cerasiformis
    186–188
oleaster 124
Ophiopogon planiscapus 34,
    35
Oregon grape 175–179
Oregon grape holly 175
Oregon holly grape 175
oriental rice paper plant 122
oriental winter box 44
Osmanthus 188–194
Osmanthus americanus 188
Osmanthus armatus 189, 192
Osmanthus decorus 188
Osmanthus ×*fortunei* 188,
    189, 192
Osmanthus fragrans 188,
    189, 190, 192
Osmanthus fragrans f.
    aurantiacus 190
Osmanthus heterophyllus
    188, 190–192
Osmanthus serrulatus 193
Osmanthus suavis 193
Osmanthus yunnanensis 193
Osmaronia cerasiformis 186
oso berry 186
Oven's wattle 86
Ozark witch hazel 157, 158

P

pampas grass 62

Panicum virgatum 64

paper birch 47

paperbush 122

paper daphne 114

Parrotia 194–197

Parrotia persica 45, 132, 139, 194–197, 214, 215

pendulous ironwood 95

Pennsylvanian maple 48

Pernettya mucronata 76

Persian ironwood 45, 132, 139, 194–197, 214

Phormium 28

Phormium tenax 42

Phyllostachys aureosulcata 64, 65, 66

Phyllostachys bambusoides 66

Phyllostachys nigra 64

Phyllostachys vivax f. *aureocaulis* 65

pink winter forsythia 83

Pinus mugo 54

Pittosporum crassifolium 55

Pittosporum dallii 55

Pittosporum patulum 55

Pittosporum ralphii 55

Pittosporum tenuifolium 55, 56, 191

Pittosporum undulatum 55

Platanus ×*hispanica* 45

privet 54

Prunus 187

Prunus laurocerasus 54

Prunus maackii 49

Prunus rufa 38, 39, 49

Prunus serrula 38, 39, 40, 49, 87

purple moor grass 36

Q

quinine bush 133

R

red-stemmed dogwood 32, 50

Rhododendron 15, 18, 82, 197–208

Rhododendron arboreum 198, 199

Rhododendron arboreum subsp. *arboreum* 199

Rhododendron arboreum subsp. *cinnamomeum* 199

Rhododendron arboreum subsp. *cinnamomeum* var. *album* 199

Rhododendron arboreum subsp. *cinnamomeum* var. *roseum* 199

Rhododendron ciliatum 202, 203

Rhododendron dauricum 112, 203–204

Rhododendron eclecteum 201

Rhododendron fulgens 199

Rhododendron ×*geraldii* 199, 200

Rhododendron grande 200

Rhododendron lapponicum 201

Rhododendron leucaspis 202, 203

Rhododendron lutescens 202

Rhododendron moupinense 201–202, 203

Rhododendron mucronulatum 203, 204–205

Rhododendron mucronulatum var. *chejuense* 204

Rhododendron mucronulatum var. *taquetii* 204

Rhododendron praevernum 199, 200, 201

Rhododendron ririei 200

Rhododendron sichotense 204

Rhododendron spinuliferum 202

Rhododendron strigillosum 200

Rhododendron sutchuenense 200, 201

Rhododendron watsonii 200, 201

Ribes 187

river birch 46, 47

Rosa sericea subsp. *omeiensis* f. *pteracantha* 34, 36

rosemary grevillea 136, 137

royal grevillea 136, 138

Rubus biflorus 51

Rubus cockburnianus 34, 35, 51, 52, 74

Rubus peltatus 51, 52

Rubus thibetanus 51

Ruscus aculeatus 37

Russian olive 124

Russian rock birch 37, 46

S

sacred bamboo 66

Salix alba 52

Salix alba var. *vitellina* 53

Salix babylonica 53

Salix daphnoides 53

Salix fragilis 53

Salix ×*rubens* 53

Salix ×*sepulcralis* var. *chrysocoma* 7, 53

Salix udensis 53

Sambucus cerulea 71

Sambucus nigra 71

Sarcococca 43, 118, 127, 208–211

Sarcococca confusa 38, 40, 208

Sarcococca hookeriana 209

Sarcococca hookeriana var. *digyna* 209

Sarcococca hookeriana var. *humilis* 209

Sarcococca orientalis 44, 209

Sarcococca ruscifolia 208, 210

Sarcococca ruscifolia var. chinensis 210
Sarcococca saligna 211
Sarcococca wallichii 211
sasanqua camellia 94, 95, 99
sasanqua tea bush 95
Scotch heather 89
Scotch ling 89
Scots heather 89
silk tassel bush 133
silky-tassel 133
silverberry 124, 126
silver wattle 85
snake-bark maple 48, 49
snapping hazelnut 159
snowdrop 36
snow heather 126
Spanish fir 54
Spanish oat grass 63
spindleberry 71
spotted alder 159
spotted laurel 56
spring heather 126
spring witch hazel 157
spurge 38
spurge laurel 117
Stachyurus 211–214
Stachyurus chinensis 211–212, 213
Stachyurus praecox 211, 212–213
Stewartia pseudocamellia 38
Stewartia pseudocamellia Koreana Group 49
Stipa gigantea 63
strawberry tree 87
sweet gum 139
switch grass 54
×*Sycoparrotia* 214–215
×*Sycoparrotia semidecidua* 214, 215
Sycopsis 214–215

Sycopsis sinensis 214, 215
Syringa suspensa 130

T
tassel bush 133
Taxus baccata 54
tea bush 99, 104
tea bush camellia 99
tea oil camellia 94, 95
tea olive 192
Tibetan cherry 38, 39, 49
timber bamboo 66
Tsuga heterophylla 54

V
vernal camellia 101
vernal witch hazel 141, 157–159, 161, 162
Viburnum 215–222
Viburnum ×*bodnantense* 43, 215, 216, 217, 222
Viburnum calvum 57, 58
Viburnum cinnamomifolium 57
Viburnum cylindricum 57
Viburnum davidii 57, 58
Viburnum farreri 14, 21, 216, 217, 218, 221
Viburnum fragrans 216, 218
Viburnum ×*globosum* 58
Viburnum grandiflorum 216, 219, 222
Viburnum grandiflorum f. foetens 219, 222
Viburnum propinquum 58
Viburnum rhytidophyllum 58
Viburnum tinus 57, 216, 220, 221
Viburnum tinus subsp. rigidum 220
violet willow 53
Virginian witch hazel 141, 157, 159–160

W
wattle 12, 85
weeping willow 53
western hemlock 54
western leatherwood 121
white-stemmed bramble 51
white willow 53
white winter forsythia 83
wicopy 121
winterberry 80
winterbloom 159
winter box 30, 43, 208
winter daphne 117, 119
winter-flowering dogwood 108
winter-flowering forsythia 83, 130
winter-flowering jasmine 163
winter-flowering honeysuckle 19, 30, 38, 43, 165
wintergreen 75
winter hazel 111, 132
winter heath 124
winter heather 124
winter honeysuckle 38, 165
winter jasmine 163
wintersweet 7, 30, 43, 104
witch hazel 8, 11, 14, 16, 18, 30, 38, 40, 43, 44, 104, 132, 139

Y
yellowbell 130
yellow bells 130
Yunnan camellia 91, 101
Yunnan osmanthus 193

Z
zebra grass 6